# SHAKESPEARE'S
# OCCASIONAL PLAYS

*Their Origin and Transmission*

by

J. M. NOSWORTHY, M.A., F.R.S.L.

EDWARD ARNOLD (PUBLISHERS) LTD.
41 Maddox Street, London W.1

First Published 1965

Printed in Great Britain by
The Camelot Press Ltd., London and Southampton

# SHAKESPEARE'S OCCASIONAL PLAYS

# CONTENTS

# Preface

It may reasonably be asked why the ensuing study of four of Shakespeare's plays presents them in what is probably the exact opposite of their correct chronological order. The answer is that, in seeking somewhat unfamiliar solutions to familiar problems, I found that the order employed here offered the best scope for effective presentation. It will, I hope, be evident that not all of my conclusions are advanced with an equal measure of conviction, but certain incidental findings have been admitted on the ground that they may conceivably prove helpful to other investigators.

I wish here to express my deep gratitude to the Trustees of the Lord Leverhulme Research Fund, who, in 1952, awarded a grant which enabled me to make an exhaustive examination of the *Macbeth* music and related problems. I owe an enormous debt to the advice, criticism and encouragement of two great scholars, unhappily no longer with us—Sir Walter Greg and Professor F. P. Wilson. Dr. Alice Walker has been more than generous in supplying me with information and in keeping me abreast of her own highly significant findings, and I am also greatly indebted to Mr. Bernard Harris for a number of shrewd and stimulating suggestions.

J. M. N.

# Introduction

The ensuing chapters are concerned with the problems presented by four of Shakespeare's plays—*Hamlet, The Merry Wives of Windsor, Troilus and Cressida* and *Macbeth*. The collocation is undeniably an extraordinary one, and its justification rests on the claim that these plays can all be classified as occasional in the sense that, irrespective of such currency as they may have achieved on the popular stage, they were, in the first place, designed for presentation before particular audiences on particular occasions. They present a fairly comprehensive range of familiar Shakespearian problems—such as dating, collaboration, adaptation, revision and textual variation—and the main purpose of the book is to suggest that the resolution of these, and of several isolated and specific problems, becomes possible when due attention is given to their occasional character.

The study of occasional plays is subject to numerous limitations, and a measure of uncertainty is inevitable. Even if we knew when and where such plays were first performed, our knowledge of the performances themselves would remain extraordinarily inadequate, and speculation on this, as on so many matters concerning the Elizabethan stage, would be worse than useless. Moreover, it is extremely difficult to decide which of Shakespeare's plays can reasonably be assigned to the 'occasional' genre. Little doubt attaches to *Macbeth, Troilus and Cressida* and *The Merry Wives of Windsor*, and the evidence presented by H. N. Paul, Peter Alexander and others has won general acceptance. A similar claim for *Hamlet* is here made apparently for the first time and is based on evidence, both internal and external, which is perhaps sufficient but certainly no more than that. If the present enquiry is limited to just these four plays, it is because there is an almost total lack of firm evidence to justify additions to the range. It is, of course, inherently probable that both *The Taming of the Shrew* and *Love's Labour's Lost* belong to the category of occasional plays. The induction of the one, with its local allusions and apparent scope for audience participation, suggests that it was designed for presentation at the house of some nobleman, while the unusual plot of the other, combined with its apparent wealth of topical allusion, may indicate that it was intended for a sophisticated private audience. But neither play can be related to any specific occasion and it therefore seems undesirable to press claims which, in any case, appear to have little bearing on the attendant problems. Moreover, the kind of internal evidence deriving from these and other plays can be highly misleading. Thus we might argue that extensive use of legal material testifies that certain plays were originally commissioned for performance at the Inns of Court. In that case, we start with *The Merchant of Venice*, *2 Henry IV* and *Measure for Measure* (not to mention the assured claims of *Troilus and Cressida*) and where we stop there is no telling. No play better illustrates the difficulties of such diagnosis than *As You Like It*, whose legal allusions seem directed at one of the Inns of Court, whose Hymen ending suggests the gracing of some notable wedding, and whose 'All the world's a stage' speech virtually establishes that it was simply written for the new Globe Theatre. That the Folio text preserves a version that was performed at some nuptial celebration is a likelihood that few critics would deny, but there is no ground for supposing that *As You Like It* was occasional in origin.

To say that Shakespeare was primarily a public entertainer is a platitude, yet its validity should not be overlooked. If the canon yields only some three or four plays which can confidently be designated occasional, the reason is that he and his company were seldom presented with a private occasion such as demanded a play never before acted. Their appearances at Court after 1603 were, of course, quite numerous and the Chamber and Revels accounts name most of the plays that were presented. The significant thing is that not one of these appears to have had its *première* at Court. Cope's letter to Cecil in 1604 offers some relevant information: 'Burbage ys come, & Sayes ther ys no newe playe that the quene hath not seene, but they have Revyved an olde one, Cawled *Loves Labore lost*, which for wytt & mirthe he sayes will please her excedingly.' It may be remarked in passing that this ten-year-old play was still considered a thoroughly diverting one, so that the alleged topicalities, which seem to relate it to some particular occasion and audience, may well be less compelling than has often been supposed. The important point, however, lies in the implication that Queen Anne preferred new (that is, recent) plays, and the Court accounts testify that this preference was often met. The obvious conclusion is that, for Court purposes, the King's Players normally selected plays which, though new, had been thoroughly rehearsed and had already proved successful in the public theatres—a procedure which is, after all, thoroughly logical. Hence, if we designate *The Merry Wives of Windsor* and *Macbeth* 'Court occasional' plays, they stand as an exception to the general rule. The one clearly came into existence because a play was needed to grace a Garter ceremony and perhaps because, as tradition has it, Elizabeth wished to see more of Falstaff: the other because King James favoured something bearing on his Scottish ancestry and his taste for demonology.

The nuptial 'occasional' play was, so far as we can judge, an even rarer phenomenon. Again the Court accounts are relevant, since these establish that not one of the 'fowerteene severall playes' presented at the marriage of Princess Elizabeth and the Elector Palatine was devised expressly for that most memorable of occasions. Nor are we justified in supposing that any particular kind of play was accounted especially appropriate to the business in hand, for the repertoire included *Othello*, *Julius Caesar*, and *The Maid's Tragedy*, together with other material that sorts oddly with wedding festivities. Certainly we are not justified in affirming that Shakespeare wrote *A Midsummer Night's Dream* especially for some important wedding in 1596 when the available evidence shews that the needs could as easily have been met by a revival of even *Titus Andronicus*. In short, the hymeneal endings of *A Midsummer Night's Dream*, *As You Like It* and *The Tempest* do not prove all that they have often been held to prove. It is reasonably safe to conclude that the surviving texts of all three preserve versions specially adapted for use at weddings, but there is no good reason for supposing that the plays were originally anything other than contributions to the company's general repertory. If so, the category of 'nuptial occasional' can hardly be said to exist.

Plays were, of course, a regular feature at the feasts held at the Inns of Court, and it is known that *The Comedy of Errors* was presented as part of the Gray's Inn Revels at Christmas 1594 and that *Twelfth Night* was given at the Candlemas Feast at the Middle Temple in 1602. It has been held that both plays were specially written for the occasion, but this view has found few supporters. There is no firm evidence for the composition date of either play, but critics are understandably reluctant to place *The Comedy of Errors* as late as 1594 since both tone and style point to the very beginning of Shakespeare's dramatic career. Such considerations have no bearing on the dates usually proposed for the later comedy, but it is not easy to see why a play allegedly written for

4

INTRODUCTION

performance at Candlemas should have carried the capricious title of *Twelfth Night, or What You Will. Troilus and Cressida*, then, emerges as the only play which can confidently be regarded as having been devised especially for Inns of Court presentation, but, as suggested in a later chapter, even this may have been a fairly comprehensive adaptation of material that Shakespeare originally intended for the public theatre.

The present claim that *Hamlet* was addressed, in the first place, to a university audience, rests in part on our certain knowledge that, some time before 1603, it had achieved the unusual distinction of having been performed 'in the two Vniuersities of Cambridge and Oxford'. The claim, if correct, is not one that can be extended to any other play, so far as can be judged. Dramatic records for the two university towns, especially Cambridge, are fragmentary. Acting companies visited Oxford on at least twelve occasions between 1589 and 1616, and it is likely that there were other visits which have not been recorded. Performances may have been civic rather than university ones (though the distinction would not have been a significant one at that period), but various colleges certainly made payments to professional entertainers and sponsored public performances.[1] Though such visits usually occurred when plague drove the acting companies out of London, it is not clear that this was invariably the case. Enforced provincial tours cannot have been remunerative, but it is reasonable to assume that Oxford and Cambridge were among the handful of places where fair profits are likely to have accrued, for, apart from London itself, they must obviously have offered greater scope for dramatic activity than any other town. Their comparative accessibility warrants the surmise, though no more, that dramatic companies came to regard them as regular centres. It is relevant to observe that the King's Players visited Oxford at least seven times between 1603 and 1616, though four of those visits admittedly coincided with outbreaks of plague in London. There is, of course, no justification for supposing that Shakespeare normally wrote plays especially for such occasions. If *Hamlet* constitutes the exception, the explanation must be that its author had foreknowledge of his company's intention to visit Oxford and Cambridge. It may be remarked that if Shakespeare's company took to the road, as it appears to have done, in or about 1600-1, it was not because plague forced them out of London. Their 'inhibition' may, as the play suggests,

[1] R. E. Alton, *The Academic Drama in Oxford* (Malone Society Collections V), pp. 29-95.

have been due to 'the late innovation', which surely refers to the absurdly popular boy-actors. If so, their decision to travel must have been the outcome of careful, maybe prolonged, deliberation, and it would not be surprising if their principal playwright for once fashioned the material on which he was working to suit the tastes of an academic audience rather than a Bankside one.

Several problems arise, and such individual ones as collaboration, adaptation and so forth are dealt with in the discussions of the plays themselves. The one general issue which calls for preliminary discussion is that of revision, since the first question relevant to all such plays is: what happened to them once they had fulfilled the needs of the occasion? The inevitable answer is that they were transferred to the Globe where they normally became part of the company's stock repertory, but this raises the further question: were they revised for the purpose and, if so, by whom? The answer to this involves a consideration of both Shakespeare's attitude and that of his Globe audience. Our knowledge of the dramatist and the promptings of common sense alike necessitate the conclusion that, if he did write plays for single occasions, he would have taken good care, from the outset, that those plays should, with a greater or lesser measure of revision, be suitable for general use. Proof of such competence, if proof is needed, is supplied by the fact that all plays written after 1608 were artfully contrived to meet the needs and conditions of both Blackfriars and the Globe. The attitude of the public audience is less easy to gauge, but certain conclusions may be drawn. There are no grounds for believing that the texts of the two royal plays were materially altered at the time of their transfer to the Globe (the changes in *Macbeth* were made later) and this is readily understandable since the original royal patronage would have contributed considerably to their success on the public stage—snob-appeal being what it is. The prospect of seeing *Hamlet* as it was presented 'in the two Vniuersities of Cambridge and Oxford' would doubtless have been less alluring, and it is extremely doubtful whether the academic version, as represented in the good texts, would have been either practicable or acceptable at the Globe—though it was clearly necessary that the play should reach Shakespeare's regular audience in some form or other. The same may have held in theory for *Troilus and Cressida*, but it appears that the transfer was never made. Shakespeare, for once, gratified the tastes of a sophisticated audience with a play which, despite its surpassing merit, lacked, and will always lack, popular appeal. The Folio text suggests that a half-hearted attempt was made to adapt the play for general use, but evidently Shakespeare soon came to realise the hopelessness of such an undertaking.

Revision in general is a complex and controversial issue which lies outside the scope of the present enquiry. There is ample and varied evidence to shew that Shakespeare (predictably) revised his manuscripts before they reached the theatre, and this and other composition methods are touched on in the discussions of *Hamlet* and *The Merry Wives of Windsor*. The extent to which a play might be revised after it had gone into actual performance raises graver problems, but it is reasonable to postulate scrupulous avoidance of any changes that would have confused the actors or brought chaos to the prompt-book. This principle, which excludes the once fashionable myth of 'continuous copy', must certainly have applied even when revision was comparatively extensive, as it appears to have been with at least two of the plays considered here. The conclusions reached in this book were emphatically not governed by this assumption, yet they do much to endorse it. The augmentation of *Macbeth* and the abridgement of *Hamlet* alike point to extraordinarily skilful revision which cannot have placed the slightest strain on actors, book-holder or anyone save the reviser. The identifiable alterations in *Troilus and Cressida* are so few as to give us pause, but the play's category has always been an uncertain one and, in any case, the sometimes narrow distinctions between comedy and tragedy can often disappear in actual performance. The possibility that a few strokes sufficed to convert a comical satire into a serious heroic, if not wholly tragic, play cannot be ruled out.[2]

The identity of this masterly reviser should not be far to seek. When all has been said that can be said of book-holders and hack-poets, it remains in the highest degree probable that the author would have made his own revisions. Shakespeare's connexion with the company,

---

[2] I am indebted to Bernard Harris for the valuable suggestion that the general argument of this and the preceding paragraph would be strengthened by reference to other plays of the period, notably *The Spanish Tragedy*, *The Malcontent* and *Bussy d'Ambois*. These, with the possible exception of the first-named, strike me as relevant examples of double-purpose (i.e. private and public) plays, but all of them raise problems, both textual and circumstantial, which I do not at present feel competent to handle. The provision of alternative endings, which I have here invoked in the case of *Troilus and Cressida*, is applicable, on Schücking's evidence, to *The Spanish Tragedy*, and my impression is that several other examples have survived. I have, therefore, risked a few desperate conjectures (see Appendix 1) in the hope that they may contain some shred of plausibility which will prove helpful to more able critics.

as playwright, actor and sharer, was practically a unique one. Far from justifying the assumption that he suffered others to make major changes, it might reasonably be held to confirm that he was himself responsible for the minor ones. The book-holder's activities, in other words, may well have been considerably less than has been generally supposed.

one

# Macbeth

## Date, Scope and Integrity

i

It now seems certain, in the face of previous editorial doubts, that *Macbeth* was written in 1606. Muir, in 1951, offered a full and reasoned argument for accepting that date,[1] and since then several important scraps of evidence have been adduced. Muir notes that in *Lingua*, published in 1607, there are possible echoes of II.i and an apparent parody of the sleep-walking scene, and refers to the familiar references to Banquo's Ghost in *The Puritan Widow*, published in 1607, and in *The Knight of the Burning Pestle*, which was first performed in that year. These serve to establish 1607 as the absolute forward limit for dating. The references to the King's Evil and to the two-fold balls and treble sceptres argue that the play was written after the accession of James the First in 1603, though some critics regard these as later interpolations. The Porter's remarks about equivocators in II.iii are generally held to refer to the trial of Father Garnet, who was executed on March 28th, 1606, but the evidence is not quite final, as Father Strange had invoked the Jesuit doctrine of equivocation a year earlier. The fact that Garnet went under the alias of Master Farmer does not justify the supposition that the farmer who hanged himself on the expectation of plenty refers to him, since the Porter is obviously talking about a farmer. Nor has a reference to the hanging of traitors in IV.ii any necessary connexion with the Gunpowder conspiracy, for it was not only in 1606 that treason was punished so.

This evidence, not conclusive in itself, gains strength from two other demonstrations. Paul, in his comprehensive study of the play,[2] presents striking evidence for the view that it was first performed at Hampton Court Palace on August 7th, 1606, in connexion with the visit of Christian of Denmark. Among other things he notes that the First Witch's reference, in I.iii, to the master of the *Tiger* was probably based

[1] *Macbeth* (New Arden Shakespeare), ed. Kenneth Muir, pp. xvi-xxvi.
[2] H. N. Paul, *The Royal Play of 'Macbeth'*, pp. 317-31 *et passim*.

on the misfortunes of Sir Edward Michelbourne's ship of that name, which sailed for the East on December 5th, 1604, and, after a remarkable series of calamities, arrived back at Milford Haven on June 27th, 1606. Thanks to Loomis's arithmetical ingenuity, it now emerges that the *Tiger* was away from England for 567 days—that is precisely 'Sen'-nights, nine times nine'.[3] It is clear, then, that Shakespeare was actively engaged on *Macbeth* in the summer of 1606, and this evidence suggests that actual composition may have extended from c. June 25th to c. August 1st, allowing about a week for rehearsal. This is not impossible, though Paul assumes that the play occupied rather more than six months.

There are several fairly close parallels between *Macbeth* and Marston's *Sophonisba*, which was first registered on March 17th, 1606, and these have been held to indicate an earlier date for Shakespeare's tragedy. Muir, however, argues persuasively that Shakespeare was Marston's debtor. If *Sophonisba* made some impact on Shakespeare, one would expect to find echoes in other plays of the *Macbeth* period, and there are such echoes, albeit faint ones, in *Antony and Cleopatra*. Thus *Sophonisba* mentions the 'sheeld of *Telamon*' and 'That seeven fold shield', uses such apostrophes as 'Right worthy!', 'Roialest!' and 'O very woman!', which inevitably recall the form of address used by Iras and Charmian, and yields one or two passages, such as:

> Th'allarum beates necessitie of fight,
> Th'unsober evening drawes out reeling forces,
> Souldiers halfe men, who to their colors troupe
> With fury, not with valor: whilst our ships
> Unrigd, unusd, fitter for fier then water
> We save in our bard haven from surprise.

and:

> Me thinkes I heare him cry. O fight for *Carthage*,
> Charge home, wounds smart not, for that so just so great
> So good a Citty: me thinks I see him yet
> Leave his faire bride even on his nuptiall night
> To buckle on his armes for *Carthage*.

which clearly resemble *Antony and Cleopatra*. It is legitimate, too, to conclude, since *Sophonisba* was readily available in print and *Macbeth* was not, that Shakespeare was the debtor.

*Antony and Cleopatra* is decisive for the dating of *Macbeth* on other

[3] E. A. Loomis, 'Master of the Tiger' *Shakespeare Quarterly*, VII (1956), p. 457.

BSP

grounds. It was from Plutarch's Life of Antony, in North's translation,
that Shakespeare drew the information that the Roman soldiers in the
Parthian War were forced to "tast of rootes that were never eaten
before; among the which there was one that killed them, and made
them out of their wits. For he that had once eaten of it, his memorye
went from him, and he knew no manner of thing', and this he transformed into Banquo's:

> Were such things here, as we doe speake about?
> Or haue we eaten on the insane Root,
> That takes the Reason Prisoner?[4]

Likewise, Macbeth's words:

> There is none but he,
> Whose being I doe feare: and vnder him,
> My *Genius* is rebuk'd, as it is said
> *Mark Anthonies* was by *Cæsar*.

clearly derive from North's version of the Soothsayer's remarks to
Antony:

> For thy Demon, said he, (that is to say, the good angell and spirit that
> kepeth thee), is affraied of his: and being coragious and high when he is alone,
> becometh fearefull and timerous when he commeth neere vnto the other.

It has been pointed out, by Holger Nørgaard,[5] that the peculiar simile
in the Bleeding Captain's first speech in I.ii:

> Doubtfull it stood,
> As two spent Swimmers, that doe cling together,
> And choake their Art.

is drawn from a speech in Samuel Daniel's *Cleopatra*, where Cleopatra
meditates on the way in which she and Antony have brought about
their own ruin:

> And since we tooke of either such firme hold
> In th' overwhelming seas of fortune cast,

---

[4] Holinshed relates that, during Duncan's wars with Sueno, the Scots 'tooke the
iuice of mekilwoort berries, and mixed the same in their ale and bread', which
berries 'spread in such sort through all parts of their bodies, that they were in the
end brought into a fast dead sleepe, that in manner it was vnpossible to awake
them.' This may have prompted Banquo's lines, but the additional debt to North
is palpable.
[5] 'The Bleeding Captain Scene in *Macbeth* and Daniel's *Cleopatra*', *The Review
of English Studies*, October 1955, pp. 395-6.

> What powre should be of powre to reunfold
> The armes of our affections lockt so fast,
> For grapling in the Ocean of our pride,
> We suncke each others greatnesse both together;
> And both made shipwracke of our fame beside,
> Both wrought a like destruction unto either.

Another common element is evident in the circumstances of Macbeth's death. Naturally it cannot be asserted that the lines:

> Why should I play the Roman Foole, and dye
> On mine owne sword?

refer specifically to Antony, since the allusion could apply equally to Cassius and Brutus, but the possibility cannot be ruled out, especially as Antony is "the Roman Foole" in a sense in which the others are not. More certainty attaches to Macduff's:

> Then yeeld thee Coward,
> And liue to be the shew, and gaze o'th'time.
> Wee'l haue thee, as our rarer Monsters are
> Painted vpon a pole, and vnder-writ,
> Heere may you see the Tyrant.

together with Macbeth's rejoinder:

> I will not yeeld
> To kisse the ground before young Malcolmes feet,
> And to be baited with the Rabbles curse.

There is nothing of this in Holinshed, but the thought of gracing Caesar's triumph haunts Cleopatra, both in Plutarch's account and in *Antony and Cleopatra*, and the resultant Shakespearian realisation is basically the same as that in *Macbeth*:

> Thou, an Egyptian Puppet shall be shewne
> In Rome as well as I: Mechanicke Slaues
> With greazie Aprons, Rules, and Hammers shall
> Vplift vs to the view. In their thicke breathes,
> Ranke of grosse dyet, shall we be enclowded,
> And forc'd to drinke their vapour.

The precise parallel, though not developed in quite the same way, occurs earlier in Antony's words:

> Let him take thee,
> And hoist thee vp to the shouting Plebeians,

Follow his Chariot, like the greatest spot
Of all thy Sex. Most Monster-like be shewne
For poor'st Diminitiues, for Dolts . . .

What these passages clearly imply is that Shakespeare wrote *Macbeth*,
including the disputed I.ii, at the time when he was already assembling
his principal material for *Antony and Cleopatra*, so that the composition
of the two tragedies must have been practically simultaneous. This
seems intrinsically probable on linguistic and metrical grounds. Such
parallels as:

> We will proceed no further in this Businesse:
> He hath Honour'd me of late, and I haue bought
> Golden Opinions from all sorts of people.
> > *Macbeth*, I.vii.31-3

> I did not think to draw my Sword 'gainst *Pompey*,
> For he hath laid strange courtesies, and great
> Of late vpon me.
> > *Antony and Cleopatra*, II.ii.156-8

and:

> Hence horrible shadow,
> Vnreall mock'ry hence.
> > *Macbeth*, III.iv.106-7

> Hence horrible Villaine, or Ile spurne thine eyes
> Like balls before me: Ile vnhaire thy head.
> > *Antony and Cleopatra*, II.v.63-4

argue for propinquity, as do most of the statistics given in Chambers's
metrical tables.[6] Hence, the claim that to know the date of the one play
is to know that of the other is probably very near the truth.

*Antony and Cleopatra* was entered in the Stationers' Register on May
20th, 1608, but an earlier composition date is clearly required since the
'newly altred' version of Daniel's *Cleopatra* which appeared in 1607
shews signs of having been revised in the light of Shakespeare's
tragedy. Echoes of *Antony and Cleopatra* have been traced in *Nobody and
Somebody* (registered in 1606), in Barnabe Barnes's *The Devil's Charter*
(acted on February 2nd, 1607, registered on October 16th, 1607, and
printed as "revised, corrected and augmented") and in Chapman's
*Bussy d'Ambois* (published in 1607). None of these is entirely convincing,
but some weight attaches to their joint testimony. R. H. Case, whose

[6] *William Shakespeare*, II, pp. 398-402.

judicious handling of this dating problem has been accepted by Ridley without modification, argues that 'we should finally exclude 1608 in considering *Antony and Cleopatra*, and admit 1606 to competition with 1607'.[7]

The implication is that both *Macbeth* and *Antony and Cleopatra* were written in 1606, the former having been completed by August and the latter by about December. The general pattern of evidence certainly supports the view, not hitherto presented, that the one play was laid aside while the other was written. If, as seems likely, *Macbeth* was the result of a royal command, it could well have been a hasty assignment. Its brevity suggests as much. The sheer quality of writing might argue for more leisurely composition, but there is no means of checking the white heat of inspiration that may have been at Shakespeare's command. There are several loose ends in the early acts which are often cited as proof of abridgement, but may equally well indicate that the dramatist was working against time. So, too, may the naming of certain characters. The customary designation, "Lady Macbeth', is strictly a solecism, based on '*Lady*' in stage-directions and speech-headings. She is '*Macbeths Wife*' at the head of I.v and, except in the dialogue, is not invested with the title of Queen. Shakespeare did not even trouble to discover her name, which, according to Holinshed, was Gruach. Lady Macduff, too, is merely '*Macduffes Wife*' at the head of IV.ii and '*Wife*' in speech-headings. In I.ii '*a bleeding Captaine*' enters, but is reduced to 'Seriant' in the ensuing dialogue. The short scenes in Act V, with their numbing couplets and their general air of inferiority, suggest either that Shakespeare was growing bored with the play or that time was running out.

The evidence, then, is virtually decisive for composition within a fairly restricted time-limit in 1606. The Folio text, however, contains material that is clearly subsequent to both Jonson's *Masque of Queens* and Middleton's *The Witch*. This means that two dates are required, one for the original and one for the revision. The latter date may be provisionally fixed as 1612 for reasons that will be made apparent.

## ii

It is generally assumed that the Folio text of *Macbeth* preserves a shortened version of the original tragedy, though with some compensating additional material by an alien hand. This has resulted in a

[7] *Antony and Cleopatra* (The New Arden Shakespeare), ed. M. R. Ridley (based on the edition of R. H. Case), pp. xxvi-xxxii.

bewildering diversity of theories, many of them completely irresponsible. The most that can legitimately be claimed is that the text appears to offer isolated instances of abridgement, and that two early accounts afford somewhat dubious evidence of omission.

The first of these is Simon Forman's report of a performance of *Macbeth* at the Globe on April 20th, 1611:

> In Mackbeth at the Glob, 1610,[8] the 20th April, ther was to be obserued, firste, howe Mackbeth and Bancko, 2 noble men of Scotland, Ridinge thorowe a wod, the(r) stode before them 3 women feiries or Nimphes, And Saluted Mackbeth, sayinge, 3 tyms vnto him, haille Mackbeth, king of Codon; for thou shalt be a kinge, but shalt beget No kinges, &c. then said Bancko, What all to mackbeth And nothing to me. yes, said the nimphes, Haille to thee Banko, thou shalt beget kings, yet be no kinge. And so they departed & cam to the Courte of Scotland to Dunkin king of Scots, and yt was in the dais of Edward the Confessor. And Dunkin bad them both kindly wellcom, And made Mackbeth forth with Prince of Northumberland, and sent him hom to his own castell, and appointed Mackbeth to prouid for him, for he wold Sup with him the next dai at night, & did soe. And mackbeth Contrived to kill Dunkin, & thorowe the persuasion of his wife did that night Murder the kinge in his own Castell, beinge his gueste. And ther were many prodigies seen that night & the dai before. And when Mack Beth had murdred the kinge, the blod on his hands could not be washed of by Any meanes, nor from his wiues handes, which handled the bloddi daggers in hiding them, By which means they became both moch amazed & Affronted. the murder being knowen, Dunkins 2 sonns fled, the on to England, the (other to) Walles to saue them selues. they being fled, they were supposed guilty of the murder of their father, which was nothinge soe. Then was Mackbeth Crowned kinge, and then he for feare of Banko, his old Companion, that he should beget kings but be no kinge him selfe, he contriued the death of Banko, and caused him to be Murdred on the way as he Rode. The next night, beinge at supper with his noble men whom he had bid to a feaste to the which also Banco should haue com, he began to speake of Noble Banco, and to wish that he wer ther. And as he thus did, standing vp to drincke a Carouse to him, the ghoste of Banco came and sate down in his cheier behind him. And he turninge About to sit down Again sawe the goste of banco, which fronted him so, that he fell into a great passion of fear & fury, vtterynge many words about his murder, by which, when they hard that Banco was Murdred they Suspected Mackbet.
>
> Then Mack dove fled to England to the kings sonn, And soe they Raised

[8] Evidently a slip of the pen since the performance was on a Saturday which did not fall on April 20th, in 1610. The error is quite understandable as the New Year began on Lady Day.

an Army, And cam into scotland, and at dunston Anyse overthrue Mackbet. In the meantyme whille macdouee Was in England, Mackbet slewe Mackdoues wife & children, and after in the battelle mackdoue slewe mackbet.

Obserue Also howe mackbets quen did Rise in the night in her slepe, & walke and talked and confessed all, & the docter noted her wordes.

This, with its faulty dating, its confusion, its obvious supplementation from Holinshed, and its associations with Collier, has been confidently held to be a forgery, but its authenticity has now been established.[9] It does not, in itself, offer much evidence for abridgement of the original play. On the contrary, it implies rather that certain scenes in the Folio were added after 1611. In view of Forman's notorious interest in astrology, it is at least surprising that his account makes no mention of the Cavern scene or of the later prognostications and their fulfilment.

The other early account which may have some relevance is that given by Peter Heylyn in the second and subsequent editions of his *Microcosmos*.[10]

*Duncan* King of *Scotland*, had two principall men whom hee emploied in all matters of importance; *Machbed* and *Banquho*. Those two trauelling together through a forrest, were met by three Fairies, or Witches (*Weirds* the *Scots* call them) whereof the first making obeisance vnto *Machbed*, saluted him *Thane* (a title vnto which that of Earle afterward succeeded) of *Glammis*; the second, *Thane* of *Cawder*; and the third, King of *Scotland*. This is vnequall dealing said *Banquho*, to giue my friend all the honors and none vnto me: to whom one of the *Weirds* made answere, that he indeed should not be King, but out of his loines should come a race of kings, that should for euer rule *Scotland*. And having thus said they all suddenly vanished. Vpon their arriuall to the court, *Machbed* was immediatly created *Thane* of *Glammis*: and not long after, some new seruice of his requiring new recompence, he was honoured with the title of *Thane* of *Cawder*. Seeing then how happily the prediction of the three *Weirds* fell out in the two former; he resolued not to bee wanting to himselfe in fulfilling the third: and therefore first hee killed the King, and after by reason of his command among the Souldiers and common people, he succeeded in his Throne. Being scarce warme in his seat, he called to mind the prediction giuen to his companion *Banquho*: whõ herevpon suspecting as his supplanter, he caused him to be killed, together with his whole kindred; *Fleance* his son only with much difficulty escaping into *Wales*. Freed now from his feare, he built *Dunsinane* Castle, making it his ordinary seat: and afterward on new feares consulting with certaine wizards about his future

[9] By J. Dover Wilson and R. W. Hunt in *The Review of English Studies*, July 1948.
[10] I have used the edition of 1627.

estate; was by one told that he should neuer be ouercome till *Bernane* wood (which was some few miles distant) did come to *Dunsinane* Castle: and by the other, that he neuer should be slaine by any man borne of a woman. Secure then, as he thought, hee omitted no kinde of libidinousnesse or cruelty, for the space of 18 years, for so long he raigned, or to say better, tyrannized. *Mackduffe* gouernour of *Fife*, ioining to himselfe some few Patriots, which had not yet felt the tyrants sword; priuily met one night at *Bernane* wood, and early in the morning marched, euery man bearing a bough in his hand the better to keepe them from discovery; toward *Dunsinane* Castle; which they presently tooke by scaladoe. *Machbed* escaping, was pursued, ouertaken, and vrged to fight by *Mackduffe*; to whom the tyrant halfe in scorne replied, that in vaine he attempted his death: for it was his destinie neuer to be slaine by any man borne of a woman. Now then is thy fatall houre come, said *Mackduffe*, for I was neuer borne of a woman, but violently cut out of my mothers belly, she dying before her deliuery: which words so danted the tyrant, though otherwise a man of good performance, that he was easily slaine; and *Malcolme Conmor* the true heire of the Crowne, seated in the throne.

This does not claim any necessary connexion with Shakespeare's *Macbeth*, but there is reason for supposing that Heylyn had a performance of the play in mind. The story is admitted to *Microcosmos*, not because it is vital to the presentation of Scottish history, but because it is 'a history then which for variety of action, or strangeness of euent, I neuer met with any more pleasing', and it may well be that 'variety of action' here tells its own tale. It may certainly be questioned whether Heylyn owed very much to the chroniclers, all of whom he trenchantly denounces, though his narrative may have been coloured by occasional recollections. The wording of 'This is vnequall dealing said *Banquho* to giue my friend all the honours and none vnto me' suggests that Heylyn recalled the relevant lines in Warner's *Albion's England*:

> To whom my father laughing, said they dealt vnequall dole,
> Behighting nought thereof to him, but to his Friend the whole,

but there is little else that he can possibly have derived from Warner's fragmentary account. Warner's version, like that in Heywood's *Hierarchie of the Blessed Angells*, treats Macbeth simply as the means to an end—the establishment of the Stuart dynasty—and, after the murder of Banquo, the interest is diverted to Fleance. Heylyn, on the other hand, keeps his attention firmly fixed on Macbeth, and in this respect is nearer to the chroniclers, whom he repudiates, and Shakespeare. His assurance that Dunsinane was taken 'by scaladoe' suggests that he was recalling a performance of Shakespeare's play, and his uncertainty about the process whereby Macbeth became thane of Glamis and Cawdor may have resulted from the truncation of I.ii. The process is quite explicitly defined by Holinshed, but it is questionable whether it would have emerged clearly from a single performance of *Macbeth*. It is pertinent to add that an adaptation of Heylyn's narrative was used as the 'Argument' in the altered version of *Macbeth* published by Chetwin in 1674, since this suggests that there may have been some kind of recognised connexion between Shakespeare's play and the *Microcosmos* account.

Where Forman, Heylyn and Holinshed agree on details which are presented differently in the Folio, it is legitimate to surmise that alterations were made in the play.[11] Two such correspondences call for consideration, but neither can be taken as evidence of abridgement:

(i) *Ridinge thorowe a wod* (Forman)
*trauelling together through a forrest* (Heylyn)

In the Folio the Witches proclaim, in I.i, that their meeting with Macbeth is to be 'Vpon the Heath', and I.iii is accordingly located 'Vpon this blasted Heath'. It is strange, therefore, that both Forman and Heylyn should concur in setting the meeting in a wood. Holinshed writes of Macbeth and Banquo 'passing thorough the woods and fields, when suddenlie in the middest of a laund, there met them three women in strange and wild apparell." The wood or forest is implicit in Holinshed's 'laund', which *O.E.D.* glosses as 'an open space among woods': 'a glade': 'untilled ground': 'pasture': When all considerations have been weighed, the fact remains that Forman's impression was that I.iii represented a wood.

(ii) *3 women feiries or Nimphes* (Forman)
*three Fairies, or Witches* (Weirds *the* Scots *call them*) (Heylyn)

Here there is common agreement with Holinshed: 'But afterwards the common opinion was, that these women were either the weird sisters, that is (as ye would say) the goddesses of destinie, or else some nymphs or feiries, indued with knowledge of prophesie by their necromanticall science'. In the woodcut which accompanies Holinshed's text they are by no means ill-favoured, and few versions of the story present them as earthly hags of the cauldron. In *Albion's England* they are 'Three Fairies' and 'Weird Elfes', while *The Hierarchie of the Blessed Angells*,

[11] I no longer adhere to most of the examples cited in my article, '"Macbeth" at the Globe', *The Library*, Sept.-Dec, 1947.

which classifies them as white nymphs, that is spirits of water, shadows them forth as

> three Virgins wondrous faire,
> As well in habit as in feature rare.

and accords them impeccable manners.

It is possible that Shakespeare, leaning on Holinshed's noncommittal report, was content to let things sort themselves out, but there is, even so, nothing essentially inconsistent in the Folio presentation. The one thing which is clear is that it is ludicrously impossible to speak of Shakespeare's Weird Sisters, 'secret, black, & midnight Hags', with their choppy fingers, skinny lips and beards, their demonic speeches and eldritch incantations, as either fairies or nymphs. Yet Forman, at the Globe in 1611, saw what he took to be fairies or nymphs. This is odd in view of his interest in witches and all that concerns them, and the suggestion that he recalled Holinshed to the exclusion of Shakespeare raises more difficulties than it solves. All in all it seems likely that the Witches in the performance which Forman witnessed were in fact fairies or nymphs, rather than hags. If so, it follows that what was presumably the original version was altered at some time after the spring of 1611. This, however, can scarcely have resulted in abridgement, since there must have been generous compensation for any cuts made in the original. What Forman's report, with possible support from Heylyn, implies is that the three fairies or nymphs in a wood of the 1606 version were transformed into the hags of the blasted heath in the revision. It may be added that the character of the Folio Witches is, perhaps, best viewed as deriving from *The Masque of Queens* and *The Witch*, while the supernatural agents of the original tragedy were conceivably akin to the 'tres quasi Sibyllae' who greeted King James on his visit to Oxford in 1605.[12]

The two accounts cited, then, offer very little evidence for abridgement, as distinct from revision. Collier supposed that part of Forman's account: 'the blod on his hands could not be washed of by Any meanes, nor from his wiues handes, which handled the bloddi daggers

---

[12] It is wholly possible that the Witches were originally played by boys who were replaced by men only after the Hecate material had been added. This, since most Elizabethan adult actors wore beards, which they would have been unlikely to dispense with in the interests of a single performance, would have changed the whole appearance of the Witches. References to their beards and the like m?y therefore be late insertions.

in hiding them, By which means they became both moch amazed & Affronted', refers to 'a mob-accordant incident' which is deleted from the Folio text, but it is abundantly clear that all great Neptune's ocean will not wash the blood clean from Macbeth's hand, and that Lady Macbeth, in retrospect, is amazed and affronted that these hands will ne'er be clean. Macbeth's hangman's hands can have lost nothing in actual performance and are, in themselves, sufficiently 'mob-accordant'.

Dover Wilson's complex theory of abridgement envisages a whole series of lost scenes or episodes.[13]

(i) An original plan for murdering Duncan discussed by Macbeth and his Lady, which resolves the existing difficulties of I.vii.

(ii) Macbeth calling at Inverness on his way to Forres to relate to the Lady his encounter with the Weird Sisters, and confessing that thoughts of murder have crossed his mind.

(iii) Lady Macbeth going to Duncan's bedchamber, knife in hand, but recoiling from the deed.

(iv) A dialogue between Macbeth and the Lady which leads to a change of plan.

(v) A scene in which Banquo, after Macbeth's coronation, expounds and justifies his ambiguous position.

(vi) A scene which resolves the mystery of the Third Murderer.

(vii) A scene which rationalises Macduff's desertion of his wife and children.

Wilson's hypothesis is open to serious objections. It attributes to Shakespeare a positively Bradleian preoccupation with motive and character on the one hand, while, on the other, it assumes abridgement so fierce that a good deal of supposedly vital information was surrendered. If the scenes which Wilson specifies were in the original play, it would have been altogether more logical to have cut, in whole or part, such things as the Porter scene, the dialogue between Ross and the old man, much of IV.iii, and parts of the sleep-walking scene. There is a sense in which even Macbeth's great speech at V.v.17-28 is expendable. It has already been pointed out that the loose ends from which Wilson's hypothesis derives may in fact be evidence of hasty composition, and they can also be accounted for on the wholly warrantable assumption that, for Court performance, a short play was required.

Wilson's case for abridgement in I.ii is altogether more credible, though his suggestion that it was the work of Middleton is gratuitous.

[13] *Macbeth* (The New Shakespeare), ed. J. Dover Wilson, pp. xxxiii-xlii.

Too much is made of the need to clarify Cawdor's treacherous alliance
with Norway. Treason is rarely shouted from the housetops, and Angus
in I.iii admits ignorance of the exact nature of Cawdor's defection.
Even so, some nine passages in I.ii are metrically irregular:

    (i) Who like a good and hardie Souldier fought
       'Gainst my Captiuitie: Haile braue friend . . .

    (ii) (Like Valours Minion) caru'd out his passage,
       Till hee fac'd the Slaue:
       Which neu'r shooke hands, nor bad farwell to him. . . .

    (iii) As whence the Sunne 'gins his reflection,
       Shipwracking Stormes, and direfull Thunders:
       So from that Spring, whence comfort seem'd to come,
       Discomfort swells . . .

    (iv) Dismay'd not this our Captaines, *Macbeth* and *Banquoh*?

    (v) I cannot tell: but I am faint,
       My Gashes cry for helpe.

    (vi) Who comes here?
       *Mal.*   The worthy *Thane* of Rosse.
       *Lenox.*  What a haste lookes through his eyes?
       So should he looke, that seemes to speake things strange.

    (vii) Where the Norweyan Banners flowt the Skie,
       And fanne our people cold.
       *Norway* himselfe, with terrible numbers . . .

    (viii) Assisted by that most disloyall Traytor,
       The *Thane* of Cawdor, began a dismall Conflict . . .

    (ix) That now *Sweno*, the Norwayes King,
       Craues composition:
       Nor would we deigne him buriall of his men . . .

All of these, with the exception of (v), which is in character, suggest
cutting. The irregularities could conceivably be laid to the charge of a
compositor working from difficult copy, but this is unlikely. Since
Wilson's view that the botching was done by Middleton is no longer
tenable, and since it is hard to believe that Shakespeare himself would
have been guilty of such untidy abridgement, it virtually follows that
the book-keeper must have been responsible, unless the Master of
Revels himself scored out certain lines to which he took objection.

    Of the extent and character of one of the cuts (iii) we can be reason-
ably certain. Here, to all appearances, a single word has been lost, and

that through the carelessness of the compositor. Hence, nearly all editors print the second line of the passage as:

> Shipwracking storms and direful thunders break,

and ignore the possibility of a more considerable omission. It is obvious, however, that the formula here proposed is that of the Homeric simile, but 'So from that spring' follows far too closely upon 'As whence', so that there is little of the requisite magnitude. The Pyrrhus speeches in *Hamlet* exemplify the identical simile presented at a suitable length:

> But as we often see against some storme,
> A silence in the Heauens, the Racke stand still,
> The bold windes speechlesse, and the Orbe below
> As hush as death: Anon the dreadful Thunder
> Doth rend the Region. So after *Pyrrhus* pause,
> Arowsed Vengeance sets him new a-worke.

On rhetorical grounds, therefore, we must assume that some two or three lines at least have been deleted, while recognising at the same time that the cut cannot very well have comprised more than half a dozen lines. Whether the remainder were more extensive it is impossible to say, but the general continuity of the scene suggests that they were not. The asperity at (i) results probably from the omission of certain details about the capture and delivery of Malcolm. At (ii) the irregularity is both metrical and syntactical, but only a fragment of the sense pattern appears to be missing. In the Folio, (iv) is printed as prose, but the rest of the scene is in verse, and Duncan does not elsewhere use prose. It is legitimate to conclude that Duncan originally spoke several lines of verse which were botched in such a way that the compositor was left with little to guide him. It is a curious coincidence that no less than five of these defective passages, (iv), (vi), (vii), (viii) and (ix), contain proper names, and that these seem directly identifiable with the dislocation. In some cases they may have been substituted by the book-keeper for more periphrastic descriptions of the 'Bellona's bridegroom' kind, but it is perhaps safer to assume that they originally fitted quite neatly into regular lines. On the supposition that some two or three lines have been scored out, (iv) might, for instance, have read something like:

> Dismay'd not this our Captaines, brave Macbeth,
> And Banquo, no less worthy to be named,
> Our first in battle, who with force renewed
> Promis'd the mere confusion of the foe.

In each case the omission must have been a relatively trivial one, and it seems that the total losses for the scene are unlikely to exceed fifty lines.

It is not easy to justify abridgement of this kind, especially as there is little real evidence of cutting elsewhere in the play. Deletion of very short passages is found in other plays, and, as Greg has shewn, the average cut in *Edmond Ironside* is only four and a half lines.[14] There are, however, thirty-eight such cuts, which shorten the play by one-twelfth and therefore offer a consistent and intelligible abridgement. The petty mutilations in *Macbeth*, which affect little more than one scene, can scarcely have served any useful purpose.

A satisfactory explanation is possible in the light of other apparent cuts in Act I. Two later passages reveal the kind of irregularity that arises from careless deletion. The first of these is Angus's report of Cawdor's treachery in I.iii:

> Who was the *Thane*, liues yet,
> But vnder heauie Iudgement beares that Life,
> Which he deserues to loose.
> Whether he was combin'd with those of Norway,
> Or did lyne the Rebell with hidden helpe,
> And vantage; or that with both he labour'd
> In his Countreyes wracke, I know not:
> But Treasons Capitall, confess'd, and prou'd,
> Haue ouerthrowne him.

and the second, Malcolm's report to Duncan of Cawdor's death at the beginning of I.iv:

> *King.* Is execution done on *Cawdor*?
> Or not those in Commission yet return'd?[15]
> *Mal.* My Liege, they are not yet come back.
> But I haue spoke with one that saw him die:
> Who did report, that very frankly hee
> Confess'd his Treasons, implor'd your Highnesse Pardon,
> And set forth a deepe Repentance:
> Nothing in his Life became him,
> Like the leauing it. Hee dy'de
> As one that had beene studied in his death,
> To throw away the dearest thing he ow'd
> As 'twere a carelesse Trifle.

14 *The Shakespeare First Folio*, pp. 145-6.
15 'Or'—emended in F2 to 'Are' and by most editors. If, however, there was deletion, the emendation is by no means certain.

Neither passage is metrically satisfactory, and attempts at adjustment by Pope, Capell and Malone are anything but successful. There are syntactical difficulties, and the punctuation looks odd, even by Jacobean standards.

Dryden recalled that 'in reading some bombast speeches of *Macbeth*, which are not to be understood, he [Ben Jonson] used to say that it was horrour'. It might, then, seem that the purpose of the deletions was to eliminate extravagant rhetoric.[16] But alterations made on aesthetic grounds would not result in such disorder, and in any case plenty of Jonsonian 'horrour' was allowed to stand elsewhere in the play.

The obvious explanation is that these local and trivial cuts were due either to censorship or anticipation of it. The scenes involved deal with rebellion and treason, and the available evidence suggests that Sir George Buc was no less vigilant than his predecessor, Tilney. It happens that a good deal in these scenes could have been taken, rightly or wrongly, as alluding to recent events. The account of Cawdor's behaviour on the scaffold, as Steevens pointed out, 'corresponds in almost every circumstance with that of the unfortunate Earl of Essex, as related by Stowe', Macbeth's succession to the thaneship of Cawdor recalls certain features of the Gowrie conspiracy, and the King's players had already, in 1604, incurred displeasure through presenting the 'Tragedy of *Gowry*'.[17] In November 1605, both the national security and the Stuart dynasty had been seriously threatened. There are possible mild allusions to the Gunpowder plot elsewhere in *Macbeth*, but clearly too comprehensive an account of rebellion, treason and the punishment of traitors would have seemed highly topical and far from acceptable.

The general conclusion must be that *Macbeth*, in its original form, was a short play, with brevity imposed by its special or 'occasional' character and, presumably, by the short space of time at Shakespeare's disposal.[18] The source material, too, may be taken as restricting scope, and it is significant that *Macbeth*, unlike several of the great tragedies, has no sub-plot and is sparing in its use of incidentals. There is evidence of deletion at certain points in Act I, but this has a particular reason, and nothing that can really be termed abridgement is apparent.

[16] See the chapters on *Troilus and Cressida* in the present volume.
[17] E K. Chambers, *William Shakespeare*, II, p. 330.
[18] *Macbeth* (2,106 lines in the Folio version) corresponds satisfactorily with other Folio texts that appear to have been abridged for use on particular occasions —*The Comedy of Errors* (1,777 lines). *A Midsummer Night's Dream* (2,174 lines) and *The Tempest* (2,062 lines).

iii

The complicated process of disintegration to which *Macbeth* has been subjected during the past hundred years originated with Steevens's publication of Middleton's tragi-comedy, *The Witch*, in 1778. The immediate consequence, however, was a series of enquiries into relative dates and relative obligations, pursued by Steevens himself, then by Malone, Dyce, Lamb, Collier and others, and nearly a century elapsed before the Clarendon editors, Clark and Aldis Wright, assigned three hundred lines of *Macbeth* to Middleton. Coleridge had earlier rejected the 'low soliloquy of the Porter', but otherwise the Romantic critics appear not to have harboured any doubts. Hazlitt, in fact, received as authentic certain passages which were interpolated into Shakespeare's tragedy from the Davenant adaptation.[19]

The main sections which Clark and Aldis Wright attributed to Middleton comprise the Bleeding Captain scene (I.ii), the dialogue of the Witches (I.iii.1-37), the Porter episode (II.iii.1-47), the Hecate portions (III.v: IV.i.39-47, 125-32), the King's Evil passage (IV.iii. 140-59), the dialogue between Menteith, Caithness and Lennox (V.ii), the Siward episode and the closing lines (V.viii.35-75). Small additions were made by F. G. Fleay, Henry Cuningham added the opening scene to the list, and latterly G. B. Harrison,[20] presumably influenced by Conrad's dubious metrical evidence, has pronounced the conversation between Ross and the Old Man (II.iv.1-20), and the whole of V.ii.vi, and viii spurious. The general tendency, however, had been to reduce the admissible alien matter. Coleridge's views on the Porter were accepted by the Clarendon editors but have found no other adherents, while, on the other hand, his brilliant comment on the Bleeding Captain scene, developed successively by A. C. Bradley[21] and the present writer,[22] has removed all doubt about its authenticity. Very few critics nowadays question Act V as it stands, and the King's Evil passage has won a somewhat indefinite kind of recognition. The general consensus of opinion is that the sections which involve Hecate and rationalise the songs and dance interpolated from *The Witch* are the

[19] Cf. his citation of 'We should rejoice when good kings bleed' in *Characters from Shakespeare's Plays*.
[20] *Macbeth* (The Penguin Shakespeare), ed. G. B. Harrison, pp. 15-16.
[21] *Shakespearian Tragedy*, pp. 389-90.
[22] 'The Bleeding Captain Scene in *Macbeth*', *The Review of English Studies*, April 1946, pp. 126-30.

work of an alien hand. Chambers thought that they might reasonably be assigned to Middleton,[23] and Sisson dogmatically asserts that they are his.[24] Dover Wilson holds the same view and develops a complex theory which involves Middleton as reviser and interpolator.[25] The present writer's case against Middleton is accepted by Muir, who favours an anonymous writer.[26] The authenticity of these sections, and *ipso facto* of the whole play, was stoutly maintained by Verity,[27] though with little basis other than blind faith, and no more can be claimed for Flatter's[28] acceptance of them since this is inseparable from an untenable general hypothesis. The only concrete evidence in favour of Shakespeare's authorship is that put forward by Wilson Knight,[29] though here again the relevant data are obscured by a comprehensive symbolical method of interpretation which has been denounced by many critics.

Since incredulity nowadays attaches only to the Hecate scenes (III.v: IV.i.39-47, 125-32), these alone call for serious consideration here. They are clearly late interpolations, and the fact that they involve two songs which originally belonged to Middleton's play, *The Witch*, has gained wide acceptance for the belief that he was the interpolator. The fatuity of this hypothesis is testified by *The Witch* itself. Middleton's Hecate is coarse, brusque and colloquial: her speeches are written mainly in blank verse, with occasional recourse to an irregular rhyming measure, but never in octosyllabic couplets. In all these respects she is radically unlike the Hecate of *Macbeth*. Her dozen or so lines of rhyme afford a sufficient demonstration:

> there take this vn-baptized-Brat:
> Boile it well: preserve the ffat,
> you know 'tis pretious to transfer
> Our 'noynted fflesh into the Aire,
> in Moone-light nights, or Steeple-Topps,
> Mountaines, and Pine-trees, that like pricks, or Stopps,
> seeme to our height: High Towres, and Roofes of Princes
> like wrinckles in the Earth: Whole *Prouinces*
> appere to our sight then, ev'n leeke
> a russet-Moale, vpon some ladies cheeke.

[23] *William Shakespeare*, I, p. 472.
[24] William Shakespeare, *The Complete Works*, ed. C. J. Sisson, p. 969.
[25] *ed. cit.*, pp. xxii-xlii.          [26] *ed. cit.*, p. xxxvi.
[27] *Macbeth* (The Student's Shakespeare), ed. A. W. Verity, pp. xxxvii-xlviii.
[28] *Shakespeare's Producing Hand*, pp. 95 foll.
[29] *The Shakespearian Tempest*, pp. 326-32.

When hundred Leagues in Aire, we feast, and sing,
Daunce, kisse, and Coll, vse every thing;
what yong-man can we wish, to pleasure vs
but we enjoy him in an *Incubus*?

Apart from this she has just one rhyming couplet:

Come my sweet Sisters: let the Aire strike our Tune
whilst we show Reverence to yond peeping Moone.

Comparison with *Macbeth* will shew the full justice of Greg's observa-
tion that 'there does not appear to be any particular resemblance
between the alleged interpolations and Middleton's work'.[30]

One general conclusion which the study of both the Folio and the
good Quartos establishes is that Shakespeare did not, as a general rule,
permit indiscriminate tampering with his work. Subject to the
reservation that his role as interpolator was governed possibly by
retirement in or about 1613 and certainly by his death in 1616, there is
no *prima facie* reason for supposing that he was not the author of the
Hecate sections. There are, in fact, very strong grounds for claiming
that he was.

Wilson Knight's defence of Hecate, ignoring his controversial
'theories of Shakespeare's symbolisms', rests on two main theses—the
similarity between Hecate and other Shakespearian theophanies, and a
suggestive set of parallels with *A Midsummer Night's Dream*.[31] He finds
that Hecate's speech in III.v is 'very similar to the speeches of other
gods and goddesses in Shakespeare', and that 'in all we can detect
the same apparent faults'. Further, 'Hecate, Hymen, Diana, and
Jupiter, all have a certain strangeness about them which marks them off
from the more firmly actualised figures of the Weird Sisters, the Ghost
in *Hamlet*, Oberon and Puck.'[32]

There are three principal affinities between *A Midsummer Night's
Dream* and the first Hecate scene (III.v) of *Macbeth*. Wilson Knight
observes that 'Acheron' appears at the end of a line in each:

And at the pit of Acheron
Meete me i'th'Morning. . . .

[30] *The Shakespeare First Folio*, p. 397 (Note E).          [31] *op. cit.*
[32] It has, of course, been contended that Hymen, Diana and Jupiter are also non-
Shakespearian interpolations, but even scepticism must end somewhere. For a
defence of Jupiter, incorporating the evidence of Meyerstein and Wilson Knight,
see *Cymbeline* (New Arden Shakespeare), ed. J. M. Nosworthy, pp. xxxiii–xxxvii.

cf. *A Midsummer Night's Dream*, III.ii.355-6:

> The starrie Welkin couer thou anon,
> With drooping fogge as blacke as *Acheron*.

and that a time-limit is set on the 'business' that is to be performed. Thus Hecate's:

> This night Ile spend
> Vnto a dismall, and a Fatall end.
> Great businesse must be wrought ere Noone.

echoes Oberon's words in the scene already cited (lines 393-4):

> But notwithstanding haste, make no delay
> We may effect this businesse, yet ere day.

Further, the agents of mischief in both plays are associated with Hecate, so that Puck, at V.i.390-5, proclaims:

> And we Fairies, that do runne,
> By the triple *Hecates* teame,
> From the presence of the Sunne,
> Following darkenesse like a dreame,
> Now are frollicke. . . .

Finally, Wilson Knight remarks that, in the song with which the fairies lull Titania to sleep (II.ii.9-24), the 'evil and ugly forms of life' which are charmed away include snakes, hedgehogs, blind-worms, spiders, beetles and snails, and 'this touches the evil life-forms in the Cauldron scene of *Macbeth*'. This, of course, extends the parallelism to a section of *Macbeth* (IV.i.1-38) whose authenticity is not challenged by any responsible critic, but the salient point is that the same order of thought and imagery, deriving from the same play, is present in both the disputed passage and the accepted one.[33]

It may be objected that all the similarities which Wilson Knight presents are commonplaces of the fairy way of writing, such as could suggest themselves equally to Shakespeare, Middleton or any other poet. There is, however, a passage in *Titus Andronicus* whose relevance appears to have gone unnoticed, though it offers even stronger parallels, and that in a context which is wholly unconnected with the world of faery. At II.iii.89-91 of that play Demetrius enters to Tamora and asks:

[33] The snake and hedgehog are, in fact, the only common features, but their validity as evidence is attested by the imagery of the *Titus Andronicus* passage discussed below.

How now deere Soueraigne
And our gracious Mother,
Why doth your Highnes looke so pale and wan?

and Tamora's immediate response is:

Haue I not reason thinke you to looke pale.

In *Macbeth* III.v the First Witch says to Hecate:

Why how now *Hecat*, you looke angerly?

and Hecate replies:

Haue I not reason (Beldams) as you are?

This linkage, common to both plays, of 'how now', 'looke' and 'Haue
I not reason' does not give the impression of being something that an
imitator would readily seize upon, and it is relevant to remark that in
both plays it is part of what may be termed a monarch–subject relationship and is presented in a context of projected evil. There are two other
suggestive verbal parallels. Hecate uses the Senecan adjectives 'dismal'
and 'fatal' at line 21:

Vnto a dismall, and a Fatall end,

and both are used by Tamora:

Vnto the body of a dismall yew (line 107)

and:

Vnlesse the nightly Owle, or fatall Rauen. (line 97)

There is, moreover, 'this abhorred pit' in Tamora's speech to set against
'the pit of Acheron' in Hecate's.

Tamora's lines are instructive, and may be quoted in full:

Haue I not reason thinke you to looke pale.
These two haue tic'd me hither to this place,
A barren, detested vale you see it is.
The Trees though Sommer, yet forlorne and leane,
Ore-come with Mosse, and balefull Misselto.
Heere neuer shines the Sunne, heere nothing breeds,
Vnlesse the nightly Owle, or fatall Rauen:
And when they shew'd me this abhorred pit,
They told me heere at dead time of the night,
A thousand Fiends, a thousand hissing Snakes,
Ten thousand swelling Toades, as many Vrchins,

Would make such fearefull and confused cries,
As any mortall body hearing it,
Should straite fall mad, or else die suddenly.
No sooner had they told this hellish tale,
But strait they told me they would binde me heere,
Vnto the body of a dismall yew,
And leaue me to this miserable death.
And then they call'd me foule Adulteresse,
Lasciuious Goth, and all the bitterest tearmes
That euer eare did heare to such effect.
And had you not by wondrous fortune come,
This vengeance on me had they executed:
Reuenge it, as you loue your Mothers life,
Or be ye not henceforth cal'd my Children.

There is an unmistakable connexion between this and a considerable part of *Macbeth*. The 'barren, detested vale' itself has an obvious affinity with the scene of Macbeth's second meeting with the Weird Sisters, and, in sense if not in form, recalls the 'blasted heath' of Act I. Various patterns of imagery tally—notably, of course, 'the nightly Owle' and 'the fatall Rauen'. More significant, however, is the way in which so many of the evil life-forms mentioned by Tamora—owl, raven, snakes, toads, urchins and yews—find their way into the Hell-broth in Macbeth, IV.i:

Lizards legge, and Howlets wing.

Fillet of a Fenny Snake.

Toad, that vnder cold stone,
Dayes and Nights, ha's thirty one

Thrice, and once the Hedge-Pigge whin'd.

Gall of Goate, and Slippes of Yew.

These parallels, especially with the yew, which is the exception in both passages, can hardly be dismissed as coincidental, and the whole matter may be expressed in terms of a *reductio ad absurdum*: if Middleton wrote the Hecate speech (III.v), he must also have written the opening section of IV.i and the *Titus Andronicus* passage: if Peele wrote *Titus Andronicus*, he must also have written the *Macbeth* passages. But, for the most obvious of reasons, it is impossible to associate Middleton with the events of 1592 or Peele with those of 1612, whereas Shakespeare, unlike the majority of Elizabethan dramatists, is known to have been alive and active at both these dates.

Evidence for the authenticity of Hecate's short speech at IV.i.39-43 comes from an even stranger source. The purpose of this interpolation is, of course, to allow Hecate and the Witches to sing a song whose opening line is

> Black Spiritts, and white: Red Spiritts, and Gray.

and this may have led Shakespeare to recall, consciously or unconsciously, that he had once made Mistress Quickly, in *The Merry Wives of Windsor*, address

> Fairies blacke, grey, green, and white

for the formal link between the nocturnal incantations, however much they may differ in purpose and degree, is a close one. And thus it came about that he made Hecate bid the Witches:

> And now about the Cauldron sing
> Like Elues and Fairies in a Ring,

a couplet which palpably recollects Quickly's

> And Nightly-meadow-Fairies, looke you sing
> Like to the *Garters*-Compasse, in a ring.

Subject, phrasing and rhyme alike testify to common authorship, and there is obviously no question of Middleton or anyone else having been the borrower since no imitator in his right mind is likely to have chosen the Fairy scene in *The Merry Wives of Windsor* as a suitable model for Hecate's speech. Indeed Hecate's couplet is so inappropriate to the occasion that even Shakespeare's sanity might be doubted, but the probable explanation is that he scribbled a few lines to justify the song without giving very much thought to the matter.

The fact that lines 39-43, though authentic, are uninspired and *mal à propos*, goes some way towards dispersing any doubt that attaches to lines 125-32. These lines, spoken by the First Witch, are undeniably feeble:

> I sir, all this is so. But why
> Stands *Macbeth* thus amazedly?
> Come Sisters, cheere we vp his sprights,
> And shew the best of our delights.
> Ile Charme the Ayre to giue a sound,
> While you performe your Antique round:
> That this great King may kindly say,
> Our duties, did his welcome pay.

Here there is a certain difficulty in the fact that the third of these couplets echoes Hecate's lines in *The Witch*,

> Come my sweet Sisters: let the Aire strike our Tune
> whilst we show Reverence to yond peeping Moone.

but these are the lines which introduce the Witches' Dance, and it seems reasonably likely that they caught Shakespeare's eye when he glanced at the prompt-copy of Middleton's play. Or he may, of course, have remembered them from the actual performance. The idea of charming the air to give a sound accords with Shakespeare's habit of justifying a consort of viols in unlikely localities.[34]

Verse tests offer little evidence for or against authenticity. Shakespeare uses octosyllabics elsewhere, especially for charms, but these, like the speeches of the Weird Sisters, are invariably trochaic. The fact that Hecate's lines are iambic does not prove them spurious. On the contrary, the subtle distinction between Hecate and her minions is one that might be looked for from Shakespeare. Hecate's use of such rhymes as *he / Destinie, Security / Enemie, see / me* (all in III.v) may be noted since Shakespeare shews a marked predilection for similar rhymes in octosyllabics in *A Midsummer Night's Dream, As You Like It, The Merry Wives of Windsor* and *The Tempest*.

Any theory of non-Shakespearian interpolation which assumes imitation of sporadic lines from the remote corners of *Titus Andronicus* and *The Merry Wives of Windsor* stands self-condemned, and the inevitable conclusion, however wounding it may be to aesthetic sensibilities, is that the Hecate is Shakespeare's. Whether the lines are worthy of him is another matter, though, as Muir shrewdly observes, they are the work of a writer 'not without poetic ability'.[35] As mere interpolations they are not likely to have stimulated Shakespeare's interest or enthusiasm, and it suffices that they meet the needs.

It has been necessary to labour this demonstration of authenticity because it is a crucial one. It establishes that Shakespeare was the sole author of *Macbeth* and that the revising hand was also his. The implications, both for aesthetic judgments and textual criticism, are far-reaching.

---

[34] Cf. *Cymbeline*, where Belarius's 'ingenuous instrument' is made accountable for solemn music in the Welsh mountains, and *The Tempest*, where Prospero's magic is responsible for sounds and sweet airs.

[35] *ed. cit.*, p. xxxvi.

two

# Macbeth

## The Scope and Nature of Augmentation

### i

Though it has now been shewn that Middleton has no direct connexion with *Macbeth*, he was, in a sense, ancillary to the revision. The whole Middleton fabric rests on the mere fact that the two songs named in the stage-directions of *Macbeth* at III.v.35 and IV.i.43 were originally used in his tragi-comedy, *The Witch*, which has survived in a transcript that remained unpublished until 1778. Several problems attach to these songs which, surviving in name only in the Folio and in full only in a non-theatrical transcript, were nevertheless available to Davenant when he produced his Restoration adaptation of *Macbeth*. Cademan's pirated Quarto of 1673 prints the full text of one of the songs, and both are given in Chetwin's 1674 edition of Davenant's play. The only conceivable solution, which proves verifiable for the one song, is that musical transcripts had survived.

The 'received' music to *Macbeth* was brought to the press in 1760 by William Boyce and attributed by him to Matthew Locke, presumably on the strength of Downes's account of the Davenant adaptation:

> The Tragedy of *Macbeth*, alter'd by Sir William Davenant; being drest in all it's Finery, as new Cloath's new Scenes, Machines, as flyings for the Witches; with all the Singing and Dancing in it: THE first Compos'd by *Mr. Lock*, the other by *Mr. Channell* and *Mr. Joseph Preist*; it being all Excellently perform'd being in the nature of an Opera, it Recompenc'd double the Expence; it proves still a lasting Play.[1]

Downes is notoriously unreliable, and several competent musicographers have doubted Locke's claim to the music published by Boyce. A dance tune printed as 'A Jig called Macbeth' in *Musick's Delight on the Cithren* (1666) and, with the initials 'M.L.' appended, as 'The Dance in the Play of *Macbeth*' in *The Pleasant Companion* (1682) establishes that

[1] John Downes, *Roscius Anglicanus* (1708), p. 33.

Locke did write incidental music for the play.[2] Malone gives 1663 as the date of Davenant's adaptation and this is rendered credible by Pepys's description of performances witnessed by him on November 5th, 1664, December 28th, 1666 and January 7th, 1667. On the second of these occasions he found *Macbeth* 'a most excellent play for variety' and on the third 'a most excellent play in all respects, but especially in divertisement, though it be a deep tragedy; which is a strange perfection in a tragedy, it being most proper here, and suitable.' Downes's attribution, then, is probably correct.

Locke's dance tune unfortunately bears no resemblance to anything in the Boyce recension, but this latter clearly derives, in whole or part, from earlier music. A setting of the song indicated in the Folio text of *Macbeth* as '*Come away, come away, &c*' was printed in 1812 by John Stafford Smith in his *Musica Antiqua*. Smith describes this as being printed 'from an MS. of that age in the editor's possession' and representing 'the original music in the Witches scene in Middleton's comedy of the Witch'. He adds that 'Matthew Locke, or whoever was the author of the music to "Macbeth", had evidently seen this composition.' There are palpable resemblances between the two settings, and Smith's claim is endorsed by Richard Clark,[3] Rimbault[4] and Cummings.[5] Rimbault, who acquired the manuscript after Smith's death in 1836, ascribes the setting to Robert Johnson (1582?-1633), and Cummings agrees. This is also the view of Cutts, who claims that Johnson, as King's Musician, wrote incidental music to plays by Shakespeare, Beaumont and Fletcher, Webster, Thomas May and, probably, Middleton, Tourneur and Jonson over the period 1608-1616.[6]

The residual certainty is that this song, originally belonging to *The Witch*, was transferred, words and music, to *Macbeth*, and the same obviously applies to the other song, 'Blacke Spirits &c', of which no musical copy appears to have survived. In Crane's transcript of *The Witch*, made c. 1625 at Middleton's behest for presentation to Thomas

---

[2] It was also included, without title or ascription, in *Musick's Recreation on the Viol* (1682). The British Museum copy has a note claiming that 'this is evidently the original rendering of "Let's have a dance" (probably Locke's) afterwards altered and improved by J. Eccles as it is now sung'.

[3] In Birchall's 1822 edition of the 'Locke' music.

[4] In D'Almaine's edition of the music (1843) and *Ancient Vocal Music of England* (1850).

[5] In *The Musical Times*, May 1st, 1882, pp. 259 foll.

[6] John P. Cutts, *The Contribution of Robert Johnson, King's Musician, to Court and Theatrical Entertainments* (University of Reading M.A. thesis, 1953).

Holmes, the dedicatory epistle refers to the play as having long lain 'in an imprisond-Obscuritie' and the title-page proclaims that it had been 'long since Acted, by his Ma^{ties}. Seruants at the Black-Friers'.[7] This implies that it had failed to hold the stage, so that the transfer of the songs was evidently from an unsuccessful play to an established one. The exact date of this transfer is uncertain, but several useful conclusions can be drawn. The King's Players' negotiations for the lease of Blackfriars began in 1608, *The Witch* itself clearly incorporates material from Jonson's *Masque of Queens*, which was presented at Whitehall on February 2nd, 1609, and Robert Johnson's service with the company apparently dated from 1608. Lawrence's conjecture that *The Witch* was the opening play of the Blackfriars season in December 1609 is therefore plausible.[8] The songs could have been transferred at any time after about the beginning of 1610, and since Shakespeare himself has been shewn to be the author of the speeches which justify their insertion, they must have been introduced before *c.* 1613. The whole process, as will be shewn, is related to augmentation which does not appear to have figured in the Globe performance witnessed by Forman on April 20th, 1611. Hence, 1612 seems a reasonable date.

ii

*The Witch*, styled on the title-page of the transcript a 'Tragi-Coomedie', was obviously designed to satisfy the sophisticated Jacobean demand for sensational drama tricked out with music, dancing and spectacle. The musical components, excluding Hecate's opening lines which, though copied in italic, are dubious and 'a Catt (playing on a Fidle)', which is unlikely to have been more than a few discordant scrapings, amount to four:

1. Song: 'In a Maiden-time profest' (lines 589-97),[9]
2. Song: 'Come away: Come away' (lines 1331-71).
3. Song: 'Black Spiritts, and white' (lines 1998-2014).
4. Dance 'here they Daunce y^e witches Dance & Ex^t' (line 2022).[10]

Early copies of the first two are extant, the first in a manuscript folio copied by John Wilson *c.* 1650 (Bodleian MS. Mus.b.L. f. 21) and in

---

[7] See Introduction to the Malone Society reprint of *The Witch*.
[8] W. J. Lawrence, 'The Mystery of *Macbeth*' in *Shakespeare's Workshop*.
[9] Line numeration follows the Malone Society reprint, as do all quotations.
[10] See J. P. Cutts, 'The Original Music to Middleton's *The Witch*', *Shakespeare Quarterly*, Spring 1956, pp. 203-9.

John Gamble's Commonplace Book (New York, Drexel MS. 4257, No. 32) and the second in the manuscript owned successively by Stafford Smith and Rimbault (New York, Drexel MS. 4175). No copy of the third has survived. A collection of nearly a hundred and fifty tunes belonging to Jacobean plays, masques and entertainments which is preserved in the British Museum (Add.MS. 10444) contains two items headed 'The First Witches Dance' and 'The Second Witches Dance'. Since several of the compositions in this volume are known to be the work of Robert Johnson, and since others certainly belonged to plays by Shakespeare, it seems likely that one, or both, of these dances figured in Middleton's play.

Lawrence's ingenious and plausible theory[11] is that the first Witches' Dance, which apparently achieved some popularity,[12] was originally composed for the performance of *The Masque of Queens* on February 2nd, 1609, and that the King's Men, who performed the antimasque of twelve witches on that occasion, commissioned Middleton to supply a play in which it could be utilised again. The obvious corollary is that, consequent upon the failure of *The Witch*, all its music, except for the unsuitable 'In a Maiden-time profest', was transferred to *Macbeth*. It may have been decided to add a second dance. There is no stage-direction in the Folio relating to anything of the kind, but the opportunity presents itself at I.iii.32-4:

> The weyward Sisters, hand in hand,
> Posters of the Sea and Land,
> Thus doe goe, about, about.

and at IV.i.4:

> Round about the Caldron go.

In *The Witch* all these musical embellishments centre upon Hecate, who bears a part in the songs and is named by name. 'Come away' is in fact an action song from which she could not very well have been eliminated. A few lines had, therefore, to be added to *Macbeth* in order to rationalise her sudden appearance and these, on the evidence given in the preceding chapter, were supplied by Shakespeare.

[11] *op. cit.*, and 'Notes on a Collection of Masque Music', *Music and Letters*, 1922. III. i. 53.

[12] Transcriptions survive in B.M.Add.MS. 17786-9, William Ballet's Lute Book, Dowland's *Varietie of Lute Lessons* and Brade's *Neuer Ausserlesene*. The date of Robert Dowland's book, 1610, is suggestive.

### iii

Davenant's adaptation, containing the 'divertisement' that so appealed to Pepys and, in Downes's words, 'being in the nature of an Opera', has a certain relevance. Downes specifies 'new Scenes, Machines, as flyings for the Witches; with all the Singing and Dancing in it'. This suggests a most ambitious transformation, and the Epilogue to Duffet's *Macbeth* travesty of 1673 throws some light on the actual performance:

> A new fancy, after the old and most surprising way of *Macbeth*, perform'd with new and costly *Machines*, which were invented and managed by the most ingenious operator, Mr. Henry Wright, 'P.G.Q.' Heccate and Three Witches, 'according to the famous mode of Macbeth, commence the most renowned and melodious Song of John Dory, being heard as it were in the Air, sung in parts by Spirits, to raise the expectation, and charm the audience with thoughts sublime, and worthy of that Heroick scene which follows.' Then the scene opens—'Thunder and lightning is discovered, not behind painted Tiffany to blind and amuse the senses, but openly, by the most excellent way of Mustard-bowl and Salt-Peter.' Three Witches fly over the pit, riding upon besoms. Then Heccate descends over the stage 'in a glorious Charriott adorn'd with pictures of Hell and Devils, and made of a large Wicker Basket'.

This reveals that the contraptions employed were more ambitious than anything that is likely to have been available in Shakespeare's day, but the supposition that Davenant's version differed in kind, as well as degree, from the revised version preserved in the Folio is almost certainly fallacious. Analysis shews that Davenant man-handled the text, making certain cuts, but adding several new scenes mainly intended to contrast the incorruptibility of the Macduffs with the depravity of the Macbeths, and to weigh Macbeth's reception of Banquo's ghost against Lady Macbeth's reaction to Duncan's. These scenes add two songs only to the music taken over from *Macbeth*. There are several stage-directions additional to those given in the Folio:

(I.i)   *A shriek like an Owl.*
        *Ex. flying.*
(I.iii)  *Enter three Witches flying*
(III.iv) *the Ghost descends.*
        *the Ghost of* Banq, *rises at his feet.*
(III.v)  *Machine descends.*
(IV.i)  Cauldron *sinks.*
        *The Cave sinks.*

Few of these, if any, are indicative of elaboration. Sound effects for the Witches' familiars were no doubt used at the Globe, and the Folio:

> Houer through the fogge and filthie ayre

suggests the use of some kind of flying machine. A windlass was certainly used in the Hecate scenes:

> Hearke, I am call'd: my little Spirit see
> Sits in a Foggy cloud, and stayes for me.

The ascent and descent of Banquo's Ghost may also have figured in the Globe performances since this implies reliance upon a device that Shakespeare had already used in *Hamlet*. Such an assumption gives point to Macbeth's 'let the earth hide thee'. His question at IV.i.106:

> Why sinkes that Caldron? & what noise is this?

establishes that the descent of the cauldron was not one of Davenant's innovations, which it now seems, amounted to no more than the descent of the cave itself. Any such gain is offset by the apparent loss of sound effects. Davenant's directions make no provision for the familiar 'Hoboyes, and Torches', and the 'Drums and Colours', etc., of the battle-scenes are also omitted. This may imply the loss of a few scraps of incidental music.

The most surprising feature of the Davenant version is its elimination of the Armed Head, the Bloody Child and the Child Crowned in IV.i and its tame substitution of Hecate as the speaker of the three equivocal prophecies. This may be a reversion to the original Shakespearian practice.[13] The Folio Apparitions scarcely accord with Shakespeare's practice in 1606, and the fact that Forman, in 1611, made no mention of them may be significant.

All that can justly be claimed for Davenant is that he turned *Macbeth* into a longer play, greatly to its disadvantage. The addition of two songs may have resulted in a more 'operatic' effect, but any such gain was made at the expense of three sensational and picturesque apparitions, The legitimate conclusion is that fundamentally Davenant's adaptation was no more 'operatic' than the revised Shakespearian version preserved in the Folio.

---

[13] Except, of course, that Hecate could not have been the speaker. But there is no reason why the prophecies should not have been given to the Weird Sisters as in I.iii.

iv

The play, as set down in the Folio, is in fact a highly spectacular affair. Stage-directions establish that sound and other effects, comprising thunder and lightning, oboes, torches, bells, knocking, sennets, drums, alarums and flourishes were numerous. Other effects, in addition to those mentioned in the last section, are implicit in the dialogue:

> I heard the Owle schreame, and the Crickets cry . . .
> Hearke, I heare Horses . . .
> Ring the Alarum Bell, blow Winde, come wracke . . .

In view of Lennox's speech at II.iii.59-68 it is reasonable to conclude that a wind-machine and other devices were much in evidence at the end of II.ii.[14] In I.i the "fogge and filthie ayre' implies the use of a smoke-curtain which may have lingered, not inappropriately, over part of the battle-field scene which follows. Further use of this device is suggested by 'So foule and faire a day' in I.iii, and the 'Foggy cloud' in III.v. A flying machine must have been used in III.v and, presumably, for Hecate's entry and unmarked exit in IV.i. At I.iii.78 the stage-direction reads 'Witches vanish' and that at IV.i.132 runs 'The Witches Dance, and vanish'. These contrast oddly with Hamlet, I.i: 'Exit Ghost' and I.iii 'Exeunt Ghost and Hamlet' but tally with 'Vanish' in Cymbeline, V.iv and '. . . with a quaint deuice the Banquet vanishes' in The Tempest, II.iii. It is reasonable to assume that, by c. 1610, quaint devices were available for the exits of supernatural characters. The use of several properties is clearly indicated. These include the cauldron, Lady Macbeth's taper, the 'leauy Skreenes' in V.vi and 'Th'Vsurpers cursed head' in V.vii (viii). Malcolm's directions to his soldiers in V.iv suggest that the 'leauy Skreenes' were merely part of a much more elaborate scenic effect. The songs and dances call for no further comment, and the evidence for costume and choreography, since this does not derive from the Folio, will be considered later.

[14] Commentators have, in general, done less than justice to the storm in Macbeth, though it is probably as significant as that in King Lear. The point is that, prior to the murder of Duncan, the night is so still that the owl and cricket are audible, but the act of murder brings pandemonium. The storm, apart from the sharp dramatic contrast, shews how man's attempt to overthrow existing order or degree is accompanied by
>          . . . raging of the sea, shaking of earth,
> Commotion in the winds, frights, changes, horrors.

The sum total of elaborate effects and devices which the Folio provides is impressive. In both number and quality it closely corresponds with the spectacular provisions of the late romances and, like them, shews the impact of the Court masque and similar entertainments on Shakespeare's dramatic practice. At the same time, it isolates *Macbeth* from all the other tragedies except, perhaps, the unfinished *Timon of Athens*. The tragic sequence from *Julius Caesar* to *King Lear* affords no parallel example of spectacular emphasis. The richness of *Antony and Cleopatra* is mainly verbal and *Coriolanus* seems almost a deliberate rejection of the opportunities that lay to hand at the time when it was written. The inference to be drawn from the inclusion of materials and effects current in 1612, but not apparently in common use in 1606, is that the main purpose of revision was to convert *Macbeth* into a tragedy of spectacle or a melodrama.

v

Most of the effects enumerated belong to Shakespeare's later practice, and it is clear that the songs and dances were a legacy from *The Witch*. What now appears most likely is that in 1612 *Macbeth* had to accommodate many other things that had been used for Middleton's play. Lawrence's supposition that Middleton had been commissioned to supply a play in which the antimasque of the *Masque of Queens* could be utilised again does not really go far enough. Jonson's masque had evidently entailed heavy expenditure for special equipment and it is merely natural to assume that the company wanted, as soon as possible, a stage-play to which anything that had cost good money could be transferred. Comparison with the *Masque of Queens* shews that *The Witch* could well have added quite a substantial sum to the costs already incurred. The King's Men must have been fairly confident that the new play would prove a 'get-penny', but their hopes, it seems, were soon shattered. The obvious course thereafter was to transfer everything that could reasonably be transferred to a popular play that made provision for witchcraft. *Macbeth*, then, in revision, drew heavily on *The Witch* and more lightly on the *Masque of Queens*. It is superfluous to add that Shakespeare, as shareholder, manager and original author, was the person best suited to undertake, or even to propose, such revision.

Middleton's debt to Jonson calls for consideration mainly because it has some bearing on the date of *Macbeth*, IV.i.1-38. The song, 'Come away: Come away' clearly borrows from the opening lines of the masque:

Sisters, stay; we want oᵗ Dame.
Call vpon her, by her name,
And the Charme we vse to say,
That she quickly anoynt, and come away:

## I. CHARME.

Dame, Dame, the watch is set:
Quickly come, we all are met.
From the lakes, and from the fennes,
From the rockes, and from the dennes,
From the woods, and from the caues,
From the Church-yards, from the graues,
From the dungeon, from the tree,
That they die on, here are wee.

Middleton takes over the 'Come away' formula and the reference to anointing:

I will but noynt, and then I mount. (1343)

and follows the Charm fairly closely in:

Ouer Woods, high Rocks, and Mountains,
Ouer Seas, our Mistris Fountaines,
Ouer Steepe Towres, and Turretts,
we fly by night 'mongst troopes of Spiritts. (1363-6)

This affords some assurance that the song was Middleton's own work and not something from the common stock, available equally to him and to Shakespeare. Middleton's other main debt is in his third song, 'Black Spiritts, and white', where Hecate's hags prepare a hell-broth similar to that in *Macbeth*, IV.i.[15] The debt is one of detail, however, since, in *The Masque of Queens*, the hags merely exhibit trophies contributory to the devising of a charm.

Shakespeare's debt to Jonson is almost wholly an indirect one through Middleton,[16] and comprises the Witches' Dance, several costumes and perhaps a few of the ingredients of the hell-broth. Jonson's own account of the antimasque suggests that it was novel and sensational, and it is reasonable to surmise that it was perpetuated in full in the 1612 *Macbeth*:

[15] See Appendix 2 for the text of both songs.
[16] The sole verbal similarity, that between the Dame's 'Well done, my *Hagges*' and Hecate's 'O well done: I commend your paines' is probably coincidental and, in any case, insignificant.

At w^ch, w^th a strange and sodayne Musique, they fell into a *magicall Daunce*, full of praeposterous change, and gesticulation, but most applying to they^r property: who at they^r meetings, do all thinges contrary to the custome of Men, dauncing, back to back, hip to hip, they^r handes ioyn'd and making they^r *circles* backward, to the left hand, w^th strange phantastique motions of they^r heads and bodyes. All w^ch were excellently imitated by the Maker of the *Daunce Mr. Hierome Herne*, whose right it is, here to be nam'd.[17]

It may be said of the costumes for Hecate and her hags that they were obviously very costly, that, in Jonson's learned way, they were based upon unimpeachable classical authority and that they confer authority in their own right. All of these are very good reasons for transferring them to a popular play. Jonson's account of Hecate runs thus:

> At this, the *Dame* entered to them, naked arm'd, bare-footed, her frock tuck'd, her hayre knotted, and folded w^th vipers; In her hand a Torch made of a dead-Mans arme, lighted; girded w^th a snake.

and of the other witches:

> These Witches, w^th a kind of hollow and infernall musique, came forth from thence. First one, then two, and three, and more, till they^r number encreasd to Eleuen; all differently attir'd; some w^th ratts on they^r heads; some on they^r shoulders; others w^th oyntment-potts at they^r girdles; All w^th spindells, timbrells, rattles, or other *veneficall* instruments, making a confused noyse, w^th strange gestures. The deuise of their attire was *m^r Iones his.* w^th the Invention and *Architecture* of the whole *Scene*, and Machine: only, I praescribd them they^r *properties*, of vipers, snakes, bones, herbes, rootes, and other ensignes of they^r *Magick*, out of the authority of antient & late *Writers*.

Not all of these costumes and properties found their way into *Macbeth*. Shakespeare, it seems, was content to limit himself to Hecate and the three Weird Sisters. The stage-direction at IV.i.38 suggests that there may have been six subsidiary witches on the stage at this point, but this is probably an error. Mutes could, of course, have been utilised according to taste and the resources of the company.

Shakespeare's direct legacy from *The Witch* would appear to comprise the two songs written by Middleton and set to music by Robert Johnson, the flying-machine and the cauldron, with, perhaps, a few of the unpleasant things that went into it. The flying device was evidently quite elaborate. In *The Witch* Firestone tells Hecate that the other witches are

---

[17] Herne was, of course, the choreographer and not, as Lawrence supposed, the composer of the music.

aboue the Steeple alredy, flying
over your head with a noyse of *Musitians*,

and in the song which follows, 'Come away: Come away', the parts of
Stadlin and the rest are specified as being performed '*in y^eaire*'. Halfway
through the song '*A Spirit like a Cat descends*', and a subsequent direction
reads '*Hec. going vp*'. That some kind of flying device was involved is
attested by various lines in the song itself:

> . . . Now I am furnished for the Flight . . .

> . . . Now I goe, now I flie . . .

> . . . oh what a daintie pleasure' tis
> to ride in the Aire
> when the Moone shines faire . . .

> . . . we fly by night, 'mongst troopes of Spiritts . . .

There is finally a residue of spectacular matter which Shakespeare
may have introduced at the revision stage, utilising properties and
devices that had been available since about the time of *Cymbeline*.
Improvements of already existing devices might reasonably be
inferred for the presentation of Banquo's ghost, the dumb-show in
IV.i, if this figured in the original play, Birnam Wood, the capture of
Dunsinane, if Heylyn's reference to 'scaladoe' is relevant, and the final
duel. This last item presents difficulties since the stage-direction at
V.vii (viii) 34 is perplexing:

> *Exeunt fighting. Alarums.*
> *Enter Fighting, and Macbeth slaine*

Greg conjectured, rightly no doubt, that there was a change in the
staging in order that a more elaborate duel might be presented, with
Macbeth's death taking place on the stage.[18] Shakespeare's actual
innovations in the 1612 version could have included a 'quaint device'
for the vanishing of the Witches, the smoke-curtain and the severed
head, a property which seems first to have come into prominence as
'*Clotens* Clot-pole' in *Cymbeline*. The Cavern Scene as a whole may
have been based on an elaborate property such as could have been used
in the romances,[19] and the three Apparitions commend themselves as

---

[18] *The Shakespeare First Folio*, pp. 394-5.
[19] Henslowe's inventory of 1598 shews that the Earl of Nottingham's men
owned many elaborate properties including a rock, a Hell-mouth and several
tombs.

spectacular novelties, especially as they involve the cauldron which was apparently taken over from *The Witch*. The dumb-show, with its seemingly superfluous eighth king, may have been altered in revision but to what purpose it is not clear. The Weird Sisters appear to have been more drastically altered. They are fairies or nymphs in all other accounts of *Macbeth* and it is generally held that Shakespeare based his original presentation of them on the 'tres quasi Sibyllae' who greeted James I when he visited Oxford in 1605. Forman certainly took them to be '3 women feiries or Nimphes' in the 1611 Globe performance. There are, therefore, reasonable grounds for concluding that it was only in 1612 that they were converted into 'secret, black & midnight Hags' with choppy fingers, skinny lips and beards.

### vi

The kind of revision outlined must obviously have affected the existing dialogue and stage-directions. If the Weird Sisters were radically altered, it follows that I.iii.43-7 were added in 1612, as was IV.i.48-9 if that scene figured at all in the original. The change in presentation, combined with the use of flying-machines and the smoke-curtain, argues that the whole of I.i belongs to the revision. At V.vii. 57-8:

> Behold where stands
> Th'Vsurpers cursed head

may be an addition, and the speech certainly reads more easily without it. The whole of III.v is clearly additional and intended to justify the interpolation of the first song.

The Cavern Scene (IV.i) raises problems. The song, together with Hecate's lines, are clearly interpolations. The stage-direction relating to the dumb-show may have been augmented and obscured. If the Apparitions were innovations, Macbeth's remarks to and about them must have been added. The real difficulty, however, is that attaching to lines 1-38, which are not susceptible of dating on purely stylistic grounds but may, on other evidence, be reasonably assigned to the revision. The song, casually set down in the Folio direction as '*Musicke and a Song, Blacke Spirits, &c.*', reveals its full character only in the stage-direction in *The Witch*: '*A Charme Song: about a Vessell*'. It necessitates the use of a cauldron, apparently one of the legacies from Middleton's play, and, being in itself a charm song, achieves its effect only as the culminating point in a reasonably extended process of witchly concoction.

There is a certain correspondence between the ingredients of Middleton's hell-broth and those of Shakespeare's. The common elements comprise parts of wolf, adder, unbaptised infant, frog, toad and bat, but these are not necessarily significant since most of them would have been likely to find their way into any witch's brew. In view of the basic link with Middleton, they are, however, suggestive. Much more relevance attaches to the fact that five of Shakespeare's ingredients— owl, snake, toad, hedge-pig and yew—figure among the evil life-forms in *Titus Andronicus*, II.iii.91-115, a passage which, as has already been seen, establishes the authenticity of *Macbeth*, III.v, which certainly belongs to the revision. It is possible that Shakespeare unconsciously echoed the *Titus Andronicus* passage in 1606 and again in 1612, but this does not seem likely, especially in the light of the other evidence.

The stage-directions in IV.i.1-38, which have given editors considerable trouble in the past, seem to clarify the position. The initial one, '*Thunder. Enter the three Witches*', cannot easily be reconciled with that after line 38, '*Enter Hecate, and the other three Witches*'. The most obvious explanation is that lines 39-43 represent Shakespeare's first addition and that lines 1-38 were an afterthought. In other words, having first written the few lines to justify the song, he realised that the hell-broth would be an attractive, even a necessary, part of the whole process, and therefore added lines 1-38, forgetting, however, to amend the stage-direction after line 38.[20]

vii

What the Folio text preserves, then, is fundamentally the original tragedy of *Macbeth* with such alterations and additions as were necessary to bring the play into line with the theatrical taste prevalent in or about 1612—that taste which led to the enthronement of Beaumont and Fletcher. Shakespeare himself, after 1608 or 1609, had concentrated entirely on material that offered full range to the sensational and the spectacular, and it is doubtful whether the revision of *Macbeth*, with its change of emphasis, worried him unduly. The apparently unfinished

[20] Many editors emend '*and*' to '*to*', but this creates an anomalous stage-direction since '*Enter Hecat*' would be quite sufficient. The objection that Hecate was not a witch is purely academic. She is, after all, *the* Witch in Middleton's play, and even Jonson had no scruples about making his Dame 'to beare the person of *Ate*, or *mischiefe*'.

tragedy of *Timon of Athens*, with its music, banquets, masque, cave, wood, walls and so forth, evidently represents a conscious attempt to write spectacular tragedy. The moral for aesthetic critics and also for stage historians is that *Macbeth* must be viewed both in relation to the great Shakespearian tragedies and to such spectacular enterprises as *The Duchess of Malfi.*

## three

# *Macbeth*

## Prompt-Book and Folio Copy

i

It is generally agreed that the Folio text of *Macbeth* rests on the prompt-book, but the general line of transmission is disputed, and the notion that Middleton was involved, in some capacity or other, has led editors to suppose that the prompt-book itself was untidy and markedly different from Shakespeare's foul papers. Thus Wilson, who attributes a considerable measure of alteration and addition to Middleton, argues that 'a prompt-book, with a second dramatist intervening between Shakespeare and the book-keeper, is not likely to retain many traces of Shakespeare's original MS.' and postulates a special transcript, 'probably made for the printers in 1622 or 1623'.[1]

The case for late transcription is not well founded. Wilson isolates four readings (I.ii.13 *Gallowgrosses*; I.ii.14 *Quarry*; I.iii.97-8 *Tale/Can*; IV.i.97 *Rebellious dead*) and comments that these 'seem more likely to be due to a transcriber than a compositor'. The first three errors, however, belong to scenes in which there there were evidently several deletions, with consequent obscurities, and not all critics are agreed that 'Rebellious dead' is a corruption at all. Wilson's further claim, that 'the famous corruption'

> Cleanse the stufft bosome, of that perillous stuffe.

and 'the seeming tautology'

> And the Crow makes wing toth' Rookie Wood

are best explained as 'the blunders of actors which have been inadvertently reproduced by a scribe familiar with the play of the stage' is tenable only on the assumption that these are corruptions.[2] The trans-

---

[1] *ed. cit.*, pp. 87-91.
[2] The first example turns in fact on the kind of pun fairly common in the play. Cf. Banquo/Banquet; surcease/Successe; guild/Guilt; throat is cut/Cut-throats; meate/Meeting; *Seyton*/dis-eate.

script, then, can be disregarded, and so, it would appear, can Middleton or any other 'second dramatist'.

## ii

The prompt-book, on the present shewing, is likely to have been the concern of Shakespeare and the book-keeper and of no one besides. The various small deletions in I.ii, iii and iv may have been made by the Master of Revels but it is at least equally possible that, anticipating possible offence, either author or book-keeper was responsible for them. All that seems certain is that they caused dislocation and untidiness which gave Jaggard's Compositor A some little trouble.

The prompt-book envisaged, then, is the body-text, written in a single hand, with the prompter's markings added, and dating from 1606. The later additions would almost certainly be inserted foul papers, similarly marked, and there would be the one or two small alterations and additional stage-directions, all of them more likely to be the work of the reviser than of the book-keeper. This yields the following analysis:

*Body-text*

| | |
|---|---|
| I.ii | Some eight or nine small deletions. |
| I.iii | One or more deletions. Stage-direction *Witches vanish* at line 78 possibly a replacement. |
| I.iv | One deletion. |
| I.v–vii | Unaltered. |
| II.i–iv | Unaltered. |
| III.i–iv | Unaltered. |
| III.vi | Unaltered. |
| IV.i.45–124 | Apparitions added with appropriate marginal alterations in dialogue. Original stage-direction altered. Stage-direction for dumb-show possibly altered. |
| IV.i.133–56 | Unaltered. |
| IV.ii–iii | Unaltered. |
| V.i–iii | Unaltered. |
| V.iv | Possible marginal addition resulting from augmented scenic effect. |
| V.v | Unaltered. |
| V.vi | As V.iv. |
| V.vii | Altered stage-direction at line 34. Stage-direction added at line 55. Lines 57-8, 'Behold . . . head' added in margin. |

*Additions*

I.i             Inserted foul sheet, apparently unmarked.

III.v           Inserted foul sheet. Stage-direction at line 33, '*Musicke,
                and a Song*', presumably Shakespeare's but duplicated by
                book-keeper at line 35, '*Song within. Come away, come
                away, &c.*'

IV.i.1-43       Probably two foul-sheet insertions. Stage-direction after
                line 38 Shakespeare's, uncorrected. Stage-direction after
                line 43 possibly conflated, '*Musicke and a Song*' being
                Shakespeare's and '*Blacke Spirits, &c.*' being the book-
                keeper's.

IV.i.125-32     Inserted foul sheet. Stage-direction '*The Witches Dance,
                and vanish*' presumably the book-keeper's, though again
                it is conflated, since '*Dance*' is evidently a substantive.

There is nothing to prove that the insertions were Shakespeare's original foul-papers, but there is no conceivable reason why they should have been anything else. The book-keeper's markings seem very light and may be more apparent than real. The absence of directions relating to the cries of the familiars in I.i and to machines, cave and cauldron in the later additions is surprising, and the names of the two songs, together with 'The Witches Dance', would have been as accessible to Shakespeare as to the book-keeper. That Shakespeare himself made the alterations in the body-text is suggested by the curious spelling '*Apparation*' which is identical with that found in *Cymbeline*, V.iv.30.

### iii

The remaining problem is the body-text itself since this goes back ultimately to the foul papers of 1606. Most critics assume that a transcript was made for actual theatrical use, and the position finally assumed by Greg was

> That behind F there lies a prompt-book of some sort is placed beyond reasonable doubt by two further considerations. One is that the record of entrances and exits is almost complete, such deficiences as there are being, if necessary, attributable to scribe and compositor. The other is that there is practically no inconsistency, much less ambiguity, in the designation of the characters. It is difficult to believe that any text printed from Shakespeare's foul papers could show such regularity.[3]
>
> [3] *The Shakespeare First Folio*, p. 395.

Greg does, however, remark that the misplacing of the torches and oboes at the beginning of I.vi is suggestive of foul papers and considers that certain of the author's directions might have been made more specific in a specially prepared prompt-book.[4] The appropriate comment on his conclusion would appear to be that regularity of marking in foul papers would be largely dependent on the use to which they were put.

Various points which have arisen in the preceding discussion argue somewhat against a theatrical transcript. If, as seems likely, the play was written at short notice for a special occasion, it is questionable whether there was sufficient time for a complete transcript to be prepared. A partial one may be admitted as a possibility and could account for the apparent discrepancy between the final act and the first four. The deletions, with dislocation, in I.ii and elsewhere, might, with caution, be cited as favouring foul papers, especially on the assumption that they were due to misgivings on the part of Shakespeare or the book-keeper. For I.ii to have assumed its present shape in a fair copy virtually entails that that copy was submitted to the Master of Revels, was marked by him, and was otherwise left unamended. Greg's remark about the consistent designation of characters can apply both ways. If foul papers were used as prompt-copy such adjustments as were necessary in the interests of clarity would certainly have been made. The designations are consistent and unambiguous, but they are, at the same time, extraordinarily casual. The scene-headings relating to Lady Macbeth and Lady Macduff have already been discussed. Had the consistency of *Coriolanus* or *2 Henry IV* prevailed the stage-direction '*Enter Macbeth as King*' in III.i would have conferred on him a different speech-heading throughout the remainder of the play, while his lady could, with advantage, have been designated 'Queen'. The discrepancies between 'Captaine' and 'Seriant' in I.ii, and between Witches and Weird Sisters are suspicious. There is no nominal distinction between the doctor of IV.iii and the 'Doctor of Physicke' of V.i and V.iii, though they are obviously not the same person. Various characters who might have been given names—the sergeant, the old man and the waiting gentlewoman—are left undefined, while new names are piled up oddly and almost unnecessarily in the last act. The whole of IV.ii is suggestive of foul papers. Here the dialogue is distributed between Ross, Wife and Son. The Messenger is unnamed, and the murderers' lines at the end of

---

[4] Not all commentators agree that the oboes and torches are misplaced. Cf. C. J. Sisson, *New Readings in Shakespeare*, II, p. 194.

the scene are not distributed as they are in III.i, and III.iii. Such irregularities are more in keeping with foul papers than fair copy, and the
book-keeper's failure to alter them could have been due simply to the
fact that they are not really misleading.

A number of stage-directions that are evidently of foul-paper origin
are preserved in the Folio and it seems doubtful whether these would
have survived both editing and transcription. Greg isolates the following as almost certain survivals:

I.ii.1        *meeting a bleeding Captaine.*
I.v.1         *Enter Macbeth's Wife alone with a Letter.*
I.vii.1       *Enter a Sewer, and diuers Seruants with Dishes and Seruice*
              *ouer the Stage.*
III.iv.1      *Banquet prepar'd.*
V.v.7         *A Cry within of Women.*
V.vi.1        *their Army, with Boughes.*

and adds several others which he thinks exhibit the vagueness that
sometimes occurs in foul papers:

II.iv.1       *Enter Rosse, with an Old man.*
III.1.44      *Exeunt Lords.*
III.iv.121    *Exit Lords.*
III.vi,1      *Enter Lenox, and another Lord.*
V.i.1         *Enter a Doctor of Physicke, and a Wayting Gentlewoman.*

These, taken in conjunction with the cursory use of proper names in
many of the other stage-directions and in speech-headings, represent a
substantial body of evidence.

If it could be shewn that the Folio preserves a large number of author-
spellings, the case for foul-paper origin would be considerably strengthened. Unfortunately our knowledge of Elizabethan and Jacobean
spelling habits is, at present, slight. There is irony in the fact that the
germ of Willoughby's important enquiry into the printing of the Folio
and of all that has followed therefrom was Satchell's orthographical
analysis of *Macbeth*. It was from this that the distinctive habits of
Jaggard's compositors A and B emerged, but a comprehensive account
of their respective orthographies remains a desideratum. Neither
compositor is likely to have retained MS. spellings deliberately, except
in proper-names and unfamiliar words, and these could, in any case,
also survive transcription.

Greg admits only one author-spelling,—that of 'Banquoh' (for

Holinshed's 'Banquho') at I.ii.34—but, if the spellings in the three pages of *Sir Thomas More* are relevant evidence, his view seems unduly pessimistic. Comparison between *Macbeth* and the three pages yields the following results:

i. *Preference for y over i*

Typical lines in *More* are:

> and that yo$^u$ sytt as kings in your desyres
> aucthoryty quyte sylenct by yo$^r$ braule.

The same preference is shewn in 'Aroynt', 'Ronyon', 'Syue', 'sayle' and 'tayle' in I.iii.6–9 and these lines are fairly representative. Several proper-names in both dialogue and stage-directions apparently represent Shakespeare's own deviations from Holinshed: 'Glamys' (H:˙Glammis'), 'Byrnan(e)' (H: 'Birnane'), 'Seyward' (H: 'Siward') and 'Seyton'. The compositorial variants 'weyward' (A) and 'weyward' (B) are conclusive for a MS. spelling 'weyard' or 'weyerd'.

ii. *ns(nc) for nce*

'Fleans' is analogous to such *More* spellings as 'obedyenc', 'insolenc' and 'scilens'.

iii. *s for ss*

'Envernes' and 'Cathnes' resemble *More*: 'stilnes' and 'trespas'.

iv. *ea for e*

*Macbeth* has 'Least' for 'Lest' at II.iv.38: cf. *More*, 'hearing' (sc. herring) and 'sealf'.

v. *ff for f*

'Fiffe' at I.ii.48 (elsewhere 'Fife' as in Holinshed) reflects the same habit as 'Beeff' and 'loff' (sc. loaf) in *More*.

vi. *o for oa*

*Macbeth* has 'rost' (sc. roast) at II.iii.18 and elsewhere 'Approch' and 'approches': cf. *More*, 'loff', 'costs' (sc. coasts) and 'throt'.

vii. *Single consonant for double*

*More* has single medial consonants in 'Comaund' and 'topt'. *Macbeth* V.vii.6 'hoter' is analogous, as are 'Glamys' and 'Glamis' (Holinshed:

'Glammis'). The same holds for 'Lenox', though Holinshed's form is 'Leuenox'.

Obviously little reliance can be placed on isolated spellings of commonplace words, but there can be little doubt that the Folio preserves Shakespearian spellings of most of the proper-names. One curious and not insignificant feature is that Shakespeare evidently began with the Holinshed form but thereafter followed his own inclinations. Thus 'Banquoh' appears only at I.ii.34 and is thereafter replaced by 'Banquo',[5] 'Fleance' becomes 'Fleans' after III.i, and 'Glamis' yields to 'Glamys' at I.iii.116. At IV.i.93 Shakespeare corrects Holinshed's 'Bernane' and 'Birnane' to 'Byrnam', but thereafter lapses into 'Byrnan', 'Birnane' and 'Byrnane'. The important point is that the same habit applies to three Folio texts which are held to have been set from foul papers. In *Antony and Cleopatra* 'Camidius' (for Plutarch's 'Canidius') degenerates into 'Camidias' and 'Camindius', 'Cleopatra' lapses for a while into 'Cleopater' and 'Scarus' becomes 'Scarrus'. 'Ventidius' is named correctly at first but is subsequently 'Ventigius', and the character of the same name in *Timon of Athens* also starts correctly but afterwards varies between 'Ventigius', 'Ventiddius' and 'Ventidgius'. 'Apemantus' in the same play becomes 'Apermantus'. In *Coriolanus*, 'Auffidius' yields to 'Auffidious' and 'Sicinius' to 'Scicinius',[6] and the characters are given their full style at the outset but are thereafter referred to by a single name. In this respect, then, *Macbeth* closely resembles three Folio texts of foul-paper origin.

It is highly probable that author-spellings of certain unfamiliar words are preserved in the Folio. The clearest example, despite compositor A's fatuous attempt at emendation, is 'weyard'. Other possible forms are 'Herbenger', 'Lymbeck' 'Centinell', 'schreame', 'Nonpareill', 'Grewell', 'Cesterne' and 'Rubarb'. It is likely too, that such corruptions as 'Gallowgrosses', 'Barlet', 'Banke and Schoole', 'sowre and firme-set' and 'Cyme' arose from abnormal spellings which baffled the compositors.

This body of evidence, though anything but decisive, does at least afford some support to the view that the body-text of the Folio *Macbeth* was a fairly orderly set of foul papers, edited systematically but not exhaustively, and used as prompt-copy. There is, strictly, little or no

---

[5] 'Banquoh', *pace* Greg, is not really likely to be an author-spelling. It is more probably compositor A's error for 'Banquho.'

[6] The 'sc' is Shakespearian: cf. 'Scicion' and 'Scilens' and, of course, 'scilens' in *Sir Thomas More*.

evidence in favour of an intervening transcript, and to assume anything of the kind is probably to assume more than the necessities of Jacobean production would warrant.

iv

In so far as the preceding findings prove acceptable, editorial procedure must inevitably proceed along lines different from those which have hitherto prevailed. Foul-paper origin must be admitted as a possibility that has at least parity with the theory of an intervening transcript, and the present case that both original play and revisions were solely the concern of Shakespeare and the book-keeper establishes an altogether more straightforward and reassuring view of the Folio text, whose imperfections must, in the main, be attributed to Jaggard's compositors. It is permissible to express the provisional view that, on the whole, both compositors dealt reasonably faithfully with their copy. Compositor B, whose settings from Quarto copy are negligent and high-handed, appears to have been more attentive when dealing with MS. and it is not easy to convict him of more than about three dozen errors in eleven and a half pages (f. 135: ff. 141b-51). The majority of his errors were evidently due to carelessness, and his treatment of final -e and final -s is notably erratic. Compositor A evidently found the MS. harder to decipher, and his stints (ff. 131-4; ff. 136-141a) include several of the major cruxes. His errors for the nine and a half pages would seem to total about twenty, but there may be more. It is clear that he found I.ii heavy going, possibly because of the deletions, and editorial vigilance is called for.

On the assumption that there were deletions in I.ii, iii and iv, the present-day editor would be justified in using dots freely, but it is questionable whether he is at liberty to add to the existing number of emendations. There is every reason why the two songs should be incorporated in the main text since they were clearly an integral part of the play in its later form, and since songs, whether or not Shakespeare wrote them, are normally set out in full in both quartos and Folio. Supplementation of the Folio stage-directions is justifiable.

# four

# *Troilus and Cressida*

## The Multiplicity of Problems

### i

*Troilus and Cressida* is exceptional in that two of its main problems, those of performance and category, were troublesome even to Shakespeare's contemporaries. The first record of the play is that of the Stationers' Register for 1603:

> 7 februarii. Master Robertes. Entred for his copie in full Court holden this day to print when he hath gotten sufficient aucthority for yt, The booke of Troilus and Cresseda as yt is acted by my lord Chamberlens Men vj$^d$

A second entry was made in 1609:

> 28$^{vo}$ Januarii. Richard Bonion Henry Walleys. Entred for their Copy vnder thandes of Master Segar deputy to Sir George Bucke and master warden Lownes a booke called the history of Troylus and Cressida. vj$^d$

Nothing appears to have come of Roberts's entry, but Bonian and Walley promptly followed theirs with a quarto whose title-page announced:

> The/Historie of Troylus/and Cresseida./As it was acted by the Kings Maiesties/seruants at the Globe./Written by William Shakespeare.

Prior to publication this title-page was replaced by a cancel which amended the main title to:

> The/Famous Historie of /Troylus and Cresseid./Excellently expressing the beginning/of their loues, with the conceited wooing/of Pandarus Prince of Licia./Written by William Shakespeare.

The cancel also added a curious epistle, headed 'A neuer writer, to an euer reader. Newes.', claiming that 'you haue heere a new play, neuer stal'd with the Stage, neuer clapper-clawd with the palmes of the vulger' and referring airily to 'the scape it hath made amongst you', which was apparently contrary to 'the grand possessors wills'. There is, finally, the Folio text with the head-title 'The Tragedie of Troylus and Cressida', which also serves for the running-title on the two pages following. Thereafter the style for the running-title is simply 'Troylus and Cressida'.[1]

Whatever difficulties existed at the Folio stage it is clear that Heminge and Condell, or whoever was responsible for breaking the plays down into three categories, had no doubt that the rightful place for *Troilus and Cressida* was among the tragedies, but this is strangely at odds with the 1609 Epistle's claim that it is 'passing full of the palme comicall' and that among Shakespeare's comedies 'there is none more witty then this'. Equally perplexing is the Epistle's insistence that this was 'a new play' since Roberts, who should have known, entered it as part of the Chamberlain's current repertoire and since the original title-page is even more specific in stating that it was performed 'at the Globe'. On the face of things it does look as if the cancel was inserted because Bonian and Walley discovered that they had been misinformed, but, disregarding other difficulties for the moment, it is not easy to see why Roberts, in 1603, should have been mistaken.

Peter Alexander's theory that the only performance had been at an Inn of Court has won general acceptance.[2] It certainly explains why the play had never been staled with the stage or clapper-clawed with the palms of the vulgar. It accords, too, with the general character of a play which, as Dr. Alice Walker excellently remarks, 'is a *tour de force* in forensic oratory', and which also contains a measure of salacious wit admirably suited to such an occasion. Moreover, the 1609 Epistle, with its series of quibbles on legal terms, obviously takes cognisance of such a performance. Alexander's explanation, then, commands acceptance though it does leave one problem unresolved, namely the connexion between the play written and presumably performed *c.* 1602 and the highly legal Epistle of, apparently, 1609.

It is possible that the Epistle relates to an Inn of Court revival of *Troilus and Cressida* in or about 1608, but this seems unlikely in view of the fact that the play, whatever its enduring qualities, contains much that was allusive and highly topical in 1602 but very doubtfully so in 1608. This applies especially if, as many critics have believed, it was at

---

[1] At the Folio stage it was first proposed that the play should follow *Romeo and Juliet*, and the first three pages were set. Copyright difficulties arose and *Timon of Athens* was substituted. The difficulties were resolved only after the *Catalogue* had been printed and *Troilus and Cressida*, mainly unpaged, was inserted at the last minute between *Henry VIII* and *Coriolanus*. The pages previously set, though in part reset, retained the original head- and running-titles: the remainder were given the abbreviated running-title.

[2] 'Troilus and Cressida 1609,' *The Library*, 4 (1948), ix, p. 267.

one stage connected with the War of the Theatres which had quite run its course by 1603. The alternative explanation is that the Epistle belongs rather to the original performance than to the 1609 publication, and this, though nothing can be established, merits consideration.

The early plays of Jonson, Marston and others shew that at the turn of the century it was a common habit for plays to begin with a certain type of prologue or induction which skimmed lightly but topically over the activities of actors and playwrights, and the Epistle, with its extended and not wholly serious appraisal of Shakespeare's comedies and its special commendation of what may be a temporary phase of *Troilus and Cressida*, conforms with this practice. If, in fact, it was originally not an Epistle at all but a special prologue, spoken by an actor dressed as a lawyer, it would have been reasonably analogous to, for instance, the prologue to *The Two Angry Women of Abingdon*, in which 'a poore Scholler' commends the author and his play.

The Epistle, with one or two trivial changes, would certainly have fitted the occasion. Its legal puns, 'commedies . . . Commodities', 'Playes . . . Pleas', 'a new English Inquisition', 'the grand possessors wills', would all have been apt, and the insistence on the novelty of the play would have had purpose. The assurance that 'it is a birth of your braine, that neuer vnder-tooke any thing commical, vainely' has a colloquial tone better fitted to the stage than to an elegant epistle,[3] and the reference to 'his representations' points to performance rather than print. It is legitimate to submit that in 'had I time I would comment vpon it', 'time' is what is required for the stage convention as opposed to 'space' for the epistolary. Even the initial 'neuer stal'd with the Stage' links the Epistle with the theatre rather than the printing-house.

Such a view imposes the not very difficult assumption that the title of the Epistle, together with 'Eternall reader', resulted from adjustment, and that the syntactically awkward parenthesis, '(for so much as will make you thinke your testerne well bestowd)', was thrust in in 1609. The references to 'the scape it hath made amongst you' and 'the grand possessors wills' are more difficult. They are usually held to indicate that publication was irregular but there appear to be no other grounds for such an assumption. All that the Epistle asks is that 'the grand possessors'[4]

---

[3] I take it that 'your' is here used colloquially. Greg, who proposed emendation to 'that', based his case on 'y$^t$' being misread as 'y$^r$'.

[4] In legal terminology, which is what matters here, possession signifies taking, holding or occupying something *without ownership*. The King's Men presumably owned *Troilus and Cressida*.

shall 'bee prayd for (for the states of their wits healths)', and this seems to link them with 'those grand censors, that now stile them such vanities'. The gibe is apparently aimed at those who denounced stage plays as vanities and schools of abuse. Both phrases merely sustain the run of legal wit and it is easy to see how the mere fact of performance on a particular occasion could be likened to a 'scape'.

This interpretation may not inspire confidence, but it is at least as intelligible as the traditional view. Regarded merely as a puff, the Epistle seems ineffectual and uneconomical, and it is equally so if treated as a disclaimer. All that was needed was the substitution of some such formula as 'Never yet publicly performed' for 'As it was acted by the Kings Maiesties seruants at the Globe'. If, indeed, they deliberately sought to disclaim anything of the sort, Bonian and Walley were quite outside the general run of Jacobean publishers, several of whom made larger and wilder claims. The supposition that it was written by the person who supplied them with the manuscript has yet to account for a lapse of six years or so between the legal occasion and the legal Epistle. The whole thing, viewed in relation to 1609, has in fact a curious air of staleness about it. The allusions and the Euphuistic touches seem distinctly out of date, as does the commendation of the comedies of a dramatist who, for some six years or more, had not been exactly not-able for his 'sauored salt of witte'.

There is finally the matter of the Folio Prologue, which, since it was omitted from the Quarto, cannot have been available to Bonian and Walley or their intermediary. The 'Prologue arm'd', which, on internal evidence, must have been written c. 1602,[5] is undeniably effective as the prelude to heroic action and its informative character renders it a necessary preliminary to public performance. Its sombre and massive verse, moreover, sets the key, if not for profound tragedy, at least for serious and impressive action. But the occasion postulated by Alex-ander was essentially a light-hearted one with, as the Epistle implies, emphasis on 'the palme comicall', and the substitution of a frivolous prologue, not by Shakespeare, seems logical enough. The real difficulty, whatever view is taken of its true character, is in accounting for the omission of the Epistle in the initial Quarto printing. One possibility is

---

[5] The gibe at Jonson's *Poetaster* in the lines

> A Prologue arm'd, but not in confidence
> Of Authors pen, or Actors voyce,

would have been pointless at a later date.

ESP

that it was received after the rest of the copy, that Bonian and Walley decided to include it, with alterations, as being an integral part of *Troilus and Cressida*, and that finding it contradictory to their existing title-page they altered the latter.

This perhaps is to consider too curiously, and certain details of the whole transaction must inevitably remain shrouded in mystery. The Epistle could have been a transformed prologue, or it could equally have been written for inclusion, as a puff, in the quarto which Roberts hoped to publish in 1603.[6] The point is that there is nothing which establishes it as the product of 1609, and the evidence against so late a date is far from negligible. As testimony for or against public performance of *Troilus and Cressida*, the Epistle may therefore be entirely irrelevant.

There is a strong *prima facie* argument against the assumption that Shakespeare would have lavished so much of his finest and most careful writing on a play designed for a single occasion, however remunerative, and the criterion of common sense establishes that once a play was completed it normally went into the company's general repertoire. Chambers, who held that *Troilus and Cressida* was performed before 1604, cites echoes in Marston's *Dutch Courtesan* (c. 1603-4) and a linked reference in *Saint Marie Magdalens Conversion* (1603).[7] These suggest wider currency than a single Inn of Court performance could have provided. The introduction of Troilus and Cressida into *Histriomastix*, with an apparent pun on Shakespeare's name and what looks suspiciously like parody of V.vii and viii:

> Thy knight his valiant elboe weares,
> That When he shakes his furious Speare,
> The foe in shivering fearfull sort,
> May lay him downe in death to snort.

may also testify. The accepted date for *Histriomastix* is 1599, but it was a theatre-war play and therefore likely to have had topicalities thrust in from time to time.[8]

ii

The textual problems which confront editors are those which

[6] There would have been no need to disclaim anything in 1603, when the play was new and unstaled.

[7] *William Shakespeare*, I, pp. 442-3.

[8] Evidence for this is supplied by its abnormal division into six acts in the 1610 Quarto.

normally arise from collateral substantive texts. Many obscurities, particularly those relating to occasion and motive, remain, but the main lines of transmission appear to have been established. Alexander's contention,[9] based on comparison of the Quarto with the three pages of *Sir Thomas More*, that the former was set direct from foul papers may still have its adherents but Dr. Alice Walker has made out a formidable case for believing that the Quarto copy was in fact some kind of private transcript.[10] The view, also put forward by Alexander, that the Folio was set from a collated copy of the Quarto[11] has won general acceptance and has been confirmed by Philip Williams.[12]

These latter-day findings are editorially reassuring, but certain questions remain. It seems that future investigators will have little to add to Dr. Walker's account of the Quarto transcript, but the date and occasion of that transcript remain obscure. The supposition that it was specially prepared from the foul papers in 1608 or 1609 is, on the face of things, unlikely since it is evident that the foul papers themselves, as received by the transcriber (X), were quite free of any theatrical markings. Unless therefore the play remained unperformed in the public theatres, and with no intention on the part of the company that it should be performed, the transcript must have been made at a very early stage, probably in 1602. This does not clear up the mystery of the Epistle or of the scholarly touch, 'Pandarus, Prince of Licia', on the title-page of the cancel, but, as will be shewn, these are of a piece with the character of the transcript itself, and point to a single agent at a single time.

The general .impression appears to be that the Quarto which served as Folio copy in 1623 had been specially collated to that end, so that Jaggard, after a false start, should after all be able to print an authoritative text. Collation resulted in the recovery of a large number of stage-directions, and this might suggest that the marked Quarto had itself served as the official prompt-copy. This, however, in view of its failure to correct a number of errors and of the curious character of some of its recoveries is not tenable. Hence there is no real alternative to the view that, in the cause of presenting the plays 'absolute in their

[9] *loc. cit.*
[10] *Textual Problems of the First Folio*, pp. 68-93. See also her edition of *Troilus and Cressida* (New Shakespeare), pp. 122-34.
[11] *loc. cit.*
[12] 'Shakespeare's *Troilus and Cressida*: the Relationship of Quarto and Folio', *Studies in Bibliography*, III, pp. 131-43.

numbers, as he conceived them', the Quarto was amended carefully, but not quite carefully enough, by reference to the authoritative copy.

### iii

There has been a general tendency for critics to assume that *Troilus and Cressida* underwent some sort of revision, but no clear or convincing picture has emerged. The disintegration theories with their tenuous theories of Shakespeare as reviser of Dekker and Chettle's play; of Shakespeare collaborating with an unknown dramatist; of the early play being rehandled by Chapman and Shakespeare and so forth, can be disregarded, though they are relevant in so far as they testify that the anomalous character of the play requires some explanation, but preferably a less desperate one. Aesthetic judgements are seldom in themselves a sufficient ground for postulating revision, let alone collaboration, though their ancillary value may be considerable. The primary requirement is to determine how far revision is a tenable hypothesis in the light of Quarto–Folio relationship.

# five

# *Troilus and Cressida*

## Quarto and Folio

i

The transmission process outlined in the preceding chapter provides a firm and much needed editorial policy, but an editor, faced with the numerous small variants between the two texts, is nevertheless called upon to draw distinctions so fine as to be uncomfortable. Thus, at IV.ii.13-14, the Quarto reads:

> Beshrew the witch! with venemous wights she staies
> As tediously as hell

but the adverb in the Folio is 'hidiously'. Most editors, quite reasonably, follow the Quarto, since 'tediously' accords well with the general sense of the passage. On the other hand, both hell and witches are thought of as being hideous rather than tedious, so that the Folio cannot be disregarded and can indeed be justified on the assumption that a correction was clearly marked in the copy-text. The alternative is to suppose that the compositor (A) set up 'hidiously' simply because he was inattentive. There are many variants which work both ways, and as many as nine explanations can be invoked to account for apparent perversions of the original. Some critics hold that there were irregularities in the foul papers at the composition stage due especially to Shakespeare settling for second thoughts but failing to delete first intentions. The theory of a special transcript must necessarily allow that the transcriber (X), being but human, was liable to misread and omit. It must also allow for a measure of sophistication on his part, with deliberate alteration or omission of obscure words and phrases. To these imperfections more would be added by Eld's compositors at the Quarto stage. Revisions may have been introduced into the prompt-copy by Shakespeare or the book-keeper at any time. When the copy was being prepared for Jaggard's use, it is likely that the collator (C) overlooked various Quarto errors and introduced a number of mistakes of his own. Jaggard's compositors A and B, when setting from print, were prone to error at the rate of one and a half and eight corruptions per page respectively. Finally, it is legitimate to surmise that casting-off resulted in omissions and deliberate bodging in the Folio text.[1]

Dr. Walker's important and challenging contributions to the study of *Troilus and Cressida* have been based on a clear recognition of these issues, and the text which she offers shews, at all points, a marked advance on the irrational eclecticism of earlier editors. Its uncertainties (and they cannot justly be termed more than that) arise through a reluctance to admit certain general principles, or so it would appear.[2] As these principles relate directly to the authority of the Folio and have some bearing also upon the character of the Quarto transcript, it will be convenient to review them here.

## ii

The view that Shakespeare's foul papers contained undeleted first thoughts has to be disregarded simply because it cannot possibly serve as the basis of a working hypothesis. The testimony of Heminge and Condell that 'wee haue scarse receiued from him a blot in his papers', which even the critical Jonson remembered as something 'the Players have often mentioned', cannot be lightly dismissed, and the three pages of *Sir Thomas More*, if Shakespeare's, go a long way towards vindicating the claims of those who best knew his habits. It is true that there are blots and deletions in the three pages, but the significant point is that the second thought followed so fast upon the first that deletion is virtually a matter of syllables. The following examples are representative:

> I [sh] Charg you keep the peace.
> [But] what you will haue them.
> You that haue voyce and Credyt w$^t$ the [Mv] number.

In the last of these the first thought was evidently 'multitude', discarded in favour of 'number' almost before it was conceived. The main point about the three pages is that a competent transcriber might have had

---

[1] As the original intention was to reprint the Quarto, this presumably served as the basis for casting-off, but some dislocation doubtless ensued when the collated copy, with its several recoveries, was substituted.

[2] It has seemed to me best not to comment on Dr. Walker's choice of individual readings since this would involve a full-scale review of her edition which would be out of place here. Where her readings are cited it is because they appear to have direct bearing on my own thesis.

difficulty in deciphering certain words,[3] that he would almost certainly have come to his own terms with the puzzling adjective 'momtanish', but that first and second shots would have given no trouble at all.

One conspicuous feature of the two texts is the similarity of graphic outline which characterises the majority of the variants. The following list is fairly complete, save for the omission of obvious accidentals:

|  | Quarto | Folio |
|---|---|---|
| I.ii.260 | an eye | money |
| I.iii.27 | broad | lowd |
| 31 | godlike | godly |
| 36 | ancient | patient |
| 110 | melts | meets |
| 165 | hem | hum |
| 219 | eyes | eares |
| 252 | seat | sence |
| 263 | restie | rusty |
| 267 | feeds | seekes |
| 276 | couple | compasse |
| 301 | proue | pawne |
| 302 | for-fend | forbid |
| 305 | sir | first |
| 368 | share | weare |
| II.i.50 | thrash | thresh |
| 133 | first | fift |
| II.ii.48 | hare | hard |
| 70 | soild | spoyl'd |
| 79 | pale | stale |
| II.iii.86 | sate | sent |
| 109 | composure | counsell |
| 204 | liked | titled |
| 212 | push | pash |
| 232 | praiers | praises |
| 260 | boord | bourne |
| 275 | call | cull |
| 277 | hulkes | bulkes |
| III.i.6 | notable | noble |
| 116 | lad | Lord |
| III.ii.23 | repured | reputed |
| 25 | tun'd | and |
| 167 | age | aye |

[3] R. W. Chambers's misreading of MS. 'pvince' (i.e. province) 'as 'prince' (see *Man's Unconquerable Mind*, p. 234) affords an apt example.

| III.iii.137 | fasting | feasting |
|---|---|---|
| 141 | shriking | shrinking |
| 160 | him, most | hindmost |
| 198 | depth | deepes |
| IV.ii.14 | tediously | hidiously |
| IV.iv.26 | strain'd | strange |
| 56 | throate | the root |
| 81 | portion | person |
| IV.v.61 | ticklish | tickling |
| 73 | misprising | disprising |
| 93 | breath | breach |
| 133 | day | drop |
| 178 | earth | Oath |
| 292 | my Lord | she loued |
| V.i.4 | curre | core |
| 35 | sleiue | Sleyd |
| 62 | faced | forced |
| V.ii.10 | sing | finde |
| | Cliff | life |
| 41 | distruction | distraction |
| 82 | take | rakes |
| 118 | Court | coact |
| 134 | spoile | soyle |
| 173 | sunne | Fenne |
| V.iv.22 | scaling | scaled |
| 24 | strawy | straying |
| 41 | lust | luck |
| V.vii.10 | spartan | sparrow |

Where a Folio reading seems wholly unjustifiable, the obvious course is to hold Jaggard's compositors responsible, but the trouble is that there are very few Folio readings that cannot be justified and, to make matters worse, the same holds for the Quarto. The variant at IV.ii.14, discussed above, is a case in point, and the editorial uncertainty which this promotes extends to practically the whole list. Thus, at I.iii.301, the Quarto's

> Ile proue this troth with my three drops of bloud.

seems infinitely the better reading until we suddenly realise that the three drops of blood derive from the image of a pawnbroker's sign and that the Folio 'pawne' may well be correct. Normally, it seems, an editor should follow the Folio unless there are compelling reasons for preferring the Quarto. This, as a general principle (to which there are exceptions), rests on the fact that the vast majority of the Folio variants in this category represent *bona fide* corrections marked by C, while the graphic similarity indicates that the Quarto, though also subject to the aberrations of Eld's compositors, reproduces words which X had failed to decipher correctly.

The character of X's work now becomes apparent. Dr. Walker inclines to the view that he was 'a naïve transcriber', but this hardly fits the case. It is clear that certain words in the foul papers defeated him. He was able to decipher individual groups of letters but had to guess at the rest. The impressive feature is that, though he usually guessed wrongly, he nevertheless guessed intelligently. His readings, in short, almost always make very good sense, so much so that editors have often preferred them to what are apparently the authoritative but less attractive readings of the Folio. The extreme example of X's ingenuity is perhaps that provided by 'vnsalted leauen' at II.i.15. The Folio reading 'whinid'st' is a form of 'vinewed'st', corrupted by C or compositor B or both, and X evidently began by misreading 'vin' as 'vn', failed then to decipher the rest of the word, and ended by improvising.

X was above all concerned with extracting sense from the foul papers, and 'vnsalted' testifies to the occasional brilliance of his improvisation. But he must, at the same time, have known that it was wrong, and the further question which arises is whether he did not, from time to time, assume the role of improver. Of the readings listed above, 'restie', 'for-fend', 'curre', 'tun'd', 'strawy' and 'spartan' are all open to suspicion as representing not what Shakespeare wrote but what X thought that he ought to have written. To follow such a line is dangerous, if only for the reason that X, in this respect, would not have been so very different from the majority of editors. It will suffice to comment briefly on a handful of Quarto readings which give the impression that they may have been X's sophistications:

I.iii.92          *Corrects the influence of euill Planets*

Greg objects that the Folio 'ill Aspects of Planets euill' is jingling and tautological, and Dr. Walker concurs. This was perhaps X's view. The Folio is rhythmically more attractive.

I.iii.106          *The primogenitie and due of birth*

The Folio reads 'primogenitiue', but as 'Prerogatiue' occurs in the line which follows, X may have objected to the homoeoteleuton.

I.iii.267        *And feeds his praise, more then he feares his perill*

The Folio reads 'seekes', for which 'feeds' may be a misreading, but the latter word alliterates and adds a Euphuistic touch, so that it may be a deliberate attempt at improvement.

II.iii.185-6     *Kingdomd Achilles in commotion rages,*
                 *And batters downe himselfe.*

The Folio 'batters gainst itselfe' is vindicated by *Julius Caesar*, II.i.67-9:

> and the state of man,[4]
> Like to a little Kingdome, suffers then
> The nature of an Insurrection.

X either failed to understand the transferred pronoun or objected to the figure.

III.ii.142       *My very soule of councell*

The Quarto sounds well, but the Folio 'My soule of counsell from me' expresses the sense more clearly. X presumably objected to 'from me' following 'from my' in line 141.

IV.i.40-1                    *I constantly beleeue,*
                 *(Or rather call my thought a certaine knowledge)*

X evidently objected to the Folio 'doe thinke' as antecedent to 'thought'.

IV.v.187       *Despising many forfaits and subduments*

The Folio 'And seene thee scorning' is clearly eorrect since the whole speech turns on 'I haue . . . seene' which is several times repeated. X evidently objected to such repetition.

The impression that X was a pedantic transcriber, with his own ideas of decorum, is strengthened by the Quarto's omission of several passages which the Folio recovers. Few of these passages can be regarded as later additions to the play. The following are relevant:

(a) I.iii.70-4
    Speak Prince of *Ithaca*, and be't of lesse expect:
    That matter needlesse of importlesse burthen
    Diuide thy lips; then we are confident
    When ranke *Thersites* opes his Masticke iawes,
    We shall heare Musicke Wit, and Oracle.

                 [4] 'state of a man' (Folio).

(b) I.iii.354-6
Which entertain'd, Limbes are in his instruments,
In no lesse working, then are Swords and Bowes
Directiue by the Limbes.

(c) II.iii.59-65
*Patro.* You rascall.
*Ter.* Peace foole, I haue not done.
*Achil.* He is a priuiledg'd man, proceede *Thersites,*
*Ther. Agamemnon* is a foole, *Achilles* is a foole, *Thersites* is a foole, and as
aforesaid, *Patroclus* is a foole.

(d) II.iii.80-2
Now the dry Suppeago on the Subiect, and Warre and Lecherie confound
all.

(e) III.iii.161-3
Or like a gallant Horse falne in first ranke,
Lye there for pauement to the abiect, neere
Ore-run and trampled on.

(f) III.iii.197
Knowes almost euery graine of Plutoes gold.
(Quarto: Knowes almost euery thing)

(g) IV.iv.79
Their louing well compos'd, with guift of nature.

(h) IV.iv.146-50
*Dio.* Let vs make ready straight.
*Æne.* Yea, with a Bridegroomes fresh alacritie
Let vs addresse to tend on *Hectors* heeles:
The glory of our *Troy* doth this day lye
On his faire worth, and single Chiualrie.

(i) IV.v.165-70
But thats no welcome: vnderstand more cleere
What's past, and what's to come, is strew'd with huskes,
And formelesse ruine of obliuion:
But in this extant moment, faith and troth,
Strain'd purely from all hollow bias drawing:
Bids thee with most diuine integritie, . . .

(j) IV.v.206
As they contend with thee in courtesie.

(k) V.ii.68
I will be patient, outwardly I will.

(*l*) V.iii.20-2
To hurt by being iust; it is as lawfull:
For we would count giue much to as violent thefts,
And rob in the behalfe of charitie.

(*m*) V.iii.58
But by my ruine.

(*n*) V.x.21-2
      But march away,
*Hector* is dead.

Several of these passages are textually unsatisfactory, and allowance must be made for the possibility that crabbed marginal additions gave considerable trouble to Jaggard's compositors.[5] The final lines (*n*), like certain Folio additions reserved for later discussion, may indicate revision. The pointless half-line (*m*) looks more like a substitution than an addition, so that the compositor (A) may have misinterpreted a marginal entry directing him to print.

> Nor you my brother, with your true sword drawne
> Oppos'd, but by my ruine, should stop my way.

in place of the Quarto's inept 'Oppos'd to hinder me'. There is reason to suppose that the compositors misread or misinterpreted marginalia at other points. At IV.iv.81, neither the Quarto 'portion' nor the Folio 'person' inspires confidence, whereas 'passion' would fit the sense admirably, and similarly at V.i.62 'sauced' seems a more apt reading than either the Quarto 'faced' or the Folio 'forced'. What is perhaps the most drastic variant in the whole play occurs in IV.v.271-6 which, in the Quarto, reads:

> First all you Peeres of Greece, go to my tent,
> There in the full conuiue we: afterwards
> As *Hectors* leisure, and your bounties shall
> Concurre together, seuerally entreate him
> To taste your bounties, let the trumpets blowe,
> That this great souldier may his welcome know.

At line 275 'To taste your bounties' is replaced by 'Beate lowd the Taborins'. Since the Quarto reading is eminently sensible and Shakespearian, as attested by the tasting of bounties in *Timon of Athens*, I.i.277 and V.i.57, the obvious explanation is that compositor B mis-

---

[5] It has to be borne in mind that a Quarto does not provide much room for marginalia, especially for such extensive interpolations as (*a*), (*c*), (*h*) and (*i*).

took a stage-direction, 'Beate the Taborins', for a correction and justified the metre by adding 'lowd'.[6] The setting-up of production notes as dialogue belongs properly to revision and will be discussed later.

When all allowances have been made for printing-house irregularities there yet remains a good deal which must be laid to the charge of X, who evidently assumed the role of censor. It has already been suggested that he was not responsible for (*m*) and (*n*). The loss of a single line in (*k*) is unaccountable, and (*h*) looks more like a late addition than an omission. The remainder can all be attributed either to X's pedantry or to his bewilderment. Agamemnon's speech (*a*) is needed to break what would otherwise be an inordinately long speech by Ulysses, but it is cumbersome and contorted and its homoeoteleuton is inelegant. In (*b*), as Dr. Walker notes, there is prolonged metonymy, but the sense is again contorted, with a suggestion of oxymoron, and the obvious Folio errors suggest uncertainties in the foul papers. There is some justification for the exclusion of (*c*) on grounds of redundancy, though it may conform with the rules of disputation. In (*d*) Shakespeare's spelling of serpigo (cf. 'Sapego' in *Measure for Measure*, III.i.31) may well have baffled X completely. Some doubt attaches to (*e*) and Hanmer's 'abject rear' for the Folio 'abiect, neere' has been generally accepted. It is, however, possible to defend the Folio on the assumption that 'neere', as often, represents 'ne'er', the sense being that the gallant horse becomes a pavement for the abject creatures who, because they are abject, are never in danger of being trampled on. But in either case the rhetoric is far-fetched. The lost line (*g*) may have been an oversight since it is necessary to the sense, but the whole context is difficult and line 80 is wrongly rendered in both the Quarto and the Folio. At (*i*) X may well have decided that the welcome was excessive and distinctly obscure. In (*j*) 'contend', following 'contention' in the preceding line, smacks of oxymoron, and the same holds for (*l*).

There are, then, ample grounds for believing that X did not scruple to amend Shakespeare's meaning and to censor those rhetorical extravagances that were bound from time to time to occur in what is after all a highly rhetorical play. Jonson, it will be recalled, condemned the bombast in *Macbeth* and also cited the line

Caesar did never wrong, but with just cause.

[6] The variant is usually explained in terms of first and second thoughts, which argues remarkable mental transition on Shakespeare's part, or as revision, which assumes a certain want of discrimination.

as an example of 'those things, could not escape laughter', and it may be
conceded that several of the lines quoted above bear a family resemblance to that which Jonson stigmatised. Further light on Shakespeare's
occasional rhetorical contortions is shed by a passage in the three pages
of *Sir Thomas More*, written probably at about the time of *Troilus and
Cressida*.[7] What Shakespeare, after much apparent effort, contrived
was:

> to kneele to be forgyven
> is safer warrs, then euer yo[u] can make
> whose discipline is ryot; why euen yo[r] hurly
> cannot pceed but by obedienc what rebell captaine
> as mutynes ar incident, by his name
> can still the rout . . .

which the book-keeper, with a nice regard for what actors and
audiences can stand, promptly converted to:

> to kneele to be forgyven.
> tell me but this what rebell captaine . . .

It would seem, on the evidence of several of the Folio recoveries, that
X did exactly the same kind of thing.

### iii

On the basis of this evidence it may be claimed that the Quarto is,
in a sense, a revised text, but with X, and not Shakespeare, as the reviser.
X emerges as a critic and improver in his own right, and it may be
permissible to hazard the dangerous, but attractive, conjecture that he
was none other than Ben Jonson. The production of *Sejanus* in 1603
indicates that Jonson was in the service of the King's Men at about the
time when the transcript may be presumed to have been made, and his
subsequent break with the company would account for him retaining it.
The transcript itself shews precisely the kind of alteration and rejection
that accords with Jonson's expressed opinion of Shakespeare's style.
Dr. Walker has shewn that X tended to underline words of learned
origin, citing *Maxim, chaos, indexes, modicums, pia mater, moral philosophy, quondam* and *major*, and this habit is characteristic of Jonson's
own MSS.[8] Jonson's familiarity with *Troilus and Cressida* is suggested

[7] For the dating of the play and its additions see J. M. Nosworthy, 'Shakespeare
and *Sir Thomas More*', *The Review of English Studies* n.s. VI, pp. 12-25.
[8] *Textual Problems of the First Folio*, p. 84.

by the fact that in *Poetaster*, IV.i, he confuses Achilles with Neoptole-
mus, as Shakespeare apparently does at IV.v.142, but the gratuitous
information that Pandarus was Prince of Licia on the cancel title-page
reflects accurate classical knowledge of the true Jonsonian kind. The
Epistle is not demonstrably in his style, but the matter could well be his.
Its contempt for the vulgar is characteristic, as are also the gibe at the
critics and the reference to the Horatian salt, which figures in the
Prologue to *Volpone*.[9] The appeal to classical authority: 'It deserues such
a labour, as well as the best Commedy in *Terence* and *Plautus*' is striking
in the light of Jonson's later encomium;

> The merry *Greeke*, tart *Aristophanes*,
> Neat *Terence*, witty *Plautus*, now not please.

There is finally the question of Jonson's relationship with Bonian and
Walley in 1608-9, when they were just setting up in business. Several
of their ventures were ephemeral pamphlets, 'A most strange reporte of
Twoo monstrous births' in Devon, 'A true relacon of the birth of
Three monsters' in Flanders, together with other sensational disclosures of diabolical phenomena and God's judgment upon sinners.
Chapman's *The Tears of Peace* stands out in honourable isolation from
the bulk of their later entries in the Stationers' Register, while among
their earlier ones, three registrations made between January 26th, 1609,
and February 22nd, *The Case is Altered*, *Troilus and Cressida*, and *The
Masque of Queens* lend them an air of respectability to which they had
otherwise scanty claims. There can be little doubt that Jonson himself
supplied them with *The Masque of Queens* and also with *The Case is
Altered* of which he was apparently no more than part-author.[10] In
view of the other evidence cited, it is tempting to see him as factor for
the third play in the group.

Whether he was or not does not seriously affect the conclusion that
the transcript underlying the Quarto was, in a small measure, a
revision of Shakespeare's original. This may have some bearing on
editorial policy since, if correct, it removes authority from many of the
Quarto's most plausible readings and confers it upon the less dazzling
Folio ones. From the point of view of the present enquiry it is little
more than negative evidence, useful, however, in its segregation of
material which is not irrelevant to the theory of author-revision.

[9] I am indebted to Professor L. C. Knights for the *Volpone* parallel.
[10] For the argument that the play was a revised version of Jonson, Chettle and
Porter's *Hot Anger soon Cold* see my article 'The Case is Altered', *Journal of English
and Germanic Philology*, XV, pp. 61-70.

# six

# *Troilus and Cressida*

## The Shakespearian Versions

### i

The question of category still remains. Several critics have found *Troilus and Cressida* coherent and satisfactory as it stands, but judgments based on the assumption that Shakespeare deliberately embarked upon 'bitter' comedies or problem plays do not inspire confidence. At the same time, the student who turns to two recent editions only to find that Dr. Walker,[1] following Campbell, accepts the play as 'comical satire', while Sisson presents it as tragedy,[2] is not likely to emerge any the wiser. Nor is it possible to introduce a *tertium quid*. Unconvincing though the play may be when viewed purely as comedy or purely as tragedy, it is even less convincing as tragi-comedy.

The general impression is a contradictory one. Many of the secondary characters—Pandarus, Thersites, Ajax, Patroclus, Paris, Helen and even Cressida and Achilles—are more or less indifferent, being no more essentially comic than the secondary characters in *Hamlet*, no more essentially tragic than those in *Henry V*. In the actual presentation of them there is a perceptible emphasis on the comic, with, however, sufficient of the grotesque to admit of tragic interpretation. Troilus is, at most, a part-time comic character, but his earnestness of purpose is a permanent feature, and in the second half of the play his function seems purely tragic. The play may have been produced for the diversion of Termers, subject to the Lord of Misrule and flown with insolence and wine, but it is hard to believe that even they found anything to laugh at in Troilus's great speeches at IV.iv.35-50, V.ii.137-60 and V.x.11-31. The same holds for Ulysses, whose function is to establish and maintain a tragic fulcrum, and whose 'degree' speech is dubiously relevant to a predominantly comic action. He is consistently grave and thoughtful and the scenes in which he appears are sometimes long and serious, with little inclination towards the comic. The debate scenes, both Trojan

---

[1] *Troilus and Cressida* (The New Shakespeare), pp. x-xix.
[2] *ed. cit.*, p. 763.

and Greek, are in fact weighty in every sense, and the four main ones account for more than a thousand lines of the play. The death of Hector is unquestionably the critical moment in a tragic action, and his status as one of the Nine Worthies and principal heroic figure in what is by consent the greatest of epic stories makes it seem unlikely that Shakespeare would have presented him as anything less. Yet both Hector in V.viii and Achilles in V.vii and viii are travesties of their former selves, and the style of these scenes can only be regarded as conscious burlesque. The reader who can believe that utterances such as:

> Most putrified core so faire without:
> Thy goodly armour thus hath cost thy life.

or:

> Euen with the vaile and darking of the Sunne.
> To close the day vp, *Hectors* life is done.

or:

> Strike fellowes, strike, this is the man I seeke.
> So Illion fall thou: now Troy sinke downe;
> Here lyes thy heart, thy sinewes; and thy bone.

or:

> My halfe supt Sword, that frankly would haue fed,
> Pleas'd with this dainty baite;[3] thus goes to bed.
> Come, tye his body to my horses tayle;
> Along the field, I will the Troian traile.

represent Shakespeare's tragic practice at any period can obviously believe anything. There would be a strong case for relieving him of all responsibility for these scenes were it not for the fact that they are so palpably the work of the man who devised the 'very tragicall mirth' of Pyramus and Thisbe in *A Midsummer Night's Dream*.

Scene-by-scene analysis confirms the general impression that the play's effect is spasmodic and insecure. The prologue, despite its taunt at Jonson, promises serious action at the heroic level. The first two scenes tend towards comedy, but are otherwise non-committal, and I.iii is serious. II.i and iii are comic, with a serious scene intervening. III.i is comic, III.ii indifferent and III.iii serious, but with comedy introduced at the end. Act IV is serious throughout, save for Scene ii

[3] 'bed' Folio.

FSP

which is indifferent. Scenes i-iv of Act V are mixed, v and vi are serious, vii and viii are mainly burlesque, ix is serious, and x begins with tragedy and ends with comedy.

This insecurity is reflected in occasional peculiarities of various kinds. IV.iv.1-110 is one of Troilus's great scenes, yet, with the entry of Aeneas, Diomedes and the rest at line 111, the tone lapses deplorably. It can be argued that Shakespeare is seeking to emphasise the change that comes over Troilus but this does not wholly account for the wooden and unimaginative verse. The description of Ajax at I.ii.19-37 has a gratuitous look, and, as Chambers observed, it 'seems unnecessarily elaborate for its place, refers to "humours", and has not much relation to the character of Ajax as depicted in the play.' Such passages, once they become apparent, read rather like afterthoughts and, suspicion now aroused, the quest for other interpolations begins, with doubts, perhaps, attaching to certain speeches by Thersites which seem to exceed immediate requirements. In other words some species of revision is implied, and extreme caution becomes necessary.

ii

Such evidence as there is to support the view that Shakespeare revised *Troilus and Cressida* after 1603 has not yet been considered, and may be deferred for the moment. The immediate problem is to explain why the original play is such a bundle of contradictions and inconsistencies, and the only conceivable explanation, however unpalatable, is that Shakespeare changed his horses in mid-stream. What, then, is here envisaged is that, following upon *Hamlet*, he set to work upon another tragedy based on the pathetic story of Troilus and Cressida, utilising the Trojan War and the corruption in Greek and Trojan society as an eminently appropriate background. On the basis of the foregoing scenic analysis it is reasonable to surmise that he had written rather more than half the tragedy when he suddenly changed his plans and turned the whole thing into comedy. It is equally reasonable to suppose that the change was occasioned by a request from one of the Inns of Court for a play suitable for presentation as part of the customary Christmas revels. This, at any rate, offers a tenable working hypothesis, which is what *Troilus and Cressida*, both in its origins and its transmission, chiefly requires.

The argument for an originally tragic purpose can rest substantially on Shakespeare's source material. The Troilus and Cressida story, in whatever form, is obviously as much a cue to tragedy as that of Romeo and Juliet, and the Siege of Troy, with its ultimate Homeric authority, is no less so. Again it does no violence to probability to assume that Shakespeare's original intention was to make the death of Troilus the final catastrophe. Caxton's account shews that the circumstances attaching to the death of Hector in the play held, in reality, for Troilus, who was surrounded and held by the Myrmidons, slain by Achilles and dragged round the battle-field. The transferring of these circumstances to Hector, who, in Caxton, was speared by Achilles 'that came privily unto him', and the burlesquing of the whole episode is the clearest indication of Shakespeare's changed purpose.

If there was a change of plan, it virtually follows that Shakespeare staggered his existing tragic material, interpolating comic scenes and incidents at various points, and this procedure is credible in the light of the scenic analysis. It is impossible to offer any assured conjecture as to which passages were interpolated at this stage but the Ajax description in I.ii seems a fairly safe guess. At the beginning of II.iii both the Quarto and the Folio have the stage-direction '*Enter* Thersites *solus*', but the remaining directions in the scene are vague and defective, and lines 1-24 have the air of being something tacked on. The opening lines:

> How now *Thersites*? what lost in the labyrinth
> of thy furie?

look as if they were originally intended for some other character, though, unless there are also later irregularities, neither Patroclus nor Achilles would meet the needs. The poor lines at IV.iv.111-41 may also be additional. In the Folio they are preceded by the casual and in-accurate direction '*Enter the Greekes*', which the Quarto omits. A further addition for Thersites seems likely at V.i.95 foll. Both the Quarto and the Folio concur in printing an '*Exeunt*' after line 94. This should cover Thersites, yet he is left soliloquising, so that the scene ends without a stage-direction in the Quarto and with an absurd '*Exeunt*' in the Folio. For the rest, within the terms of reference of the present argument, it appears that Shakespeare finished off his metamorphosed tragic torso with a couple of scenes of deliberate burlesque, a few scraps of the original play, and gave the last word to Pandarus, whose appearance on the battle-field is the crowning inconsistency.

Other issues are involved. As with *Macbeth*, the occasional play may have been required at fairly short notice. This would account for the division of the final act into as many as ten short-winded scenes, and also for the cursory character of several of those scenes, which contrast so oddly with the carefully written material earlier in the play. All comical additions would inevitably embody a considerable number of topical allusions for the benefit of an audience of Termers, and it is probable that many of these would be directly to the stage-quarrel.

iii

Whether *Troilus and Cressida*, in its Revels guise, became a decisive contribution to the War of the Theatres remains obscure. In *The Return from Parnassus*, a Cambridge play of *c.* 1602 written possibly by John Day, Will Kempe is brought on to the stage (IV.iii) and made to refer to *The Poetaster* and to Shakespeare having given Ben Jonson a purge that made him beray his credit. It is generally agreed that, of Shakespeare's surviving work, *Troilus and Cressida* is the only play that could reasonably be regarded as the 'purge', and there is a fair amount of evidence, though of dubious weight. The linking of Troilus and Cressida with the name Shakespeare in *Histriomastix* has already been noted, but the point of this is by no means clear. The line at I.iii.73:

When ranke Thersites opes his Masticke iawes,

with its possible quibble on both 'mastix' and 'Marston' may imply that Thersites is a caricature of Marston, which, on linguistic grounds, he very well could be. This identification, however, would be more credible if the line were not omitted in the Quarto, which is more closely linked with the Revels performance than is the Folio. The presentation of Ajax, especially with the apparently interpolated description in I.ii, may be in mockery of Jonson whose credit, in view of the inevitable Elizabethan pun on Ajax (a jakes), would be literally berayed.

There is perhaps more in the 'purge' theory than the majority of modern critics allow but its exponents have failed to reach any generally acceptable conclusion. Thersites has been variously identified with Marston, Dekker and Jonson, Ajax with Dekker and Jonson, and Achilles with Jonson. Until firmer identifications are forthcoming, the allegorical significances, if any, must be left to take their chance.

One curious feature is that, in reshaping the play, Shakespeare appears to have gone in debt to Lyly, and especially to *Campaspe*. In both plays the conflict between love and military achievement is made central, with the triangle Troilus–Cressida–Diomedes corresponding to Alexander–Campaspe–Apelles. The subsidiary characters fall into two opposed groups, and there is a strange arithmetical correspondence since Shakespeare opposes eight Greek warriors to the five sons of Priam, while Lyly sets eight philosophers against five Macedonian warriors. Both dramatists present what is essentially a conflict of values, so that the characters are discursive rather than active, yet impatient for action. Thersites, as the privileged and irrepressible commentator, fulfils a function strangely reminiscent of that of Diogenes, and shares his capacity for abuse, cynicism and extravagant expression.

Songs are a conspicuous feature of Lyly's play, and call for no justification,[4] but the songs in *Troilus and Cressida* are difficult to account for, especially as they are assigned to Pandarus, of all people. They are quite unlike the songs that Shakespeare uses elsewhere, and can scarcely have constituted a musical embellishment. In tone and style they are distinctly Lylian, and may have been conscious parodies. It may, with caution, be urged that the general presentation of Pandarus is somewhat on Lylian lines. Lyly's interminable allusions to bees and honey inform Pandarus's speeches at various points. In the exchange with Helen in III.i, he is 'hony sweete Lord' and she, 'hony sweete Queene'', and his valedictory verses begin:

> Full merrily the humble Bee doth sing,
> Till he hath lost his hony, and his sting.
> And being once subdu'd in armed taile,
> Sweete hony, and sweete notes together faile.

For a play written *c.* 1602 *Troilus and Cressida* contains an abnormally large measure of Euphuism, notably in III.ii, IV.v, and sporadically throughout the last act. Troilus, Cressida and Pandarus all use it, and even Thersites lapses into it from time to time:

> With too much bloud, and too little Brain, these two may run mad: but if with too much braine, and too little blood, they do, Ile be a curer of madmen . . . to what forme but that he is, shold wit larded with malice, and malice forced with wit, turne him too: to an Asse were nothing; hee is both Asse and Oxe; to an Oxe were nothing, hee is both Oxe and Asse: . . . Aske me not what I would be, if I were not *Thersites*: for I care not to bee the lowse of a Lazar, so I were not *Menelaus*.

[4] Lyly's authorship of the songs printed for the first time in *Sixe Court Comedies* (1632) has been questioned, perhaps unnecessarily, since the earlier examplars shew that songs were an integral part of the original plays.

It is probable that Lyly's comedies returned to favour for a short while when the boys' companies were revived *c.* 1600, but these soon became involved in the stage-quarrel. Even so, the polemics of both Jonson and Marston leaned heavily on Lyly's earlier practice, and such plays as *Cynthia's Revels, Jack Drum's Entertainment* and *Histriomastix* have a curiously antiquated air. In the second of these Brabant Senior chides the children of St. Paul's because

> they produce
> Such mustie fopperies of antiquitie,
> And do not sute the humorous ages backs
> With cloathes in fashion.

In terms of the present hypothesis, a half-written tragedy, the apparent relics of which are maturely and consistently Shakespearian, was converted into a pasquinade which borrowed much from John Lyly and possibly from his imitators. That *Troilus and Cressida*, in this form, was, amongst other things, a general comment on the stage-quarrel is more than likely. Shakespeare, in *Hamlet*, had already referred to the quarrel, but the popularity of the 'little eyases', which for a time seems to have threatened the security of his own company, seems to have caused him graver concern. On the assumption that the Revels version of *Troilus and Cressida* developed this attitude, it is possible to see the play as a burlesque which launched specific attacks on the belligerents and which, by imitating Lyly's pattern, motives and language, provided Shakespeare's company with something which, in performance, would be received as an unflattering impersonation of the offensive little eyases. Such a function would not have been alien to Shakespeare's practice. The inner-plays in *Love's Labour's Lost, A Midsummer Night's Dream* and *Hamlet*, and such incidentals as Pistol's ranting, Nym's humours and the King Cambyses vein, all shew that his concern was to ridicule not merely a style of dramatic writing, but also performance methods.

Such an interpretation of *Troilus and Cressida* would be altogether more convincing if the play did not contain so much serious material representing Shakespeare almost at his best. The issue that has to be faced squarely is that about one-half of the play is tragedy or near-tragedy, the other half a mixture of comedy and burlesque, and that no serious attempt is made to reconcile these mutual contradictions. It is difficult to conceive any explanation that can stand as an alternative to the change of purpose proposed here, even though this hypothesis rests on so small a body of concrete evidence.[5]

## iv

All the evidence so far adduced accords with Alexander's theory. It seems that the Termers got very much the kind of play that they were accustomed to, with a full measure of salacious wit, topical allusion and pointed satire at the expense of playwrights and actors. The question is whether Shakespeare was content to let the matter rest there. The stage-quarrel was over and doubtless forgotten by 1603, so that all the topical jokes would by then have lost their point. Even so, Thersites, Ajax and the rest are made of enduring stuff, and it is natural to suppose that *Troilus and Cressida*, perhaps after a lapse of several years, found its way once again into the King's Men's repertoire, but now addressed to its original tragic purpose.

There is strong evidence for this view in the stage-directions of Quarto and Folio. The Quarto shews that in the transcript, made from what may have been a somewhat untidy set of foul papers at the time of the Revels performance, the stage-directions were extremely scanty, though doubtless sufficient to meet the needs. Yet the Folio, based on matter drawn from those same foul papers, adds more than fifty directions. It is unthinkable that X, who was a conscientious transcriber, omitted them through oversight or caprice, and it therefore follows that they were not in the foul papers at the time of transcription. The insertion of '*Enter Pandarus*' at I.ii.36, that is on one of the three un-collated pages of the Folio, may have been a happy inspiration of compositor B, but it is highly unlikely that either the compositors or the collator supplied the remainder. The character of certain amended directions rules out any such possibility. At II.ii.96 the Quarto stage-direction reads '*Enter Cassandra rauing*' whereas the Folio prints '*Enter Cassandra with her haire about her eares*' and at III.iii.37 the Quarto has 'Achilles *and* Patro. *stand in their tent*', while the Folio has '*Enter* Achilles *and* Patroclus *in their Tent*' For either collator or compositor to have made this kind of alteration would have been utterly pointless, and the inevitable conclusion is that they were

---

[5] The problem of localities in this play is one which I do not feel competent to handle in detail, but I think it possible that such confusion as exists may have arisen through one part of the play having been designed for the Globe, the other for an indoor stage.

> My selfe will straight aboord, and to the State,
> This heauie Act, with heauie heart relate.

or:

> And then to Rome. Come Dolabella, see
> High Order, in this great Solemnity.

but this may be illusory, and the small Folio addition at lines 21-2 calls for notice. Lines 23-31 are, in a sense, superfluous. Having observed that 'there is no more to say', Troilus pauses and then proceeds to utter what, for lack of implementation, seem wild and whirling threats prompted by uncertainty rather than decision. If Shakespeare had carried the play on to the death of Troilus they would be quite intelligible, but have no perceptible relevance in either the Revels play or in the assumed revision which aimed at converting the occasional comedy into something fitted to general use with as little alteration as possible. Hence it may be suggested that, in the later revision, Shakespeare noticed the futility of including a passage which gave promise of an action to which he no longer wished to proceed and accordingly made the addition at lines 21-2 in order to provide a suitable final couplet:

> Scarre Troy out of it selfe. But march away,
> *Hector* is dead: there is no more to say.

This explanation is, admittedly, not without difficulties. At line 21, the Quarto reads:

> Scarre Troy out of it selfe, there is no more to say.

so that, unless an alexandrine was intended, there must either have been deletion in the foul papers or omission by X. The distinctions are impossibly subtle but fortunately do not affect the contention that Pandarus was transferred and his epilogue omitted. Lines 32-57 were apparently not deleted in the foul papers, but Shakespeare (or the book-keeper) made the omission abundantly clear by substituting '*Exeunt*' (Folio: V.x.34[7]) for the Quarto '*Exeunt all but Pandarus*'.

Another Folio anomaly pointing to revision is that at IV.v.96. The Quarto reading:

> The yongest sonne of *Priam*, a true knight,

---

[7] It should properly appear after line 31 but was presumably carelessly entered in the Quarto copy-text.

is obviously correct, whereas in the Folio:

> The yongest Sonne of *Priam*;
> A true Knight; they call him *Troylus*;

not only wrecks the metre, but incorporates a half-line caught up from line 108. This duplication can hardly be laid to the charge of compositor A, and Dr. Walker's view that the words 'are a first thought, which Shakespeare at once discarded'[8] would account for their inclusion in the Folio but not for their omission in the Quarto, as in fact would her similar explanation of V.iii.113-15. It is altogether more likely that 'they call him *Troylus*' was added to the foul papers by Shakespeare to indicate an intended cut. Lines 97-107, like V.x.22-31, are expendable in the sense that they relate to an aspect of Troilus, his military prowess, which is not fully developed in the play as it stands. Ulysses's lines, admitting the cut, would read:

> The yongest Sonne of *Priam;* a true Knight;
> They call him *Troylus*; and on him erect,
> A second hope, as fairely built as *Hector*.
> Thus saies *Æneas*, one that knowes the youth,
> Euen to his inches: and with priuate soule,
> Did in great Illion thus translate him to me.

and this would clearly be quite adequate to the presumed needs of the revision.

It is arguable that the Folio anomalies at IV.v.96, V.iii.112 and perhaps V.x.21-2 are not the result of late revision at all, but original intentions which were discarded when the play was reshaped for the Revels performance. This would explain the extra-metrical Quarto line at V.x.21, but otherwise its cogency is very doubtful. It would imply that in the foul papers, as they reached X, there were at least two contradictions which X resolved first by looking ten lines ahead and then by looking several scenes ahead, thereby shewing a remarkable grasp of Shakespeare's intentions. It is, moreover, one thing to suppose that these anomalies stood in the original foul papers but quite another to suppose that the Folio's fifty-odd additional or amended stage-directions were there as well. There is also the handful of Quarto-Folio verbal variants to suggest later re-working of the foul papers.

[8] *ed. cit.*, p. 206.

V

It may be protested that the argument presented here heaps conjecture upon conjecture. Unfortunately the very nature of the play
makes this inevitable, and any hypothesis must stand or fall according
to its capacity for resolving the very complex problems. These are such
that conjecture begins the moment we designate the play either comedy
or tragedy. The Inn of Court performance and X's transcript, though
supported by reputable evidence, are nevertheless conjectures. Of the
various new theories propounded here those relating to the Epistle as
refashioned prologue and to Jonson as transcriber and factor are perhaps
the most vulnerable, but neither invalidates the main thesis.

The situation here envisaged is that c. 1602 Shakespeare began working on a tragedy which was to handle the love-story of Troilus and
Cressida, using the defection of Cressida and the slaying of Hector as
its principal climaxes and the death of Troilus as its catastrophe. When
the play was well advanced, but very far from complete, he was invited,
by one of the Inns of Court, to supply a comedy suited to their annual
revels, possibly at short notice. He complied by interpolating comic
material and topical allusion into his existing draft of Troilus and
Cressida and adding burlesque scenes in the final act. This play was
performed and a transcript made. In 1609 this transcript was made
available to Bonian and Walley and a quarto was published. The fact of
publication may have led Shakespeare to contemplate a stage revival, or
the idea may have come earlier. At any rate, he evidently went through
the original foul papers with that end in view, accepting the Revels
version as more or less a *fait accompli* but endeavouring to emphasise the
serious and heroic side of the story.[9] Hence, he restored the original
Prologue, marked a cut in IV.v, brought the rejection of Pandarus
forward to V.iii, indicated a possible alternative ending and dispensed

---

[9] The suggestion that Shakespeare, as a matter of convenience, was prepared both
to degrade and to rehabilitate the Homeric story may seem absurd, but, as T. J. B.
Spencer has forcibly argued ("'Greeks" and "Merrygreeks'": *Essays on Shakespeare and Elizabethan Drama in Honor of Hardin Craig*, pp. 223-33) the Elizabethans
were far from being philhellenists and Homer had 'his Scaligerian detractors'. That
the tale of Troy was the one which Shakespeare chiefly loved is inherently probable, but his affection for it doubtless derived from Latin, specifically Virgilian,
sources, and there is no reason to suppose that he regarded the *Iliad* as sacrosanct.
In short, the Troy story, like the tale of Lear or the nominally tragical history of
Henry the Fourth, was something which he felt free to trim according to mood or
the needs of the occasion.

with the Epilogue. It is possible that he made verbal changes here and there, and some, if not all, of the additional and amended stage-directions are almost certainly his.

Whether the revised foul papers became the basis of an actual revival is another matter. The scenic revision that can be deduced from Quarto-Folio comparison is not very extensive, and the augmented stage-directions, though numerous, are by no means full. Dr. Walker's view that 'they are not such as to suggest that the foul papers had been prepared for use as prompt copy' seems correct.[10] Shakespeare perhaps came to feel that he was flogging a dead horse, so that his final intentions were thwarted just as his original ones had been. It may be that Coleridge shewed an intuitive grasp of those unrealised intentions when he defined the play as 'a grand heroic piece in the robust style of Albert Dürer'.

The editorial position remains complex. Partial revision does not justify an editor in carrying out what he may assume to have been Shakespeare's abandoned intentions, so that the anomalies at IV.v.96 and V.viii.113-15 can have no claim to a place in the text. The additional stage-directions are clearly required, though supplementation is necessary. The real difficulties arise in connexion with the choice of variant readings. If the present demonstration is correct, there would appear to be no escape from the conclusion that authority rests consistently with the Folio since that text derives indirectly from both the original and the revised foul papers, and recourse can confidently be made to the Quarto only when there is reason for believing that Jaggard's compositors were guilty of error. This may impose some nice distinctions, but any editor who accepts the present thesis will at least have the comfort of knowing that he is right if he interprets *Troilus and Cressida* as comedy, and equally right if he takes it for tragedy.

[10] *ed. cit.*, p. 139.

seven

# The Merry Wives of Windsor

## Traditions and Problems

i

The main traditions attaching to *The Merry Wives of Windsor* are that the play was written at Elizabeth's command, that the Queen herself stipulated that it should portray Falstaff in love and that composition occupied no more than a fortnight. The first and third of these traditions were given currency by Dennis in 1702, the first and second by Rowe in 1709, and all three by Gildon in 1710.[1] Though such claims, made a century after the writing of the play, cannot be trusted over-far, all have won wide acceptance, possibly on the ground that, if they did not already exist, it would be necessary to invent them. The play shews signs of hurried composition and, if the generally accepted date of 1600-1 is allowed to stand, little short of a royal command can account for the resuscitation of Falstaff who had passed into Arthur's bosom in *Henry V* in 1599.

A further tradition, originating with Richard Davies of Sapperton towards the end of the seventeenth century, is that the 'dozen white Luces' in I.i alludes to Sir Thomas Lucy. Davies reports that Shakespeare was

> much given to all unluckinesse in stealing venison & Rabbits particularly from Sᵣ Lucy who had him oft whipt & sometimes Imprisoned & at last made Him fly his Native Country to his great Advancemᵗ. but His reveng was so great that he is his Justice Clodpate and calls him a great man & yᵗ in allusion to his name bore three lowses rampant for his Arms.[2]

This story, though Davies's knowledge of both Shakespeare and the play was obviously extremely hazy, was repeated by Rowe and is still current, despite the fact that it was shewn by Malone and confirmed by J. S. Smart[3] that Sir Thomas Lucy never owned a deer-park. In 1931 Leslie Hotson identified Shallow with Justice William Gardiner

[1] See E. K. Chambers, *William Shakespeare*, II, pp. 261-3, 265-8.
[2] *ibid.*, p. 257.    [3] *Shakespeare: Truth and Tradition*, pp. 94-6.

of Southwark and Slender with his stepson, William Wayte, who on November 29th, 1596, craved sureties of the peace against Shakespeare, Francis Langley, lessee of the Swan Theatre, and others.[4] Since Gardiner married a Frances Lucy and impaled three luces in his coat-of-arms, the general grounds for Hotson's identification appear to be sufficient.

A further personal allusion has been seen in the curious 'three sorts of cosen garmombles' (Quarto F4v: Folio IV.v.79, 'three Cozen-Iermans'). In 1839 Charles Knight suggested that this refers to Frederick, Count of Mömpelgart's visit to England in 1592.[5] Mömpelgart, who became Duke of Württemberg in 1593, aspired to the Order of the Garter, and his hopes were kept alive by Elizabeth's half-promises. Ambassadors were sent to urge his claim, and he was elected to the Order *in absentia* on April 23rd, 1597. Despite protests and a further embassy, he was still unable to obtain his insignia, and the investiture was eventually granted by James in November 1603. Throughout the whole proceedings the Duke or his agents appear to have had trouble over horses, so that the horse-stealing episode in *The Merry Wives*, linked with Germans and the Quarto's apparent play on the name of Mömpelgart, certainly appears to be a direct allusion. On the other hand, too much reliance cannot be placed on a single reading preserved in a carelessly printed text deriving from a garbled report, especially as the Folio supplies a natural and intelligible variant.

A further identification, that of Falstaff with Sir John Oldcastle, calls for little comment here since it relates more strictly to the historical plays. Alleged puns on the word 'castle' found here and there in the play do not carry any weight as they are used indiscriminately. Oldcastle's descendant, Lord Cobham, evidently objected to the disguised Ford's use of his family name of Brooke, so that the 'Brooke' of the Quarto appears as 'Broome' in the Folio.

ii

The composition date for *The Merry Wives of Windsor*, since it cannot entirely be dissociated from the traditions and supposed allusions, has been much disputed. Conservative opinion inclines to 1600-1, but Hotson, basing his case on the death of Gardiner on November 26th, 1597, and the Duke of Württemberg's election to the Garter in the same year, argues that the play was written for performance at the Garter

---

[4] *Shakespeare versus Shallow*, pp. 1-28, 85-92 and *passim*.
[5] *The Pictorial Shakespeare*, I, p. 144.

Feast held on St. George's Day, 1597.[6] This claim will not bear scrutiny. There is no reason why Shakespeare should not have worked off his grudge against Gardiner after the latter's death, especially if, as seems evident from Hotson's account, Gardiner's name was a by-word for infamy. The Duke of Württemberg and his ambition were a standing joke throughout the last ten years of Elizabeth's reign, and Garter Feasts were held at other times. If *The Merry Wives* was written for that of 1597 it is curious that there is no complimentary reference to George, Lord Hunsdon, who was elected on that occasion, since he had been installed as Lord Chamberlain on March 17th, 1597, and was obviously eligible for mention as the patron of Shakespeare's company.

The fact that *The Merry Wives* is not included in the list of Shakespeare's plays given by Meres in *Palladis Tamia*, published in or after September 1598, argues that the play had not yet been performed. It is true that Meres omits *Henry VI* and *The Taming of the Shrew*, but these were early pieces.[7] *Palladis Tamia*, here and elsewhere, shews clearly that its author aimed at being comprehensive and up to date, and the omission of a play presented on an exalted occasion some eighteen months previously is incredible. Certainly if *The Merry Wives* belongs to 1597 the tradition that Elizabeth imposed the theme goes by the board since she is scarcely likely to have become infatuated with a dramatic character who had not yet been created. The historical plays in fact appear to rule out any date prior to 1600 for *The Merry Wives*. The two parts of *Henry IV* are usually assigned, on good evidence, to 1597 and 1598, while the grounds for placing *Henry V* in 1599 are conclusive. Of the characters carried over to *The Merry Wives*, Pistol, Shallow and Falstaff's page first appear in *2 Henry IV*, and Nym is an innovation in *Henry V*. Unless there was a change in nomenclature this means that *The Merry Wives* was certainly later than the *Henry IV* plays. It may have preceded *Henry V*, but the general impression is that Shakespeare was turning three proven favourites, Pistol, Nym and Bardolph to further account. The revival of Falstaff is insignificant since Shakespeare was not required to fit him, or any other character, into a chronological scheme.

[6] J. Crofts in *Shakespeare and the Post Horses* also favours 1597, but his evidence, based on certain post-horse incidents and the feud between the Howards and the Earl of Essex, is inconclusive. William Green's preference for the same date in his recent *Shakespeare's 'Merry Wives of Windsor'* seems to arise from his acceptance of certain of the less happy speculations of Hotson, Crofts and Bracy.

[7] *The Taming of the Shrew* may in fact be included under the style of *Love's Labour's Won*, as Chambers (*op. cit.*, p. 326) suggests.

### iii

*The Merry Wives* was entered on the Stationers' Register on January 18th, 1602, to both John Busby and Arthur Johnson, to whom Busby assigned it. The reasons for simultaneous entry and transfer are obscure. In the same year a Quarto duly appeared bearing the flamboyant title-page:

> A Most pleasaunt and/excellent conceited Co-/medie, of Syr *Iohn Falstaffe*, and the/merrie Wiues of *Windsor./*Entermixed with sundrie/variable and pleasing humors, of Syr *Hugh/*the Welch Knight, Iustice *Shallow*, and his/ wise Cousin M. *Slender./*With the swaggering vaine of Auncient/*Pistoll*, and Corporall *Nym./*By *William Shakespeare,/*As it hath bene diuers times Acted by the right Honorable/my Lord Chamberlaines seruants. Both before her/Maiestie, and else-where.

The text, as presented here, runs to 1,624 typographical lines, that is about one-half the length of the Folio version. This brevity, combined with general incoherence, clearly shews that something is wrong, and there is no escape from the conclusion that Johnson's edition is one of those stigmatised by Pollard as 'Bad' quartos.[8]

The true character of the 1602 Quarto became apparent in 1910 when Greg, following a suggestion by Hart, closely analysed the text and found that a suspicious accuracy attaches to the Host of the Garter's part:

> Not only do we find the Host's part alone usually in more or less verbal agreement in the two versions, not only do we as a rule find the versions springing into substantial agreement when he enters and relapsing into paraphrase when he quits the stage, but when he disappears for good and all at the end of the fourth act (and the actor very likely went home or to the tavern) we find what remains of the play in a more miserably garbled condition than any previous portion.[9]

Greg concluded, therefore, that the Quarto text *in toto* was reported by the actor who had played the part of the Host, but subsequently admitted the possibility that the agent of the piracy was 'an independent reporter relying generally on mine Host's assistance'.[10]

[8] W. Bracy, *The Merry Wives of Windsor: The History and Transmission of Shakespeare's Text* (1952), claims that the Quarto is a stage-abridgement possessing independent authority. The untenability of his position is exposed in a detailed review by Greg (*Shakespeare Quarterly*, January 1953), and the theory may be disregarded.

[9] *Shakespeare's Merry Wives of Windsor 1602*, pp. xl-xli.

[10] *The Editorial Problem in Shakespeare*, p. 71.

GSP

The validity of Greg's main thesis cannot seriously be questioned, but he is wrong in speaking of the 'miserably garbled condition' of the last act. This section of the Quarto is in fact the only considerable section that is not miserably garbled for the very good reason that it clearly derives from a manuscript whose connexion with Shakespeare's comedy has not yet been defined. This warrants the tentative conclusion that the pirate, having by fair means or foul obtained a useful piece of MS., prevailed upon the Host-actor to supply a memorial report of the first four acts. Whether the resultant text served, or was intended to serve, as prompt-copy for provincial use is a moot point. In its Quarto form the play seems barely intelligible, let alone actable, and it may well have been that the stationers were answerable for the piracy. There would obviously have been a ready sale for a play presented before the Queen, especially if it was originally written at her command.

The Quarto was reprinted by Jaggard in 1619, with a reduced title-page, but neither this nor the original have any immediate connexion with the Folio version. The copy supplied to Jaggard for the Folio in 1621 is generally held to have been a transcript prepared by Ralph Crane, probably from the foul papers. Several of Crane's distinctive habits are apparent in the Folio text, namely careful division into acts and scenes, massed entries at scene-headings, free use of parentheses and lavish and illogical use of hyphens. From what can be deduced of Crane's practice, his transcript of *The Merry Wives* is likely to have introduced between thirty and sixty errors in the dialogue alone. Some of these may have been corrected by the Folio compositors, but they, in their turn, can be allotted at least fifty errors and probably many more.[11] The linguistic abnormalities of Caius, Evans and the Host are likely to have given trouble to both Crane and the compositors, and it is probable that the foul papers underlying the transcript had been well thumbed, if not mutilated. Editors have found it necessary to emend or supplement the Folio in the light of the Quarto at a number of points, and this is disturbing in view of the fact that the Quarto itself is such a hopelessly defective document. The Folio omissions, which may be numerous, could be attributed either to Crane's negligence or to actual

[11] Hinman's analysis (*The Printing and Proof-Reading of the First Folio of Shakespeare*, II, pp. 366-75) gives three pages (40-2) to A, ten (49-52, 54-6, 58-60) to B, and seven (39, 43-48) to C. Page 53 is indeterminate. The minimum estimate of fifty errors, though tentative, is based on the apparent performance of A and B with manuscript copy in *Macbeth* (see Chapter 3 *supra*), but if Dr. Walker's estimates for B are correct it is likely that allowance should be made for somewhere between a hundred and a hundred and twenty errors.

deterioration of the foul papers. In view of the length of the Folio
version it is improbable that there are extensive losses, but, all in all, the
only substantive text cannot be said to inspire confidence.

The play, as preserved in the Folio, has several unsatisfactory features.
The fact that it is almost entirely in prose can be disregarded. It is very
good prose, and if Shakespeare was working against time he may well
have decided to dispense with the laborious business of versifying. On
the other hand, the few verse passages that there are have little to
commend them save, here and there, a graceful Shakespearian touch
just sufficient to dispel any doubt about his responsibility for them.
Certain episodes, notably the post-horse incident, look as if they were
surrendered, while others are obscure. Caius and Evans plan revenge on
the Host, while Nym and Pistol plot against Falstaff, but the outcome
of these stratagems is not at all clear. Simple's visit to Falstaff to enquire
about Slender's chain in IV.v has no perceptible connexion with anything that has gone before. These cannot very well be explained as cuts
since *The Merry Wives*, as it stands, is considerably longer than any of
the comedies that precede it. There is confusion in the use of Christian
names, so that Page is Thomas in one place and George in another.
Simple and William appear and disappear quite casually, and Jack
Rugby does not survive beyond the third act. The Falstaff group has
every appearance of having been superimposed. Falstaff, despite some
uncharacteristic moments, retains much of his former glory, but Nym,
Bardolph and Pistol are reduced to mere formulas whose appearances
are spasmodic. Shallow and Mistress Quickly bear hardly any resemblance to their prototypes in the historical plays.[12] It is one thing to
transport Falstaff and his cronies to Windsor but quite another to
present the hostess of an Eastcheap tavern as a respectable inhabitant of
that town. And it is, to say the least, curious that Robert Shallow of
Gloucestershire should also have found his way to Windsor.

iv

The explanation that best covers these irregularities is that Shakespeare, working in haste, failed here and there to eliminate all traces of
episodes in his source-material which were otherwise discarded. The
basic source of *The Merry Wives* is the tale of Bucciolo and Pietro

[12] In *Henry V*, Mistress Quickly has become Mistress Pistol, but *The Merry Wives* is not necessarily inconsistent. Falstaff's remark about the 'mad Prince of Wales' (Quarto G3r) suggests that Shakespeare placed the action in the reign of Henry IV, though the allusion may have been interpolated by the Quarto reporter.

Paulo in Ser Giovanni Fiorentino's *Il Pecorone*. Other alleged sources, all of them derived from Giovanni, comprise two stories from Straparola's *Le tredici piacevoli notti*, Barnabe Riche's tale of Two Brethren and their Wives from *Riche His Farewell to Militarie Profession*, and the tale of the Two Lovers of Pisa from Tarlton's *Newes out of Purgatorie*. Since Giovanni alone refers to the buck-basket incident, which is given some prominence in *The Merry Wives*, it is unlikely that Shakespeare made use of any of the other prose versions, and there are no close parallels of thought or expression to suggest that he did. Nor is there any stronger reason for postulating his direct use of *Il Pecorone*. There can be little doubt, in fact, that Shakespeare's source already existed in dramatic form. Dover Wilson has put forward convincing reasons for his belief that Shakespeare transformed into prose something that had originally been written in verse.[13] This, of course, implies a play, for a narrative poem devoted to the theme of *The Merry Wives of Windsor* is quite inconceivable. Here and there Shakespeare's prose has rhyming words, and from these it may be inferred that the source play made occasional use of couplets. It is tolerably certain that the Falstaff of *The Merry Wives* replaces a quite different character, an affectate and youthful philanderer, and that Pistol, Nym and Bardolph were simply foisted into scenes that were quite skilfully rewritten.

An eligible source-play is therefore a desideratum, and it has often been assumed that Shakespeare used a lost play of 1593 named in Henslowe's diary as 'the Gelyous comodey'. Precisely what firm conclusions can be drawn from the fact that *The Jealous Comedy* and *The Merry Wives* handle the stock theme of jealousy it is difficult to see, but Fluellen's remark that 'there is salmons in both' seems appropriate. The same kind of blind faith attaches to the view that Shakespeare used a lost Oldcastle play, and there is no evidence to shew that such a play ever existed. The play which most closely resembles *The Merry Wives* is Henry Porter's comedy of *The Two Angry Women of Abingdon*, and the logical course is to consider whether it was to Porter that Shakespeare turned when, if tradition is trustworthy, Elizabeth peremptorily imposed the theme of Sir John in love.

---

[13] *The Merry Wives of Windsor* (New Shakespeare), ed. Sir Arthur Quiller-Couch and John Dover Wilson, pp. 93-101.

# eight

# The Merry Wives of Windsor

## Shakespeare and Porter

i

Very little is known about Henry Porter. He was named by Meres in *Palladis Tamia* as one of the 'best for Comedy amongst us', and Henslowe's diary records payments for five plays, of which Porter was wholly or partly the author, between December 1596 and March 1599. His only surviving play, *The Two Angry Women of Abingdon*, must, on the evidence of an allusion in Richard Harvey's *Plaine Percivall* (*c.* 1590), have been written not later than 1589.[1] It was revived early in 1599, in which year two quartos were published, and the fact that Porter now wrote a second part argues for popularity. That these two plays, presented at a time when domestic drama enjoyed a brief but considerable vogue, were conspicuously successful is attested by Henslowe's payment in earnest of a third play, *The Two Merry Women of Abingdon*, on February 28th, 1599, simultaneously with the signing of a contract to the effect that Henslowe should henceforth have the monopoly of Porter's work.[2] There is no record of the dramatist in Henslowe's diary after May 28th, 1599, but an indictment among the Southwark Assize records, discovered by Hotson, reveals that on June 6th, 1599, a certain Henry Porter was mortally wounded in a duel with one John Daye.[3] Date, locality and the names of victor and vanquished all serve to establish that this was an affray between two dramatists.

*The Two Angry Women of Abingdon* is a comedy of considerable distinction and if Porter's other plays were of comparable quality, he must have been an influential figure throughout the fifteen-nineties. The impact of the extant play upon Shakespeare's practice is evident during the period 1595-6, notably in *Romeo and Juliet* and *A Midsummer*

---

[1] J. M. Nosworthy, 'Notes on Henry Porter', *Modern Language Review*, XXXV, pp. 517-21.

[2] The diary also shews that receipts were very high for February 1599, the month in which the Abingdon plays were performed.

[3] *Shakespeare's Sonnets Dated*, pp. 193-203.

*Night's Dream.*[4] Thereafter occasional reminiscences occur in *The
Merchant of Venice, Much Ado about Nothing* and the two parts of
*Henry IV.*

## ii

It is legitimate to admit two initial propositions: that *The Merry
Wives*, in its broad outlines, comes very close to *The Two Angry
Women*, and that no other known play written before 1600 resembles
*The Merry Wives* in any way. The similarity between the titles of the
two plays is a consideration at least as valid as anything relating to *The
Jealous Comedy*, and the Pages and Fords, who must have been central
characters in the original play, bear family likeness to the Barneses and
Gourseys of Porter's comedy. Both plays, in other words, deal with
middle-class provincial families, and both are set in Berkshire towns
adjacent to wooded country and the River Thames. There is palpable
similarity of incident. Slender's wooing of Ann Page, though there is
no parallel episode in Porter's play, recalls nevertheless what is related
of Mall Barnes's suitor, who could 'say nothing to her, but God be with
yee', and of the russet youth who

> askt the prettie maide
> How they solde corne last market day with them,
> Saying: indeed twas very deare with them.[5]

Cousin Slender's 'fallow wit and meddow matter' are often in evidence,
notably in 'the iest how my Father stole two Geese out of a Pen'. The
comic duel arranged between Caius and Evans has an Abingdon
parallel, and both skirmishes are more productive of blood-curdling
threats than violent action. The parallel between Falstaff being thrown
into the Thames 'like a barrow of butchers Offall' and Coomes being
lured into a pond by Hodge is striking, and there are minor similarities.
Falstaff recognises that all this has come to pass through building
'vpon a foolish Womans promise', while Coomes concludes that 'a
man shall be serued thus alwayes when hee followes any of these
females.' Both characters observe that they have swallowed more water
than will do them good, and associate that water with more potent
drink such as sack and March beer; both make graphic use of animal

[4] For *Romeo and Juliet* see J. M. Nosworthy, 'The Two Angry Families of
Verona,' *Shakespeare Quarterly*, III, pp. 219-26. *A Midsummer Night's Dream*
frequently resembles Porter's play in situation, setting, character and dialogue.
[5] Quotations and line-numbering follow the Malone Society reprint.

imagery; both refer to foul stenches. There are other similarities of incident, but it is scarcely necessary to enumerate them. Verbal parallels are not particularly striking. One figure which is common with Porter occurs frequently in *The Merry Wives* in such phrases as:

> our pribbles and prabbles; If it be confessed, it is not redressed; Thou'rt an Emperor (*Cesar, Keiser* and *Pheazar*); thou shalt haue egresse and regresse; What? the Sword and the Word?; de Iack dog: Iohn Ape; Gallia and Gaule-Soule-Curer, and Bodie Curer; No, he giues me the Potions and the Motions; No he giues me the Prouerbes, and the No verbes; giuen to . . . swearings, and starings.

There is common ground in repeated use of the verb 'hang', in animal and, more especially, nautical imagery, but this is not sufficiently distinctive to merit more than passing mention.

Individual words common to the two plays but otherwise rare in Shakespeare include: *aqua vitae, Galen, horn-mad, peck* (sc. a large number), *possibilities* (sc. pecuniary prospects), *slice*, and *warrener*. There are several phrasal parallels that merit notice. Shakespeare rarely alludes to butter or cheese outside *The Merry Wives*. The following similarities, though loose, are therefore interesting:

> thinke of that, a man of my Kidney; thinke of that, that am as subiect to heate as butter. (*M.W.W.*III.v.117-18)
>
> Her wit's a sunne that melts him downe like butter (*2.A.W.A.*1087)

> Hang him, mechanicall-salt-butter rogue. (*M.W.W.*II.ii.290)
>
> . . . these russet coates cheese-cakes and buttermakers. (*2.A.W.A.*1369-70)

> I will make an end of my dinner; ther's Pippins and Cheese to come
> (*M.W.W.*I.ii.12-13)
>
> Why she, when men haue dinde and call for cheese,
> Will straight maintaine Iests bitter to disgest. (*2.A.W.A.*1106-7)

The following sets also involve expressions which are otherwise rare in Shakespeare:

> By cocke and pie, you shall not choose. (*M.W.W.*I.i.315-16)
>
> Merrie go sorrie, cocke and pye my hearts. (*2.A.W.A.*862)

> here will be an old abusing of Gods patience, and the Kings English.
> (*M.W.W.*I.iv.5-6)
>
> Ile trowle the bowles in the Buttery, by the leaue of God and maister Barnes. (*2.A.W.A.*79-80)

The better that it pleases your good Worship to aske. (*M.W.W.*I.iv.143-4)

I thanke yee I am the better for your asking. (2.*A.W.A.*2299-300)

What a taking was hee in, when your husband askt who was in the basket?
(*M.W.W.*III.iii.191-2)

Looke ye sirra where your fellow lies,
Hees in a fine taking is he not? (2.*A.W.A.*1018-19)

Well, I would not for the prize of my sword and buckler any body should see
me in this taking. (*ibid.*, 2192-4)

I that I will, come cut and long-taile, vnder the degree of a Squire.
(*M.W.W.*III.iv.47-8)

Well thou degree aboue a hackney, and ten degrees vnder a Page.
(2.*A.W.A.*1709-1)

Three of Nicholas Proverbs's saws appear in *The Merry Wives:* one of
them, 'Bought wit is the best' is paraphrased freely; another, 'As honest
as ever broke bread', occurs also in *Much Ado about Nothing;* the third
may be significant since Porter and Shakespeare employ almost
identical forms:

> ile nere put my finger in the fire, and neede not. (*M.W.W.*I.iv.90-1)
> I will not thrust my hand into the flame and neede not.[6] (2.*A.W.A.*1830-1)

There is finally the parallel between Dick Coomes's vaunt, echoed elsewhere by Shakespeare:

> ha I haue seene the day, I could haue daunst in my fight, one, two, three,
> foure and fiue, on the head of him: six, seauen, eyght, nine & ten, on the
> sides of him, and if I went so far as fifteen, I warrant I shewd him a trick of
> one and twentie. (2.*A.W.A.*2382-6)

and Shallow's:

> I haue seene the time, with my long-sword, I would haue made you fowre
> tall fellowes skippe like Rattes. (*M.W.W.*II.i.235-8)

Controlling all these incidental similarities there is a general resemblance of plot. Both plays deal with parental attempts to cross true love,

---

[6] It is, perhaps, desirable to emphasise that these parallels of word and phrase
have a validity which is not superficially apparent. Of the words cited, 'possibilities', 'slice' and 'warrener' are used by Shakespeare only in *The Merry Wives*,
and that play yields two out of four examples of 'Galen', two out of five of
'horn-mad', and one out of two of 'peck'. 'Butter' is exclusive to *The Merry
Wives* and *1 Henry IV* and its use in a term of abuse in the second parallel cited is
suggestive. 'In a taking' is exclusive to *The Merry Wives*. 'Cock and pie' is
found only in *Romeo and Juliet*.

with plans for a runaway marriage, with tricks played by wives on their husbands and with a resolution effected after nocturnal confusion in the woods. Shakespeare, like Porter, handles these matters at an everyday level and not, as in *The Two Gentlemen of Verona* and *A Midsummer Night's Dream*, in a contrived atmosphere of romance or enchantment. From all this it might appear that Shakespeare simply took *The Two Angry Women* as his model, and this conclusion would be inevitable if the Folio text were the sole basis of comparison. The Quarto, however, points to radically different circumstances.

### iii

Since the desideratum is almost certainly a play which Shakespeare was able to refashion to his own needs with the minimum effort, it is extremely doubtful whether any question of influence arises. If, as the foregoing evidence suggests, there is something of Henry Porter about *The Merry Wives of Windsor*, it seems reasonably possible that Shakespeare's immediate source was neither *The Jealous Comedy* nor an Oldcastle play but one of Porter's lost domestic comedies. Not, of course, *The Two Angry Women of Abingdon*, and almost certainly not its sequel which was duly delivered to Henslowe and performed by Nottingham's company. There remains, however, *The Two Merry Women of Abingdon* which apparently never reached Henslowe but which must have been completed, or nearly so, at the time of Porter's death in June 1599. Hence there are fairly strong *prima facie* grounds for claiming that an extremely useful set of foul papers was lying idle just at the time when Shakespeare found himself in urgent need of a ready-made comedy of provincial life.

At this point a little guarded speculation is necessary. The sequel to *The Two Angry Women* doubtless handled a second quarrel and, in view of Frank Gourney's rejoinder at 2541-2,

> Good Lord what you would doe!
> Well we shall see one day how you can woe.

it seems probable that Philip Barnes's courtship was set against this background of minor hostilities. But the third Abingdon play concerned merry women, and women's mirth in Elizabethan comedy normally spells discomfiture for the men. If Mistress Barnes and Mistress Goursey were the merry women on this occasion, their husbands can confidently be regarded as their most likely victims. Goursey, on the shewing of the extant play, is perhaps the more vulnerable for he is quick-tempered and certainly affects jealousy. So (for the sake of argument) Goursey suspects that he has been cuckolded—not by the sober and rational Barnes but by some third person who has to be duped by the merry women into such a position that jealousy and comedy are completely liberated. Against this would almost certainly be set some elementary theme of wooing and winning. Certain devices that had proved popular in the earlier plays would re-appear, and these could obviously include a comic duel and a ducking. Nocturnal confusion and its resolution might be repeated. Other incidents might be developed. If Coomes is led in error to pay court to Hodge, the idea might be so extended that one man finds that he has actually married the other. This, of course, is pure conjecture, but it does no violence to probability. *The Merry Women of Abingdon* is a fact, and one whose possibilities of plot are fairly limited. The grounds for supposing that Porter tended to repeat himself are substantial enough, for it is clear that he caught the public's fancy with the extant play and that the sequels were written in response to a demand that he had himself created. The point, then, is that one quite legitimate set of inferences claims for this lost play certain central features which, in fact, constitute the main plot, the sub-plot, the background and several of the incidents of *The Merry Wives of Windsor*.

iv

The supposition that certain happenings at Windsor originally belonged to Abingdon receives geographical support of an admittedly dubious character. The common features—a small Berkshire town, water meadows, and woodland—have already been mentioned. Maidenhead and Colnbrook are common to both *The Two Angry Women* and *The Merry Wives*. Shakespeare's 'Mother Prat' episode is one which could apply as fittingly to Abingdon as to Windsor. Reginald Scot, in his *Discoverie of Witchcraft*, refers to the witch-finding activities of Richard Gallis of Windsor and says that if any witches

> be yet behind, I doubt not, but Brian Darcie will find them out; who, if he lacke aid, Richard Gallis of Windesor were meete to be associated with him; which Gallis hath set foorth another booke to that effect, of certeine witches of Windsore executed at Abingdon.

This at least brings Abingdon within the Windsor orbit.

Two other topographical possibilities which arise from Quarto–Folio variation are indefinite, but are sufficiently interesting to bear setting out. The theft of the post-horses is presented thus in the Folio:

> *Host.* Where be my horses? speake well of them varletto.
> *Bar.* Run away with the cozeners: for so soone as I came beyond Eaton, they threw me off, from behinde one of them, in a slough of myre; and set spurres, and away. (IV.v.65-70)

The corresponding passage in the Quarto, which, since it involves the Host, may have independent authority, reads:

> *Host.* Why man, where be my horses? where be the Germanes?
> *Bar.* Rid away with your horses:
> After I came beyond Maidenhead,
> They flung me in a slow of myre, & away they ran. (F4v)

If, as Wheatley plausibly suggested, the slough of mire alludes to the town of Slough, it is quite clear that, in the Folio, the cozeners set out from Windsor, passing first through Eton and then Slough, while the Quarto, for what is it worth, implies that the starting point was somewhere west of Maidenhead—that is, from the direction of Abingdon.

The second point arises from Page's plans for the marriage of Anne and Slender. In the Folio Fenton tells the Host:

> Her father hath commanded her to slip
> Away with *Slender*, and with him, at *Eaton*
> Immediately to Marry. (IV.vi.23-5)

This, in the Quarto, becomes:

> But her father still against her choise,
> Doth seeke to marrie her to foolish *Slender*,
> And in a robe of white this night disguised,
> Wherein fat *Falstaffe* had a mightie scare,
> Must *Slender* take her and carrie her to *Catlen*,
> And there vnknowne to any, marrie her. (G1v)

The '*Eaton*' of the Folio accords naturally with the Windsor setting, but the Quarto '*Catlen*' is hard to account for. It has hitherto been explained as a misreading, but it could equally well be a variant of 'Catley', a place-name from the Abingdon district which no longer survives. The northern angle of Berkshire is remarkable for place-names compounded from names of birds and animals with 'ley' as their second element.[7] The only wild-cat survival is apparently in 'Catmore', but 'cat leage' is

---

[7] F. M. Stenton, *The Place Names of Berkshire:* An Essay, pp. 3, 19.

'this old fat-fellow'. There are no specific resemblances to Porter, save for the tendency to lapse into rhyme. Such a couplet as:

> Well lets about this stratagem, I long
> To see deceit deceiued, and wrong haue wrong.

could easily be his.


### (c) *G1r–G1v*

The dialogue between Fenton and the Host occupies thirty-four lines in the Quarto, but has much in common with the longer Folio scene of fifty-five lines. It might therefore be regarded as a reported scene, but there are difficulties. If the Host was the reporter it is strange that he interpolated a line:

> But how will you come to steale her from among thē?

and even stranger that he should have misrepresented his own opening lines which read in the Quarto:

> Speake not to me sir, my mind is heauie,
> I haue had a great losse.

as against the Folio:

Master *Fenton*, talke not to mee, my minde is heauy: I will giue ouer all.

Strangest of all is the fact that the Quarto is more apt than the Folio since, in both versions, Fenton's reply is that he will make good the Host's loss. In this matter, too, the Quarto promise of 'a hundred pound toward your losse' sounds more probable than the Folio:

> A hundred pound in gold, more then your losse.

Fenton's speeches, for the greater part, might be reported, but occasional Quarto variation, as in

> The feruent loue *I* beare to young *Anne Page*,
> And mutually her loue againe to mee.

and:

> And by thy furtherance there be married.

goes rather beyond the reporter's normal level of achievement, both in vocabulary and metre. The versification throughout is in fact surprisingly regular in view of the transpositions—that is, if the scene was reported. Again, proper-names and Caius's title result in hyper-metrical lines:

> And firme for Doctor *Cayus*, in a robe of red
> By her deuice, the Doctor must steale her thence.

which are regularized in the Folio as:

> Her Mother, (euen strong against that match
> And firme for Doctor *Caius*) hath appointed.

Falstaff once more receives the gratuitous adjective 'fat', as also in the Folio. The possible significance of '*Catlen*' has already been noted. Though there are no clear parallels between this scene and *The Two Angry Women*, such lines as

> And bring her where the priest abides our coming,
> And by thy furtherance there be married

seem to reflect the same order of expression as:

> There to morrow say that we will meete them,
> And there determine of their marriage. (1727-7)

It may, with caution, be added that the runaway marriage plan in Porter's play (lines 1722-47) utilizes various words that figure also in the Quarto scene ('appoint': 'may steale hence': 'match': 'agree': 'bound'), but the collocation is not remarkable.

## (d) *G2r-G4v*

This is by far the longest section and is separated from the preceding one only by a brief and wretchedly corrupted report of V.v.1-40. It is, for the main part, quite independent of the Folio, though there are sporadic pieces of what look like memorial reconstructions of certain Folio speeches. These, though set as verse, are in fact prose. The section begins with Mistress Quickly's instructions to the 'fairies', corresponding to Folio V.4.41-106 but quite dissimilar. The verse here is regular and competent, and is shared by Quickly and Evans, whose Welshisms are not consistent. There are a couple of interjections by Falstaff. Quickly's lines:

> About it then, and know the truth,
> Of this same metamorphised youth.

prove conclusively that this section originally belonged to a play that had nothing to do with Falstaff. There are no perceptible echoes of

Porter's comedy, though a run of octosyllabic couplets faintly recalls the Boy's lines in *The Two Angry Women*, 309-43.

The remainder corresponds to Folio V.v.107-259. Here the tokens of Porter's style are more in evidence, and it will be convenient to set the passage out in full with relevant parallels. Speeches which are imperfect reproductions of the Folio are italicised.

Fal.    Horne *the hunter quoth you: am I a ghost?*
       *Sblood the Fairies hath made a ghost of me:*
       *What hunting at this time at night?*
       *Ile lay my life the mad Prince of* Wales
5      *Is stealing his fathers Deare. How now who haue*
       *we here, what is all* Windsor *stirring? Are you there?*
Shal.   God saue you sir Iohn Falstaffe.
Sir Hu.  God plesse you sir Iohn, God plesse you.
Pa.    Why how now sir *Iohn*, what a pair of horns in your hand?
10 Ford.  Those hornes he ment to place vpon my head,
       And M. *Brooke* and he should be the men:
       Why how now sir *Iohn*, why are you thus amazed?
       We know the Fairies man that pinched you so,
       Your throwing in the Thames, your beating well,
15     And whats to come sir *Iohn*, that can we tell.

          For the form of address (12-13) cf. Porter: 'Why you man are . . .' (2518): 'Sownes man, and if . . .' (2532): 'Nay man I would' (2540).

Mi. Pa.  Sir *Iohn* tis thus, your dishonest meanes
       To call our credits into question
       · Did make vs vndertake to (do) our best,
       To turne your leaud lust to a merry Iest.

          For 'credit' in this sense cf. 216, 1233, 2109.

20 Fal.   *Iest, tis well, haue I liued to these yeares*
       *To be gulled now, now to be ridden?*
       *Why then these were not Fairies?*
Mis. Pa.  No sir Iohn but boyes.
Fal.    *By the Lord I was twice or thrise in the mind*
25     *They were not, and yet the grosnesse*
       *Of the fopperie perswaded me they were.*
       *Well, and the fine wits of the Court heare this,*
       *Thayle so whip me with their keene Iests,*
       *That thayle melt me out like tallow,*
30     *Drop by drop out of my grease. Boyes!*

cf: Her wit's a sunne, that melts him downe like
butter . . . (1087)
. . . Sheele persecute the poore wit-beaten man,
And so be bang him with drie bobs and scoffes.
(1091-2)

|  |  |
|---|---|
| Sir Hu. | I trust me boyes Sir Iohn: and I was<br>Also a Fairie that did helpe to pinch you. |
| Fal. | I, tis well I am your May-pole,<br>You haue the start of mee, |
| 35 | Am I ridden too with a wealch goate?<br>With a peece of toasted cheese? |
| Sir Hu. | Butter is better then cheese sir Iohn,<br>You are all butter, butter. |
| For. | There is a further matter yet sir Iohn, |
| 40 | There's 20. pound you borrowed of M. Brooke Sir Iohn,<br>And it must be paid to M. Ford Sir Iohn. |
| Mi. For. | Nay husband let that go to make ameds,<br>Forgiue that sum, and so weele all be friends. |

cf: Go to, imbrace and say if you be friends,
That heere the angrie womens quarrels ends. (2904-5)

|  |  |
|---|---|
| For. | Well here is my hand, all's forgiuen at last. |
| 45 Fal. | It hath cost me well,<br>I haue bene well pinched and washed. |

### Enter the Doctor

|  |  |
|---|---|
| Mi. Pa. | Now M. Doctor, sonne I hope you are. |
| Doct. | Sonne begar you be de ville voman,<br>Begar I tinck to marry metres An, and begar |
| 50 | Tis a whorson garson Iack boy. |
| Mis. Pa. | How a boy? |
| Doct. | I begar a boy. |
| Pa. | Nay be not angry wife, Ile tell thee true,<br>It was my plot to deceiue thee so: |
| 55 | And by this time your daughter's married<br>To M. Slender, and see where he comes. |

### Enter Slender

Now sonne Slender,
Where's your bride?

53. cf:
Nay stay, I doe not chide but counsell, wife. (516)

60 *Slen.*   Bride, by Gods lyd I thinke theres neuer a
man in the worell hath that crosse fortune that I
haue: begod I could cry for verie anger.

> cf: Was euer man deluded thus like me?
> I thinke some spirit leads me thus amisse. (2438-9)
> Oh, I could crie for anger and for rage. (2726)

*Pa.*      Why whats the matter sonne *Slender*?
*Slen.*    Sonne, nay by God I am none of your son.
*Pa.*      No, why so?
65 *Slen.*  Why so God saue me, tis a boy that I haue married.
*Pa.*      How a boy? why did you mistake the word?
*Slen.*    *No neither, for I came to her in red as you*
*bad me, and I cried mum, and hee cried budget, so*
*well as euer you heard, and I haue married him.*
70 *Sir Hu.*  Ieshu M. Slender, *cannot you see but marrie boyes?*

> For the blindness taunt cf:
> *Dicke Coomes,* what difference is there between
> a blind man, and he that cannot see? (2011-12)

*Pa.*      O I am vext at hart, what shal I do?

> cf:
> Go to, I am angrie at the heart, my very heart. (1267)

> *Enter Fenton and Anne*

*Mis. Pa.* Here comes the man that hath deceiued vs all:
How now daughter, where haue you bin?

> cf:
> How now minion, wher haue you bin gadding?
> (692)
> How now sirra, where haue ye beene walking? (726)
> Mistress Page's line appears to have lost a participle.

*An.*      At Curch forsooth.

> Mall Barnes also swears like a comfit-maker's wife.
> Cf: her use of 'forsooth' at 642-3.

75 *Pa.*    At Church, what haue you done there?
*Fen.*     Married to me, nay sir neuer storme,
Tis done sir now, and cannot be vndone.

> For 'never' in similar context cf:
> Growe to the house top with your anger sir.

Neare tell me, I care not thus much for it. (1261-2).
No you shall not, neere looke so big. (1269)

Ford. Ifaith M. *Page* neuer chafe your selfe,
She hath made her choise wheras her hart was fixt,
80 Then tis in vaine for you to storme or fret.

ibid. For 'chafe' cf:
Yet *Barnses* wife would chafe if that she knew. (2719)

Fal. *I am glad yet that your arrow hath glanced*
Mi. For. Come mistris *Page*, Ile be bold with you,
Tis pitie to part loue that is so true.

For 'to be bold with' cf:
How do ye meane he will be bould with me? (43)
Ile in, and let them be as bolde with vs. (1116)
For 'tis pity' cf:
Faith tis a pretty wench, and tis pitty but she should
haue him. (2963-4)
and cf. (also in connexion with lines following):
The greatest sinne wherein your soules may sinne,
I thinke is this, in crossing of true loue. (2944-5).

Mis. Pa. Altho that I haue missed in my intent,
85 Yet I am glad my husbands match was crossed,
Here M. *Fenton*, take her, and God giue thee ioy.

cf:
To it *Francis*, to it sister, God send yee ioy. (2978)

Sir Hu. Come M. *Page*, you must needs agree.

cf:
Come mistresse *Goursey*, do you first agree? (2876)

Fo. I yfaith sir come, you see your wife is wel pleased:
Pa. I cannot tel, and yet my hart's well eased,
90 And yet it doth me good the Doctor missed.
Come hither *Fenton*, and come hither daughter,
Go too you might haue stai'd for my good will,
But since your choise is made of one you loue,
Here take her *Fenton*, & both happie proue.

91. For the gesture cf:
Mother, giue me your hand, giue me yours to.
(2880)

94. cf:
M. Bar. Well may she prooue a happy wife to him.
M. Gou. And may he prooue as happy vnto her.
(2983-4)

95   Sir Hu.  I will also dance & eat plums at your weddings.

> For a similarly fatuous comment by a comic char-
> acter cf:
> And mistresse Mary, when yee go to bed, God send
> you good rest, and a peck of Fleas in your nest,
> euery one as big as Francis. (2965-7)

Ford.   All parties pleased, now let vs in to feast,
And laugh at Slender, and the Doctors ieast.
He hath got the maiden, each of you a boy
To waite vpon you, so God giue you ioy,
100    And sir Iohn Falstaffe now shal you keep your word,
For Brooke this night shall lye with mistris Ford.

> 98-9. cf, especially the rhyme:
> To it Francis, to it sister, God send yee ioy
> Tis fine to sing dansey my owne sweete boye.
> (2979-80)

As in the preceding sections, proper-names result in metrically irregular lines:

> Ifaith M. Page neuer chafe your selfe . . .
> Come mistris Page, Ile be bold with you . . .
> Here M. Fenton, take her, and God giue thee ioy . . .
> Come M. Page, you must needs agree . . .

## vi

The one absolutely certain conclusion which arises from this analysis is that part of the Quarto derives from a MS. source consisting of the final scene, together with one or two fragments, of a play that depicted the gulling of a 'metamorphised youth', under circumstances identical with those of The Merry Wives of Windsor, by characters who bore names different from the Shakespearian ones. Clearly Fenton replaces a monosyllabic name and Page a dissyllabic one, and other adjustments are evident. These fragments, in combination with a debased memorial report of the bulk of Shakespeare's comedy, evidently served as Quarto copy, and may, or may not, have been identical with Shakespeare's source-play. They are assuredly not his work.

There is no single piece of evidence strong enough to establish Porter's claim to these fragments, except perhaps the tantalising 'Catlen' variant, but the cumulative data furnish a relatively good case. In the final section (d), which comprises a hundred lines, thirty or forty of which are interpolated, there are some twenty tricks of style, thought rhyme, vocabulary and even characterisation which recall *The Two Angry Women of Abingdon* and are, by implication, tokens of Porter's style. Similar evidence appears, though less frequently, in the other sections. These parallels, moreover, accord with similarity of situation. In section (a) parental interference produces verbal echoes of the corresponding incident in Porter's play, while in (d) the denouement, which, like that of *The Two Angry Women*, resolves the elements of lovers meeting, parents thwarted, mistaken identity and nocturnal confusion, exhibits the same order of thought and expression. The parallels are not such as to admit mere influence as an explanation, nor are they, for the main part, so closely linked with the situation that they can be dismissed as inevitable commonplaces. There are, then, reasonable internal grounds for supposing that the Quarto preserves relics of a lost play by Henry Porter, and if so it virtually follows that that play was *The Two Merry Women of Abingdon*.

vii

The inclusion of these relics in the Quarto is, irrespective of Porter's supposed authorship, susceptible of alternative explanations. It is evident that those concerned in the piracy were able, by fair means or foul, to lay their hands on the remnants of a set of foul papers which ultimately formed part of the copy used by Creede's compositor. The assumption that this copy was more or less an arbitrary compilation in which the pirates fumbled their way through the best part of four acts and then luckily rounded their efforts off with a section of an entirely alien play can be disregarded. For one thing, the Quarto ending clearly stands in some sort of relationship to that of Shakespeare's comedy, and for another, the process assumed would argue resource and judgment on the part of the agents quite incompatible with the incompetence of which they stand convicted elsewhere.

A more tenable hypothesis is that implicit in Greg's view that the Quarto was the work of an independent reporter who relied mainly on the Host's assistance. A process whereby this person salvaged several sheets of what he knew to be Shakespeare's source-play and then prevailed upon a minor actor to reconstruct the remainder is intelligible enough. There are, however, several difficulties. The irregularities in the Host's speeches in section (c) have already been noted, but the main problems concern section (d) which imposes a number of subtle distinctions. Of the hundred lines quoted above, about sixty apparently belong to the source-play, the equivalent speeches in *The Merry Wives* having been completely rewritten. The remaining forty lines (those italicised) represent Folio speeches in an imperfect form. At the same time, these must stand in lieu of material in the source-play that Shakespeare had refashioned in terms of Falstaff, Evans, Caius and Slender. Under such a hypothesis this would mean that the speeches of those characters, as given in the Quarto, are memorial reconstructions imposed on the source-play MS. by the reporter. In other words, the copy for section (d) consisted of foul papers of a sustained and orderly run of verse speeches, with some deletions and marginal replacements— or possibly a transcript of them. This is, on the whole, a credible explanation, but it does not account for the Quarto preservation of four lines (27-30) which evidently derive from the source-play and not from the Folio. It is impossible to legislate for oblivion, but Pistol's absence is curious and it seems strange that a reporter who was able to recall Falstaff's.

Heauens defend me from that Welsh Fairy.[11]

should have failed to remember

Least he transforme me to a peece of Cheese.

which is, after all, the essence of the joke. His omission of all reference to the Garter, unless Folio V.v.59-80 belongs to a later revision, is incredible.

The alternative is to suppose that what came into the reporter's hands were several sections of the source-play MS. which contained Shakespeare's own markings and working notes. This would mean that the italicised parts of section (d) represent his tentative gropings towards the form which these speeches assumed in his final draft. It would also mean that he substituted his own speech-headings for those of the original and that he altered the names in the dialogue, leaving the necessary metrical adjustments until later. Pistol's inclusion in the Folio version is explicable as an afterthought, and the inclusion of the

---

[11] Quarto: God blesse me from that Wealch Fairie.
The variation in the Folio possibly resulted from the Act of Abuses of 1606, though elsewhere little attempt is made to modify profanity.

Porterian lines in Falstaff's speech (27-30) is understandable enough in a tentative jotting. The very real difficulty about such an explanation is that an author's casual working notes are not likely, in practice, to differ very much from a memorial report, so that this evidence, such as it is, is ambiguous.

There are, however, more substantial reasons for believing that these MS. fragments had passed through Shakespeare's hands. Firstly, there is the curious inconsistency, common to both the Quarto and Folio, in the treatment of Evans's verse speeches. The Folio shews that although Shakespeare paid considerable attention to Evans's Welsh pronunciation, he was by no means consistent, so that 'goot', for instance, in the early part of the play yields to 'good' in the later. In V.iv, and V.v. 136-69 Evans is very much Welshified, but there are no Welsh traces of any kind in his verse speeches in V.v.41-97, though Falstaff refers to 'that Welsh Fairy'. In the Quarto, too, Evans, still 'that wealch Fairie', temporarily sheds most of his native habits. It is true that he addresses two of the fairies as '*Peane*' and '*Pead*' and that he converts 'blue' into 'plew', but other words, 'brokers', 'bed', 'bodie' 'buck' and 'Tapers', are left unmutated. This insufficiency, common to both texts, can scarcely be coincidental, and the Quarto appears to shew that Shakespeare made a couple of perfunctory alterations in the MS. of the source-play but forgot even these when he came to the final draft.

Secondly, there are the curious stage-directions of section (d). Throughout the reported parts of the Quarto the stage-directions are emphatic and adequate as often in the 'Bad' Quartos, but in section (d) they are descriptive and extraordinarily full, thus:

> (i) *Enter sir Hugh like a Satyre, and boyes drest like Fayries, mistresse Quickly, like the Queene of Fayries: they sing a song about him, and afterward speake.*
>
> (ii) *They put the Tapers to his fingers, and he starts.*
>
> (iii) *Here they pinch him, and sing about him, & the Doc-tor comes one way & steales away a boy in red. And Slender another way he takes a boy in greene: And Fenton steales misteris Anne, being in white. And a noyse of hunting is made within: and all the Fairies runne away. Falstaffe pulles of his bucks head, and rises vp. And enters M. Page, M. Ford, and their wiues, M. Shallow, Sir Hugh.*

Such stage-directions are not characteristic of prompt-copy, nor are they of the kind normally found in reported texts. There is nothing comparable in, for instance, the 'Bad' Quartos of *Hamlet* or *Henry V*.

On the other hand, long quasi-narrative directions are common in texts based on foul papers,[12] and comparison is possible with several plays which preserve stage-directions of this kind. The Quarto stage-direction (i) bears a clear resemblance to that in *Cymbeline*, V.ii.1:

> *Enter Lucius, Iachimo, and the Romane Army at one doore: and the Britaine Army at another: Leonatus Posthumus following like a poore Souldier. They march ouer, and goe out. Then enter againe in Skirmish Iachimo and Posthumus: he vanquisheth and disarmeth Iachimo, and then leaues him.*

Such similarities as '*like the Queene of the Fayries*' and '*like a poore Souldier*', '*they sing a song*' and '*They march ouer*', and '*and afterward speake*' and '*and then leaues him*' suggest identity of authorship. The '*afterward speake*' and '*like*' techniques are reflected in *Timon* I.ii.1:

> *Then comes dropping after all Apemantus discontentedly like himself.*

while at I.ii.150 *Timon* has the same piling up of 'and' as the Quarto, stage-direction (iii):

> *The lords rise from Table, with much adoring of Timon, and to shew their loues, each single out an Amazon, and all Dance, men with women, a loftie straine or two to the Hoboyes, and cease.*

Also relevant is *Timon*, IV.iii.48:

> *Enter Alcibiades with Drumme and Fife in warlike manner. and Phrynia and Timandra.*[13]

Directions beginning with '*Here*' as the Quarto stage-direction (iii) have survived foul-paper transcription in *The Tempest*, V.i.57:

> *Here enters* Ariel *before:* etc.

and V.i.171:

> *Here Prospero discouers Ferdinand and Miranda, playing at Chesse.*

The '*noyse of Hunters*' in the same play (IV.i.257) may also be compared with the '*noyse of hunting*' in the Quarto of *The Merry Wives*.

---

[12] See Greg, *The Shakespeare First Folio*, pp. 135-7, for a full discussion of indefinite and permissive stage-directions in foul papers.

[13] The 'and' formula was evidently used extensively by Shakespeare. For notable examples see *Shrew*, Ind. ii.1, *2 Henry VI*, II.iii.59, and *Titus Andronicus*, *passim*.

These stage-directions in the final section of *The Merry Wives* Quarto thus reveal a close family likeness to what Greg terms the indefinite directions found in Shakespearian texts of foul-paper origin. The Quarto stage-direction (iii) is obviously wrong in providing an entry for Sir Hugh, who has been present almost from the beginning of the scene (stage-direction (i)), and this is the kind of careless slip that Shakespeare himself could have made, whereas it would be quite unusual in a stage-direction compiled by a reporter, assisted by the Host. Finally it may be remarked that the use of '*Hu*' as a speech-heading, once in this final section and twice in section (b), clearly distinguishes them from the reported parts of the text where '*Sir Hu.*' is the rule which admits the exception '*Hu*' once and '*S. Hu.*' twice. Again the inconsistency is quite Shakespearian.

It is relevant to recall Greg's comments on the stage-directions in *Timon of Athens*:

> It is not surprising that some of these directions are reminiscent of what may have been jottings in the author's original plot; where the drama has only half disengaged itself from the matrix of thought, it is natural that the directions should not have been fully adapted to the needs of the stage.[14]

The Quarto directions under review appear to be working notes of this kind. In (a) '*like a Satyre*', applied to Evans, suggests a loose and tentative idea. The final form of Evans's disguise is unfortunately obscured in the Folio through Crane's elimination of intermediate stage-directions, but in IV.iv., in both texts, the plan is that he shall be 'like a Iacke-an-Apes'. The same vagueness, suggestive of inchoation, applies to '*they sing a song about him*'. The song is given in the Folio, and a reporter, even if he could not recover this, would have found no difficulty in providing an adequate substitute. In (c), apart from the faulty entry for Evans, the colours of the dresses are confused in such a way as to suggest that Shakespeare simply noted the action down, leaving the correct distribution for later attention. As it stands in the Quarto this stage-direction (fol. G3r) is at variance with both Fenton's remarks to the Host (fol. G1v) and Slender's account (fol. G4r). In view of the propinquity of these passages a reporter's error seems unlikely, whereas confusion in an author's marginal jotting would probably have gone unnoticed.

Finally there is Mistress Quickly whose presence as the Fairy Queen is, as Hart observed, 'very undesirable'.[15] Shakespeare's intentions, as

[14] *The Shakespeare First Folio*, p. 410.
[15] *The Merry Wives of Windsor*, ed. H. C. Hart (Arden Shakespeare), p. 209.

represented in the Folio, are far from clear. At IV.iv.71 Mistress Page
announces

> My *Nan* shall be the Queene of all the Fairies,
> finely attired in a robe of white.

This, it might be argued, is simply to pull the wool over her husband's
eyes, but strangely enough Fenton, at IV.vi.20, is apparently under the
same impression:

> Must my sweet *Nan* present the *Faerie-Queene*.

It is clear, however, that, if Slender and Caius are to be deceived,
someone else must take Anne's place as the Fairy Queen. Whatever the
extent of the grossness of the foppery, Mistress Quickly in her own
character seems a most unlikely substitute, and the speech-headings in
V.v, '*Qui*' and '*Qu*' in the Folio and '*Quic*' in the Quarto, may therefore merely indicate that the actor who had hitherto played Mistress
Quickly now assumed the role of Fairy Queen. Such doubling is
amply provided for by the Quarto direction, '*mistresse Quickly, like the
Queene of Fayries*', and the speech-headings themselves are really non-
committal.[16] The significant thing is that the inconsistency, if such it is,
is common to both texts.

---

[16] It is relevant to remark that under any circumstances this doubling looks
more like an author's proposal than a theatrical possibility. Quickly appears in
V.i and the Fairy Queen's entry occurs some eighty-five lines later. Whether,
under Elizabethan conditions, this would have sufficed for the actor to change from
the costume of a soubrette to that of the Fairy Queen, with all its trappings, is
questionable. The whole doubling process therefore has what may be termed a
'permissive' air about it.

# nine

# The Merry Wives of Windsor

## Shakespeare's Revising Hand

### i

Greg's invaluable study of *The Merry Wives of Windsor* suffers from one serious drawback. His original position was that the Host alone compiled the Quarto, and, as he wisely pointed out, there is 'no justification for conjecturing two agents where one will suffice'.[1] Subsequently, however, he modified this view, at first in terms of actor and reporter, and finally thus:

> An outstanding feature of the report is the habitual fullness and accuracy of the Host's part and the way in which the text in general improves when he is on or near the stage. The same is true, if less noticeably, of Falstaff's. In neither case, however, is the quality of the reporting uniform, and it seems less likely that the Quarto was vamped up by the two actors themselves than that an independent reporter was able to draw on the recollection of each. The last act is much confused.[2]

Such multiplication of agents is undesirable simply because it cannot account for the general character of the Quarto, and particularly for its mingling of comparative goodness with extreme badness. It is entirely possible that a second actor was confederate with the Host, but to assume that their joint report was afterwards bullied into shape by a further agent is unnecessary. The weakness of so many theories relating to individual 'Bad' quartos has been the invocation of this external agent, variously defined as reporter or hack-poet, to account for occasional passages of more or less regular verse. That such a person was, from time to time, implicated is by no means improbable, but he should not, as a rule, be assumed unless all other explanations fail. For *The Merry Wives*, it would seem, one actor, or perhaps two, armed with a few pages of manuscript, will suffice, and there is no question of a hack's intrusion. So much appears to have been established by inductive

[1] *The Merry Wives of Windsor*, 1602, p. xli.
[2] *The Shakespeare First Folio*, p. 334.

methods in the previous chapter, and it now remains to consider the implications of Quarto–Folio relationship in the four verse passages discussed above.

ii

(a) *Quarto E4r-E4v: Folio III.iv.1-103*

Both passages are in verse but so dissimilar that the Quarto cannot reasonably be regarded as a memorial report of the Folio. In the main it must be taken as reproducing the source-play, but with the adjustments already mentioned. In rewriting the scene Shakespeare borrowed and developed occasional phrases:

> Q. Thy father thinks I loue thee for his wealth,
> Tho I must needs confesse at first that drew me,
> But since thy vertues wiped that trash away,
> I loue thee *Nan*.

> F. Albeit I will confesse, thy Father's wealth
> Was the first motiue that I woo'd thee (*Anne:*)
> Yet wooing thee, I found thee of more valew
> Than stampes in Gold, or summes in sealed bagges. (13-16)

> Q. M. *Fenton* I pray what make you here?
> You know my answere sir, shees not for you:
> Knowing my vow, to blame to vse me thus.

> F. Why how now? What does M^r *Fenter* here?
> You wrong me Sir, thus still to haunt my house.
> I told you Sir, my daughter is disposd of. (72-4)

> Q. But heare me speake sir.

> F. Sir, will you heare me? (78)

> Q. Speake to Misteris *Page*.

> F. Speake to Mistris *Page* (81)

> Q. For my part Ile neither hinder you, nor further.

> F. *Fenton*, I will not be your friend, nor enemy. (93)

The kind of resemblance apparent in these passages, that is pervasive similarity with verbal likenesses that are at best slight and spasmodic, contrasts strangely with that which informs the memorial reporting, a characteristic of which is the reporter's ability to remember many of the words of the original, but very little besides. On the other hand, to see the Quarto as the raw material and the Folio as the transformed and refined product of Shakespeare's genius makes a wholly intelligible pattern. One further parallel may be noted:

Q. How say you this was my doings?
I bid you speake to misteris *Page*

F. This is my doing now: Nay, saide I, will you cast away your childe on a Foole, and a Physitian:
Looke on M. *Fenton*, this is my doing. (99-101)

The Quarto lines cannot with confidence be assigned to the source-play, nor do they give the impression of having been reported. It therefore seems likely that they reproduce a marginal note which Shakespeare subsequently expanded into the Folio lines. Mistress Quickly was doubtless a character imposed upon the original play by Shakespeare, either as an addition or, more probably, as a replacement, so that all her speeches in the Quarto are conceivably marginalia. These, in addition to the two lines above, comprise:

> Godes pitie here comes her father.
> Speake to Misteris *Page*.

and:

> By my troth so I will, good hart.

All of these have the appearance of working notes for the Folio prose speeches.

## (b) *Quarto F3r-F3v: Folio IV.iv.6-90*

The independence of the Quarto is attested by the regularity of its verse and the comparative frequency of rhymed couplets, but Shakespeare's transformation of his material is complete, so that little of the Quarto is retained in the Folio. The following may be noted:

Q. I do not thinke heele come being so much deceiued.

F. Fie, fie, he'll neuer come. (20)

Q. Let me alone, Ile to him once againe like *Brooke*, and know his mind whether heele come or not.

F. Nay, Ile to him againe in name of *Broome*,
Hee'l tell me all his purpose: sure hee'l come. (76-7)

Q. That will *I* do, and in a robe of white
   Ile cloath my daughter, and aduertise *Slender*
   To know her by that signe, and steale her thence,
   And vnknowne to my wife, shall marrie her.

F. That silke will I go buy, and in that time
   Shall M. *Slender* steale my *Nan* away,
   And marry her at *Eaton*. (73-5)

Q. *I* will also be there, and be like a *I*ackanapes,
   And pinch him most cruelly for his lecheries.

F. I will teach the children their behauiours: and I will be like a Iacke-an-
   Apes also, to burne the Knight with my Taber. (67-9)
   And Fairy-like to pinch the vncleane Knight. (57)

Q. First he was carried and throwne in the Thames,
   Next beaten well, *I* am sure youle witnes that.

F. You say he has bin throwne in the Riuers: and has bin greeuously
   peaten, as an old o'man. (21-2)

Q. Well lets about this stratagem, I long
   To see deceit deceiued, and wrong haue wrong.

F. Let vs about it,
   It is admirable pleasures, and ferry honest knaueries. (80-1)

The last two Quarto passages look like more or less unaltered fragments
of the source-play which Shakespeare subsequently assigned to Evans
and accordingly redrafted. Presumably there was no comic Welshman
in the original. The third Quarto passage is apparently another survival.
The remainder have the appearance of working notes.

(c) *Quarto G1r-G1v: Folio IV.vi.1-55*

Though there is frequent parallelism, the Quarto clearly derives
from an independent MS. The possibility of memorial reconstruction
can be disregarded in view of the Quarto's comparative metrical
regularity and the lack of exact correspondence in the Host's speeches.
The Quarto scene is palpably non-Shakespearian. The Folio is evidently a fairly hasty adaptation, admitting some new details. It is
undistinguished, but the Shakespearian touch is apparent in occasional
lines such as

The mirth whereof, so larded with my matter

and:

> While other Iests are something ranke on foote.

In reworking his source material Shakespeare introduced minor confusions of his own. As has already been noted, the opening lines of the Quarto have a more probable ring than those of the Folio and the Quarto is at least consistent in the matter of the red dress. The Folio has a suspicious duplication at line 30:

> While other sports are tasking of their mindes

which follows hard on:

> While other Iests are something ranke on foote.

and this argues either careless composition or failure to delete. The Quarto says nothing of Anne Page representing the Fairy Queen, and this, on the evidence of the Folio and of the later Quarto stage-directions already discussed, must be accounted an unresolved Shakespearian anomaly. The Quarto proposes a reasonably logical scheme of action with everything turning on the colours of the dresses, whereas the Folio insistence on the Fairy Queen renders the colours irrelevant since, presumably, Slender, Caius and Fenton would all seek to steal away the same character. In the light of V.v. one of them should, theoretically, acquire Mistress Quickly, but Shakespeare clearly changed his plan as he went along. The page of MS. which served as the Quarto copy had evidently been adjusted by him in respect of proper names and speech-headings, but there is nothing to suggest that he added marginal notes. The Folio gives the impression of being a complete revision, with extensive borrowing and some augmentation, of the source-play.

### (d) Quarto G2r-G4v: Folio V.v.41-259

Shakespeare's adaptation of source material which the Quarto substantially preserves is again evident, and the case for regarding certain speeches and stage-directions in the Quarto as Shakespeare's working notes has already been presented. The first part of the Quarto scene (corresponding to the Folio lines 41-105) must certainly preserve a section of the source-play almost unaltered since the verse is regular, and since the 'metamorphised youth' remains. Shakespeare evidently adjusted the speech-headings and changed two or three consonants in the speeches which he decided to allot to Evans. Falstaff's two remarks can be regarded as marginal interpolations, as can Evans's

> It is right indeed, he is full of lecheries and iniquitie.

which, unlike his earlier speeches in the scene, is in character.

Shakespeare was too old a hand at writing fairy scenes to need guidance from his source, and it is likely that his refashioning of this section was spontaneous. Even so, he incorporated words and phrases from the original:

Q. You Fayries that do haunt these shady groues.

F. Fairies blacke, gray, greene, and white,
   You Moone-shine reuellers, and shades of night. (41-2)

Q. And when you finde a slut that lies a sleepe,
   And all her dishes foule, and roome vnswept,
   With your long nailes pinch her till she crie,
   And sweare to mend her sluttish huswiferie.

F. Where fires thou find'st vnrak'd, and hearths vnswept,
   There pinch the Maids as blew as Bill-berry,
   Our radiant Queene, hates Sluts, and Sluttery. (48-50)

Q. Where is *Pead*? go you & see where Brokers sleep.

F. Wher's *Bede*? Go you, and where you find a maid. (53)

Q. Spare neither legge, arme, head, nor face.

F. Pinch them armes, legs, shoulders, sides, & shins. (58)

Q. And set it to his fingers endes,
   And if you see it him offends,
   And that he starteth at the flame,
   Then is he mortall, know his name.

F. With Triall-fire touch me his finger end:
   If he be chaste, the flame will backe descend
   And turne him to no paine: but if he start,
   It is the flesh of a corrupted hart. (88-91)

Q. About it then, and know the truth.

F. About him (Fairies) sing a scornfull rime. (97)

Q. A little distant from him stand,
   And euery one take hand in hand,

And compasse him within a ring,
First pinch him well, and after sing.

F.  Pray you lock hand in hand: your selues in order set:
And twenty glow-wormes shall our Lanthornes bee
To guide our Measure round about the Tree. (81-3)

About him (Fairies) sing a scornfull rime,
And as you trip, still pinch him to your time. (97-8)

And Nightly-meadow-Fairies, looke you sing
Like to the *Garters*-Compasse, in a ring. (69-70)

What these comparisons appear to establish is that Shakespeare, though responsive to suggestion, effected a wholesale transformation of his source-material. Lines 69-70 of the Folio, with their parallel rhyme and utilisation of the Quarto 'compasse', are especially interesting as evidence that the allusion to the Order of the Garter belonged to Shakespeare's original version of *The Merry Wives*.

The remainder of the Quarto scene, which has already been set out in full, calls for little comment. The dialogue tentatively redistributed among the Pages and Fords yielded, in the reshaping process, to something more pointed and flexible, though the transformation is mainly in terms of prose. Falstaff's mutterings in the Quarto:

*Horne* the hunter quoth you: am I a ghost?
Sblood the Fairies hath made a ghost of me:
What hunting at this time at night?
Ile lay my life the mad Prince of *Wales*
Is stealing his fathers Deare. How now who haue
we here, what is all *Windsor* stirring? Are you there?

cannot reasonably be regarded as a dramatic speech, and the typographical dislocation argues that they were rough marginal jottings which Shakespeare subsequently discarded. The reference to the 'mad Prince of *Wales*' may originally have been incorporated in the Folio version. It could have given no offence in Elizabeth's reign, but was hardly likely to survive later than 1610 when Prince Henry was created Prince of Wales. All other speeches assigned in the Quarto to Falstaff, Shallow, Evans, Caius and Slender can reasonably be accounted marginal annotations, though elements of the speeches which they were intended to replace may have been retained. A portion of the source-play appears to have been caught up in one of Falstaff's speeches:

ISP

Well, and the fine wits of the Court heare this,
Thayle so whip me with their keene Iests,
That thayle melt me out like tallow,
Drop by drop out of my grease. Boyes!

The final couplet, which is practically identical with that in the Folio, must be reckoned one of Shakespeare's additions to the MS., that is, unless Ford, or some name that rhymed with 'word', was used in the source-play.

ii

The process so far discussed has been that of revision or adaptation by Shakespeare of a pre-existing comedy, possibly by Henry Porter, and the main contention here is that *The Merry Wives of Windsor*, in its Folio form, was the outcome of that process. Critics have been haunted by the idea that the play underwent some measure of revision after 1602, but no really convincing hypothesis has been put forward. Several allusions to events in the reign of James I have been alleged, but none of these will endure scrutiny. The only available evidence, therefore, is again that provided by Quarto–Folio comparison.

One peculiarity of the 'good' text is that it occasionally omits phrases or lines which are preserved in the 'bad' one. Several of these seem necessary to the sense, so that supplementation, especially by the eighteenth-century editors, has been a common practice. The passages in question are as follows:

(i) Q. I haue matter in my head against you and your cogging companions, *Pistoll* and *Nym*. They carried mee to the Tauerne and made mee drunke, and afterward picked my pocket.

   F. Marry sir, I haue matter in my head against you, and against your cony-catching Rascalls, *Bardolf*, *Nym*, and *Pistoll*. (. . . .). (I.i.127-9)

(ii) Q. I cannot abide the smell of hot meate
    Nere since I broke my shin. Ile tel you how it came
    By my troth. A Fencer and I plaid three venies
    For a dish of stewd prunes, and I with my ward
    Defending my head, he hot my shin. Yes faith.

   F. I had rather walke here (I thanke you) I bruiz'd my shin th'other day, with playing at Sword and Dagger with a Master of Fence (three veneys for a dish of stew'd Prunes) and by my troth, I cannot abide the smell of hot meate since. (I.i.293-7)

(iii) Q. Pray you do, I must not be absent at the grace.
I will goe make an end of my dinner.

F. I pray you be gon: I will make an end of my dinner. (I.ii.9-10)

(iv) Q. His minde is not heroick. And theres the humor of it.
F. He was gotten in drink: is not the humor cõceited? (I.iii.23)

(v) Q. I haue operations in my head, which are humors of reuenge.
F. I haue opperations,
Which be humors of reuenge. (I.iii.98-9)

(vi) Q. Why this is right my letter.
O most notorious villaine!
Why what a bladder of iniquitie is this?
Lets be reuenged what so ere we do.

F. Letter for letter; but that the name of *Page* and *Ford* differs: to thy
great comfort in this mystery of ill opinions, heere's the twyn-
brother of thy Letter: but let thine inherit first. (II.i.71-4)

(vii) Q. Beware, take heed, for *Falstaffe* loues thy wife:
When *Pistoll* lies do this.

F. Sir *Iohn* affects thy wife.
(. . .) (II.i.115)

(viii) Q.        And for the knight, perhaps
He hath spoke merrily, as the fashion of fat men
Are: But should he loue my wife,
Ifaith Ide turn her loose to him.

F. (. . .)
I marry do's he: if hee should intend this voyage toward my wife,
I would turne her loose to him. (II.i.188-9)

(ix) Q. I will retort the sum in equipage.

F. Why then the world's mine Oyster, which I, with sword will
open. (II.ii.2)

(x) Q. Hark van vrd in your eare. You be vn daga
And de *Iack*, coward preest.

F. By-gar, you are de Coward: de Iack dog: Iohn Ape (III.i.84-5)

(xi) Q.        By Ieshu *I* will knock your
vrinalls about your knaues cockcomes, for missing
your meetings and appointments.

F.  I will knog your Vrinal
    about your knaues Cogs-combe. (III.i.91-2)

(xii) Q.  No he giues me the prouerbes, and the nouerbes:
          Giue me thy hand terestiall,
          So giue me thy hand celestiall.

F.  No, he giues me the Prouerbes, and the
    No-verbes. Giue me thy hand (Celestiall) so. (III.i.106-7)

(xiii) Q.  (*Doc.*) And dere be ven to, I sall make de tird:
           (*Sir Hu*) In your teeth for shame.

F.  (*Ca.*) If there be one, or two, I shall make-a-the turd. (. . .)
                                                          (III.iii.251)

As evidence for revision most of these passages are insignificant. The Quarto additions at (i), (ii), (iv) and (xiii) look suspiciously like actors' gags. Those at (vi) and (vii) are evidently contaminations from *Henry IV*. The Act of Abuses may, with caution, be held to account for the Folio omission in (iii). The change in Pistol's reply to Falstaff in (ix) is something of a mystery, and may in fact have been an afterthought. The remaining Quarto additions are all desirable and their omission from the Folio must be accounted accidental. In (v) the Folio lines are typographically odd and it would seem that the compositor (A) inadvertently failed to fit the requisite half-line into his composing stick. The remaining omissions in the Folio may testify to lacunae in Crane's transcript, though (x) and (xi) on a C page and (xii) on a B page are in close propinquity at a point where the stints were divided and may on that account be due to miscalculation in the casting-off of the Folio copy. The Quarto supplement at (viii), as Hart remarked, 'is quite characteristic of Page's agreeable character, and is itself worthy of a place.'[3] Here, as elsewhere, there seems no reason to postulate revision.

The supposition that the 'Garter' passage (V.v.59-80) belongs to a later revision of the play is unacceptable in the light of evidence cited above.[4] If, as tradition has it, Elizabeth herself commissioned the play there is no reason why a Garter Feast should not have been the occasion, and the Windsor setting, in itself, argues for something of the kind. The absence of any reference to the Garter in the Quarto, incredible in a memorial report, is intelligible in the light of the hypothesis presented in the previous chapter.

There is a better case for assuming revision in the post-horse episode

[3] *ed. cit.*, p. xxiii.          [4] *supra.*, p. 121.

(IV.v), though few positive conclusions can be drawn. In the Quarto the passage runs:

*Enter Bardolfe*

*Bar.* O Lord sir cousonage, plaine cousonage.
*Host.* Why man, where be my horses? where be the Germanes?
*Bar.* Rid away with your horses:
After I came beyond Maidenhead,
They flung me in a slow of myre, & away they ran.

*Enter Doctor*

*Doc.* Where be my Host de gartyre?
*Host.* O here sir in perplexitie.
*Doc.* I cannot tell vad be dad,
But begar I will tell you van ting,
Dear be a Garmaine Duke come to de Court,
Has cosened all de host of *Branford*,
And *Redding*: begar I tell you for good will,
Ha, ha, mine Host, am I euen met you?                    *Exit.*

*Enter Sir Hugh*

*Sir Hu.* Where is mine Host of the gartyr?
Now my Host, I would desire you looke you now,
To haue a care of your entertainments,
For there is three sorts of cosen garmombles,
Is cosen all the Host of Maidenhead & Readings,
Now you are an honest man, and a scuruy beggerly lowsie knaue beside:
And can point wrong places,
*I* tell you for good will, grate why mine Host.          *Exit.*
*Host.* I am cosened *Hugh*, and coy *Bardolfe*,
Sweet knight assist me, *I* am cosened.                   *Exit.*

The corresponding section in the Folio reads:

*Bar.* Out alas (Sir) cozonage: meere cozonage.
*Host.* Where be my horses? speake well of them varletto.
*Bar.* Run away with the cozoners: for so soone as I came beyond *Eaton*, they threw me off, from behinde one of them, in a slough of myre; and set spurres, and away; like three *Germane-* diuels; three *Doctor Faustasses*.
*Host.* They are gone but to meete the Duke (villaine) doe not say they be fled: *Germanes* are honest men.
*Euan.* Where is mine *Host*?
*Host.* What is the matter Sir?
*Euan.* Haue a care of your entertainments: there is a friend of mine come to

Towne, tels mee there is three Cozen-Iermans, that has cozend all the *Hosts* of *Readins*, of *Maidenhead*; of *Cole-brooke*, of horses and money: I tell you for good will (looke you) you are wise, and full of gibes, and vlouting-stocks: and 'tis not conuenient you should be couzoned. Fare you well.

*Cai.* Ver'is mine *Host de Iarteere?*

*Host.* Here (Master *Doctor*) in perplexitie, and doubtfull delemma.

*Cai.* I cannot tell vat is dat: but it is tell-a-me, dat you make grand preparation for a Duke *de Iamanie*: by my trot: der is no Duke that the Court is know, to come: I tell you for good will: adieu.

*Host.* Huy and cry, (villaine) goe: assist me Knight, I am vndone: fly, run: huy, and cry (villaine) I am vndone.

The Quarto version is anything but reassuring. Its '*Hugh*, and coy *Bardolfe*' shews the kind of absurdity that Creede's compositor was capable of, and the wilder flights of the reporter are evident in the last three lines of Evans's speech. As has already been noted, it differs from the Folio in locating the beginning of the flight of the horse-thieves not in Windsor but somewhere west of Maidenhead. It transposes the speeches of Evans and Caius, not without confusion. One distinctive feature is the mysterious phrase 'grate why', for which editors have provided some most improbable interpretations. The most obvious explanation is that this represents the reporter's attempt to reproduce French 'gratuit', which accords with'I tell you for good will', but if so it must belong to Caius and not, as in the Quarto, to Evans. The other peculiarity is 'cosen garmombles', which certainly looks like an allusion to Mömpelgart. Even so, as Chambers remarked, '"Garmombles" may be a bit of "gag" in any case',[5] and the other divergences from the Folio are not demonstrably significant.

However, the Folio itself offers grounds for inferring revision. It gives a somewhat incomplete account of the whole episode and appears to go out of its way to introduce two disclaimers, one to the effect that '*Germanes* are honest men' and the other a straightforward denial of the German Duke's presence at Court:

> der is no Duke that the Court is know, to come.

The probability is that the play originally contained palpable allusions to Mömpelgart and his agents, all of which were quite acceptable so long as Elizabeth was on the throne, and that objections were raised during the reign of her successor. Deletions were accordingly made in the prompt-book, but were doubtless trivial. Objections raised by the

[5] *William Shakespeare*, I, p. 432.

Cobham family resulted, of course, in the alteration of Ford's assumed name from 'Brooke' to 'Broome', and the Act of Abuses led to spasmodic and inconsistent modification of oaths. Shakespeare himself may have made all the requisite changes in the prompt-book, though they could equally well have been the work of the book-keeper. Shakespeare, in *The Merry Wives of Windsor*, was assuredly a reviser in the sense that he refashioned another writer's play, but there are no substantial grounds for postulating later revision.

ten

# Hamlet

## The General Textual Problems

### i

The case presented in the chapters which follow is that *Hamlet* has features in common with the plays already discussed. It is argued that, like all of these, it was originally designed for a private occasion—one roughly analogous to that postulated for *Troilus and Cressida*—and that the needs of the public theatre subsequently necessitated some measure of revision. Since *Hamlet* has always been a happy hunting-ground for every kind of theory, it would be hazardous to claim this hypothesis as one that has hitherto remained unexplored but, so far as the present writer is aware, it has not, as yet, been related to recent developments in textual criticism. It is fitting that it should be since, if correct, it resolves several of the outstanding problems and offers a reasonably coherent pattern of transmission down to the time of the printing of the Folio.

*Hamlet* has survived in three versions—Q1, printed for Ling and Trundell in 1603; Q2, printed for Ling by James Roberts in 1604; and the Folio. There are material differences which have been variously explained, and since many of the explanations have invoked the so-called *Ur-Hamlet* it will be convenient to consider this before proceeding to review the Shakespearian versions. It may be remarked that *Hamlet*, like *The Merry Wives of Windsor*, is haunted by the shadow of a lost source-play, though it doubtless wears its rue with a difference.

### ii

The existence of the *Ur-Hamlet* is established by allusions in Nashe's Preface to Greene's *Menaphon* (1589) and Lodge's *Wit's Miserie* (1596), together with Henslowe's record of a performance given at Newington Butts on June 11th, 1594, by the combined Admiral's and Chamberlain's companies. Since Nashe's allusion occurs in the middle of what is palpably an attack on Thomas Kyd and all his works, it has been generally assumed that the *Ur-Hamlet* was Kyd's, but, as G. I. Duthie has forcibly argued, there are no firm grounds for this assumption.[1] The view that Shakespeare himself was the author of the earlier play has been advanced at various times. If it could be trusted home it would undeniably help towards the resolution of several problems but unfortunately there is a total lack of evidence. If, prior to 1589, he had exercised his prentice talents on the Hamlet story, however crude the result, it is distinctly odd that he should subsequently have plodded towards long-delayed tragic fulfilment by way of *Titus Andronicus* and *Romeo and Juliet*. No firm claim for the authorship of the *Ur-Hamlet* is therefore admissible, nor can much reliance be placed on the tentative composition date (1587 or 1588) as advanced by Boas and accepted as convenient by other critics.[2] The play may well have been earlier than *The Spanish Tragedy* which lacks a source and occasionally gives the impression of having been coloured by some version of the Hamlet story.

Such considerations are immaterial, however. One thing that can be confidently assumed is that the *Ur-Hamlet* was based on the story in Belleforest's *Histories Tragiques* which relates 'Avec quelle ruse Amleth, qui depuis fut roy de Dannemarck, vengea la mort de son père Horvendille, occis par Fengon son frère, et autre occurrence de son histoire.' An equally safe assumption is that the play was executed in the approved manner of English Seneca so that the outcome must inevitably have borne a close family resemblance to *The Spanish Tragedy*. Certain conclusions may therefore be drawn.

It is a probable, and even necessary, assumption that the early play, like Shakespeare's, ended with the completion of Hamlet's revenge purpose. Belleforest's somewhat aimless account of his hero's subsequent adventures, the 'autre occurrence de son histoire', does not impress by virtue of its dramatic potentialities. And even the most uncritical of Elizabethan dramatists, when he found Hamlet acquiring both a second uncle and a second wife, must have suspected conflation of two quite separate stories. The revenge tale itself doubtless sufficed for Kyd's needs, if Kyd it was, and, together with the basic plot and several specific incidents, he took over Hamlet's feigned madness and the general background of drunkenness and corruption. The character in Belleforest corresponding to Ophelia is an unnamed harlot, who may have been modified in the *Ur-Hamlet* but was, nevertheless, ultimately responsible for the allegation of lightness brought against Ophelia in

---

[1] *The 'Bad' Quarto of 'Hamlet'*, pp. 55-77.
[2] *The Works of Thomas Kyd*, ed. F. S. Boas, p. xlix.

Shakespeare's play. Senecan elements, in so far as inferences can be drawn from *The Spanish Tragedy*, would include Hamlet's procrastination, his insistence on a full and perfect revenge, the ghost, the dumb-show and the inner-play. It is permissible to surmise that the *Ur-Hamlet* ended, as *The Spanish Tragedy* does, with the inner-play performed by the principals, who do not poison in jest. Further than this it is not possible to go, and it may be that even these claims are excessive. To admit them does no harm, however, since the most that they imply is that, in terms of plot and incident, *Hamlet* owes just about as much to the *Ur-Hamlet* as *Measure for Measure* does to *Promos and Cassandra*.

It has sometimes been claimed that fragments of the *Ur-Hamlet* dialogue are encrusted in Shakespeare's play, but the notion that *Hamlet* owes much to its predecessor in respect of tone and style has little to commend it. One aspect of Shakespeare's methods as an adapter has already been considered in connexion with *The Merry Wives of Windsor*. The case for Porter, if tenable, makes it likely that Shakespeare inherited, in whole or part, a shapely and well-written comedy, yet the demonstrable Porterian elements in the Folio play resolve themselves into plot and situation, together with a collection of isolated words and phrases, and not a vestige of Porter's style, as revealed by *The Two Angry Women of Abingdon*, is apparent in the dialogue. Shakespeare's practice over the period 1597-1606, that which covers both *Hamlet* and *The Merry Wives of Windsor*, is elsewhere invariable. *The Famous Victories of Henry the Fifth* served as one of the sources for the later history-plays, yet the dramatist's various debts do not include any that can be termed stylistic, and the same holds for *King Lear* viewed in relation to *The History of King Leir*. Shakespeare's handling of his source, *Promos and Cassandra*, in *Measure for Measure* is particularly illuminating since his general obligations are considerable. Whetstone's play supplies the main plot, a fair proportion of the background and practically the whole of the governing morality. In the dedication he expounds a theory of comedy which goes some way towards explaining Shakespeare's own handling of the theme. *Promos and Cassandra* belongs, of course, to the infancy of Elizabethan drama and, as a stage action, has little to commend it. But much of its dialogue is shapely, meaningful and, at times, dramatic to a degree, so that there are points where Shakespeare, without any loss of face, might reasonably have settled for a close paraphrase. Yet not one line, and scarcely a phrase, of Whetstone's finds its way into *Measure for Measure*. In his Roman plays Shakespeare was content to follow North's *Plutarch* very closely indeed, but North was, after all, a great master of English prose. When the source material was itself a play it seems that quite different methods applied and it might indeed be claimed, on the evidence of *Measure for Measure*, that Shakespeare was almost pathologically concerned with covering his tracks.

There is no reason for supposing that he made any exception in the case of the *Ur-Hamlet*. The Senecan manner proved far less durable than Senecan matter, and at the time when *Hamlet* was written the rhetorical excesses of Kyd and his followers were openly derided, not least by Shakespeare himself. The *Ur-Hamlet* in this respect is not likely to have fared better than *The Spanish Tragedy* and, in fact, the references of both Nashe and Lodge hint that its stylistic absurdities had been ridiculed almost from the first. Finally, it may be argued that Shakespeare is unlikely to have treated Kyd, or whoever wrote the *Ur-Hamlet*, with a deference that he withheld from Marlowe. It is almost certain that the Pyrrhus speeches in *Hamlet* were based on Aeneas's account of the fall of Troy in *Dido, Queen of Carthage*, yet, despite palpable similarities of tone and style, it is not possible to isolate a single close verbal parallel.

The *Ur-Hamlet*, then, is likely to have been used by Shakespeare in the same general way that he used *Promos and Cassandra*. In other respects there is ample justification for regarding it as little more than a red-herring. *Hamlet* admittedly contains a fair number of passages that belong, stylistically, to the Senecan tradition, but Shakespeare was, after all, writing a revenge tragedy. Moreover, as most of the plays of his maturity shew, he was always prepared to revive outmoded patterns of style when it suited his purpose to do so.

### iii

The 1603 Quarto, formerly regarded as Shakespeare's first draft, is now generally recognised to be a pirated text based on memorial reconstruction. The case, put forward by H. D. Gray,[3] that the reporter was an actor who successively sustained the roles of Marcellus, Lucianus and a supernumerary has been used by Duthie as one of the bases for an impressive and generally convincing analysis of the Q1 problems,[4] and the present writer has attempted to shew, on the evidence of apparent

[3] 'The First Quarto Hamlet', *Modern Language Review*, pp. 171-80, and 'Thomas Kyd and the First Quarto of Hamlet', *Publications of the Modern Language Association of America*, xlii, pp. 721-35.

[4] *op. cit.*

cues, the location of the reporter's appearances in the later acts.[5] Wilson's view that the pirate had access to a copy of Voltemar's part has been widely accepted,[6] and Greg has argued persuasively that this may have been another of his roles.[7]

In the main Q1 was apparently derived from the version of *Hamlet* preserved in the Folio, but there are several interesting divergences. The Nunnery scene is brought forward so that it follows immediately upon Polonius's proposal to 'loose my daughter to him'; the opening speeches of the inner-play are radically different from those of the authentic texts but are written in tolerable couplets; the Closet scene ends with Gertrude protesting her innocence and undertaking to further Hamlet's plan for revenge; there is a scene in which Horatio relates to the Queen the circumstances of Hamlet's return to Denmark and in which she reiterates her intention of helping her son by allaying Claudius's suspicions.

These divergences might normally be regarded as improvisations by a reporter whose recollection of certain vital episodes proved virtually non-existent and who, as a result, was forced to devise a few substitutes of his own in order to achieve a coherent text. This explanation may hold for some of the differences mentioned, but certainly not for all of them. There exists another reported text, *Der Bestrafte Brudermord*, which is evidently a memorial reconstruction of *Hamlet* used by English strolling players in Germany during the seventeenth century. This certainly has no direct connexion with Q1 yet it accords substantially with that text in its placing of the Nunnery scene and, in its account of Hamlet's adventures at sea, employs the words: 'Nun begab es sich, dass wir eines Tages contrairen Wind hatten' which clearly echo Q1:

> Being crossed by the contention of the windes.

(Horatio to the Queen in the fourth of the divergences noted above.) There is no corresponding line in the authentic texts. It may be added that the *Brudermord* agrees with Q1 in substituting the name 'Corambus' (Q1: Corambis) for 'Polonius'.

Duthie's view is that these peculiarities accord with the general theory that Q1 represents an abridged memorial reconstruction designed for use in the provinces by a group of actors who had no right

[5] '*Hamlet* and the Player who could not Keep Counsel', *Shakespeare Survey 3*, pp. 74–82.

[6] J. D. Wilson, 'The Copy for *Hamlet* 1603 and the *Hamlet* Transcript 1593', *The Library*, ix, pp. 156–60.

[7] *The Shakespeare First Folio*, pp. 302, 330 (note).

to the play. Such a conclusion is not easy to resist since the great majority of Bad Quartos are thought to be of this character, but the concomitant assumption that the reporter was responsible for what seems to be quite skilful abridgement and that he tied up the loose ends with several passages of blank verse of his own devising raises difficulties. In the first place it offers no really satisfactory explanation of the connexion, if any, between Q1 and the *Brudermord*. And in the second it attributes to the reporter talents which, on other grounds, one can scarcely believe that he possessed. We may reasonably ask why, if he was capable of turning out tolerably competent and functional verse and of giving some measure of coherence to the abridgement, he was content, at the same time, to let the products of his own muddled memory survive with all their imperfections on their heads. Evidence of his illiteracy, if not downright imbecility, is apparent throughout. One specimen will suffice by way of illustration:

> To be, or not to be, I there's the point,
> To Die, to sleepe, is that all? I all:
> No, to sleepe, to dreame, I mary there it goes,
> For in that dreame of death, when wee awake,
> And borne before an euerlasting Iudge,
> From whence no passenger euer retur'nd,
> The vndiscouered country, at whose sight
> The happy smile, and the accursed damn'd.
> But for this, the ioyfull hope of this,
> Whol'd beare the scornes and flattery of the world,
> Scorned by the right rich, the rich curssed of the poore?
> The widow being oppressed, the orphan wrong'd,
> The taste of hunger, or a tirants raigne,
> And thousand more calamities besides,
> To grunt and sweate vnder this weary life,
> When that he may his full *Quietus* make,
> With a bare bodkin, who would this indure,
> But for a hope of something after death?
> Which pusles the braine, and doth confound the sence,
> Which makes vs rather beare those euilles we haue,
> Than flie to others that we know not of.
> I that, O this conscience makes cowardes of vs all,
> Lady in thy orizons, be all my sinnes remembred.

This passage, which is no better and certainly no worse than many others in Q1, is illuminating. It proves conclusively that nothing but a purely mechanical memorial process was involved and that the reporter was quite content to leave it at that. The memorial lapses are not in themselves especially significant, but what is impressive is the reporter's total disregard of Shakespeare's meaning, of anybody's meaning, of elementary syntax and of all metrical principles. If, as Duthie suggests, the reporter had some modest ability as an adapter and hack-poet it is quite inconceivable that he should have failed to give some shape and coherence to the fragments, scraps, the bits and greasy relics of his memory. It is possible, therefore, to admit the provisional judgment that Q1 rests wholly on a memorial reconstruction which alternates between the tolerably accurate and the grossly inaccurate. This, however, implies that most of the divergences noted were the outcome of fairly reliable reporting, so that the need to explain them still remains, and this is a matter to which it will be convenient to return later.

The general question of Q1 authority is also one that can best await the outcome of the present discussion. For the moment it will suffice to remark that its stage-directions, being recollections of actual performances, are sometimes illuminating and that critics are willing to admit the possibility that one or two of its variant readings may be correct. Theoretically it should reproduce the speeches of Marcellus, Voltemar and Lucianus with complete accuracy and should be generally reliable for some of the adjacent dialogue, but it would be rash to claim that this holds in practice, especially as allowance has to be made for two unverifiable possibilities, first that the reporter may even have forgotten parts of his own speeches, and second that the compositor may sometimes have misread his copy. Even so, the Lucianus section affords three variant readings—*trapically* (Q2, F: *tropically*); *must take* (Q2, F: *mistake*); *bane* (Q2, F: *ban*)—which cannot be lightly set aside. Voltemar's speech in Q1 contains a couple of indifferent variants, but the important point is that the speaker is apparently given his correct name. If, as seems likely, Voltemar is really a form of Valdemar, Q2 (*Voltemand*) and the Folio (*Voltumand*) are unacceptable. The Marcellus sections raise several problems, but the Q1 variants, of which there is a fair sprinkling, are not significant. Several of them can confidently be dismissed as printer's errors, and the impression throughout is that the reporter was not quite word-perfect.

iv

Wilson's painstaking analysis has conclusively established that Shakespeare's foul papers served as the basis for Q2,[8] though it is

8 *The Manuscript of Shakespeare's Hamlet.*

evident that reference was also made to a copy of Q1. Wilson describes it as 'one of the worst printed of all the original Shakespearian texts' and concludes that it was set by a careless and inexperienced compositor who was working against time, with the result that he was responsible for a notable crop of misreadings and omissions. It is now known, thanks to the investigations of Fredson Bowers[9] and J. R. Brown,[10] that two compositors were involved and, since the responsibility for error and omission appears to apply equally to both of them, Wilson's explanation is no longer tenable. The only alternative, so far as one can see, is that finally mooted by Greg, that 'the source of the peculiarities of Q2 may have to be sought in the copy'.[11]

All critics are agreed that Q2 was dependent to some degree on Q1, but opinions differ about the extent of such dependence. Dr. Alice Walker maintains that Q1 was used up to the end of Act I and at no other point.[12] In addition she holds that a corrected copy of Q1 served as Q2 copy for the whole of the first act. There can be no doubt about such dependence in Act I since the typographical links are numerous and irrefutable, but Dr. Walker's other contentions are vulnerable. The second of them postulates a tedious and laborious process whereby a collator transferred to the comparatively restricted margins of Q1 all the corrections and additions that were necessary to convert its version of Act I into that presented in Q2. The kind of copy that would have resulted can only be described as a compositor's nightmare compared to which fair would be too foul an epithet for the foulest of foul papers. It may be said that this whole doctrine of marked quartos serving as printing-house copy is one that calls for the most rigid control. Dr. Walker, as one of its leading exponents, is nothing if not penetrating and judicious, but in her application of it to the problems of *Hamlet* Q2 zeal seems, for once, to have outrun discretion.

The question of Q2 dependence on Q1 after the first act is a difficult one. Sporadic typographical similarities suggest that Q1 was consulted throughout, though the Q2 compositors naturally disregarded those sections which bear little perceptible resemblance to the genuine text. The following attempt to isolate sections involving consultation is

[9] F. T. Bowers, 'The Printing of Hamlet, Q2', *Studies in Bibliography*, vii, pp. 41-50.

[10] J. R. Brown, 'The Compositors of Hamlet Q2 and *The Merchant of Venice*', *Studies in Bibliography*, vii, pp. 17-40.

[11] *The Shakespeare First Folio*, p. 331.

[12] 'The Textual Problem of *Hamlet*: a Reconsideration', *The Review of English Studies*, n.s., ii. pp. 328-38.

necessarily approximate and, up to a point, impressionistic, though the evidence invoked, namely identical spelling and capitalisation, is the same as that which is conclusive for Act I. Compositor determination is in accordance with that proposed by Bowers.[13]

| | Compositor | Typographical Links |
|---|---|---|
| II.i.59–61 | Y | Tennis; Videlizet (z caught up from Q1 viz.); brothell. |
| III.i.140–54 | Y | yce; Nunry (Q1: Nunnery); madde. |
| III.ii.260–71 | Y | keene; groning; croking; ranck (Q1: rancke). Punctuation throughout Lucianus's speech (lines 266–71) shews close similarity. |
| III.iv.1–37 | X | comming; Rat; Duckat; penitrable. |
| IV.iv.1–4 | Y | Fortinbrasse (Q1: Fortenbrasse); *Craues (F: Claimes); randeuous (Q1: Randevous). |
| IV.v.52–73 | Y | dond (Q1: dan'd); dupt; Charitie; doo't; too't; too blame; sunne. (Q1: Sunne); chuse; God night (Q1: God bwy). |
| V.i.28–66 | Y | buriall; pitty; Mason; Shypwright (Q1: Shipwright); Carpenter; gallowes dooes well; Doomesday. |
| V.i.230–305 | Y | *Imperious (F: Imperiall); stoppe; Priest; ministring Angell; *wisedome feare; hold off (F: wisenesse feare. Away); Crocadile (Q1: crocadile). |
| V.i.306–22 | X | Doue; Cat; Dogge (Q1: Dog). |
| V.ii.352–414 | X | *I leaue (Q1: thou leaue. F: shall liue); bloudily; kingdome; *royall (F: royally); amisse. |

It must be conceded that some of these resemblances do not carry much weight and that others may be fortuitous. On the other hand, it would be placing an enormous strain on coincidence to suppose that such spellings as *yce, Duckat, penitrable, randeuous, chuse, Crocadile* and *bloudily*, not to mention the correspondences in capitalisation and punctuation, stood independently in the actor-reporter's manuscript and in Shakespeare's foul papers. There seems to be no escape from the conclusion that Q1 was consulted in most, if not all, of the sections listed above, and the possibility of contamination throws some doubt on the five Q1-Q2 readings marked with asterisks since the plausible variants supplied by the Folio may well have been *bona fide* corrections. In fact 'wisenesse' (V.i.286), 'shall liue' (V.ii.356) and 'royally' (V.ii.409),

[13] Bowers's full analysis is as follows: X: I.i.1–I.v.183; II.i.162–II.ii.605; III.iii.21–III.iv.210; V.i.306–V.ii.414; Y: I.v.185–II.i.161; II.ii.606–III.iii.20; III.iv.211–V.i.305.

which is metrically justifiable, have all been widely accepted. It is arguable that 'Claimes' (IV.iv.3) is the required reading since Fortinbras has no need to crave something that has already been promised and is virtually granted at II.ii.80. In view of 'Th' Imperiall *Caesar*' in *Cymbeline*, V.v.474, it is strange that editors should have been unanimous in their acceptance of 'Imperious' at V.i.236.[14]

It appears, then, that the Q2 compositors consulted Q1 whenever they could profitably do so and that they even used it at points where, in the light of present knowledge, it can scarcely be regarded as helpful in any real sense. Both compositors were equally involved since, although most of the examples cited above occur in Y's stints, X was responsible for setting the whole of Act I. When the thoroughly disreputable character of Q1 is taken into account, the whole procedure seems barely comprehensible. Yet, if we add to it the fact that X and Y were responsible, in roughly equal measure, for the manifold errors and omissions of Q2, a single, seemingly inevitable, explanation presents itself—namely, as Greg came near to asserting, that the manuscript that found its way into Roberts's printing-house was an unusually difficult one.[15] The fact that Q1 was apparently consulted in the most improbable places strongly supports this conclusion. No compositor in his right mind would have given a second glance to such things as the Q1 version of IV.v.52-73 or V.i.230-305 unless driven to dire extremes by the complexities of his primary copy. It is clear that, since Q2 makes good all the omissions of Q1, there is no question of the manuscript having been defective. It is simply that it was, in places, indecipherable.

There is no reason to suppose that Shakespeare's foul papers were unduly difficult as a general rule. Current critical opinion holds that some two dozen of the plays derived from foul papers[16] and, in the majority of cases, the compositors appear to have found them reasonably straightforward.[17] Occasionally they seem to have been orderly

[14] Malone's claim that both words had the same meaning, together with Dyce's assertion that 'imperious' was the usual Elizabethan form, may be responsible. It would seem, however, that Shakespeare distinguished clearly between 'imperious' (dominant, overbearing) and 'imperial' (pertaining to empire). Cf. also 'imperiall Votresse' in *A Midsummer Night's Dream*, II.i.163.

[15] Greg does not make his position quite clear in *The Shakespeare First Folio*, but he was evidently moving towards a number of revolutionary conclusions.

[16] Greg (*op. cit.*, p. 430) observes that 'foul papers come somehow into the picture in the case of twenty-five plays'.

[17] Consultation of a 'Bad' Quarto occurs elsewhere only in *Romeo and Juliet*, Q2, the reason being that the manuscript was defective.

KSP

enough to have stood as prompt-copies. If the manuscripts that Shakespeare normally delivered to the theatre were anything like the three
pages of *Sir Thomas More* one would judge that they can have presented
relatively few problems to a competent Elizabethan printer. The three
pages themselves contain a few deletions and alterations, sometimes
rather carelessly made, and one baffling word, 'momtanish', which a
compositor might have been tempted to emend. The three lines of
contorted rhetoric which involve deletions and substitutions by Hand
C are, of course, irrelevant since the graphic obscurities are not of
Shakespeare's making. In the last analysis there is the claim made by
Heminge and Condell that 'what he thought, he vttered with that
easinesse, that wee haue scarse receiued from him a blot in his papers'.
The extraordinary fluency here attributed to Shakespeare need not be
taken too seriously since it is quite possible that Heminge and Condell
had little first-hand knowledge of their friend's methods of composition.[18] On the other hand, no one was better qualified to speak of
the foul papers that he delivered to the company, so that the scarcity of
blots which they allege is, no doubt, substantially true in respect of all
manuscripts that can be regarded as final drafts.

   If, then, Q2 is 'one of the worst printed of all the original Shakespearian texts', the reason may be that it was based on one of the worst
of all Shakespeare's manuscripts. Q1 must, of course, have been purely
of catalytic value and cannot be regarded as a copy text. The numerous
imperfections, even if we make an unwarrantably generous allowance
for the fallibility of compositors, may be indicative of careless pen-
manship but are more likely to have arisen out of all the chopping and
changing that great poets habitually indulge in. The myth of Shakespeare's absolute fluency, for which Jonson, Milton and Pope are really
more blameworthy than Heminge and Condell, is one that will not
abide the test of common sense.[19] And least of all can *Hamlet*, perhaps
the most thoughtful of all the plays, be thought of 'as springing up with
all its parts absolute'. It is likely that our reactions to this particular
*Hamlet* manuscript, if it ever came to light, would be precisely those of

   [18] The addresses in the Folio, though based on information supplied by Heminge
and Condell, may not have been written by them. Jonson's authorship has been
plausibly suggested.
   [19] The *Sir Thomas More* addition might suggest otherwise, but it is substantially
a collection of familiar Shakespearian formulas and, though dramatically effective,
is far removed from that complexity of utterance which informs, for example,
*Macbeth* or *Antony and Cleopatra*. It is probable that *Timon of Athens* is a more
reliable guide to Shakespeare's methods of composition.

Charles Lamb, when, in expectation of 'a full-grown beauty', he examined the manuscript of *Lycidas:*

> How it staggered me to see the fine things in their ore! interlined, corrected! as if their words were mortal, alterable, displaceable at pleasure! as if they might have been otherwise, and just as good! as if inspiration were made up of parts, and these fluctuating, successive, indifferent.

Experience teaches us that this superb diagnosis covers not only such perfectionists as Milton and Tennyson but also the seemingly careless, like Wordsworth, and the seemingly facile, like Shelley. We have no justification for supposing that Shakespeare, a poet more rich and complex in utterance than any of these, differed from them in kind, however much it may please us to suppose that he differed in degree.

It is suggested, then, that the Q2 manuscript was very much an author's final draft which had been handed to the company in all its untidiness. Since a manuscript which baffled two compositors cannot possibly have been of any use for general theatrical requirements, it follows that a transcript must have been made, and it will later be argued that this served as the Folio copy. If so, it is evident that the playhouse scribe recognised certain markings in the original manuscript (brackets in the left-hand margin) as deletions and that the Q2 compositors did not. The reason for such deletions as emerge from a comparison between Q2 and the Folio is not altogether clear and, as Greg shrewdly observed, 'the omission of 225 lines out of nearly 4,000 is not very much and does not suggest any serious attempt to shorten the play'.[20] This view is supported by the fact that the Folio, in its turn, contains passages which are not in Q2. These have often been treated as inexplicable Q2 omissions. This may well suffice for two short passages (IV.v.161-3 and V.i.39-42), but there are reasonable grounds for holding that, of the longer ones (II.ii.244-76, II.ii.352-79 and V.ii.68-80), the first two were not in fact omissions but last-minute additions.

The deletions marked in the Q2 manuscript but ignored by the compositors do not call for much further comment. Several of the passages involved seem superfluous or redundant—the Lord's speech at V.ii.203, which merely repeats the message already delivered by Osric, is an obvious example—and this, no doubt, is why Shakespeare rejected them. The only omission which raises really ponderable difficulties is that at IV.iv.9-66, and the question is whether a cut was seriously

[20] *The Shakespeare First Folio*, p. 317.

intended.[21] Possibly the most interesting deletions in relation to definition of the Q2 manuscript are those at I.i.108-26, I.iv.18-38 and V.ii.110-50, 162-3. All of these give the impression, perhaps falsely, of having been surrendered in the actual process of composition. The first of them is evidently a fairly close paraphrase of some lines in Lucan's *Pharsalia*, which Shakespeare may have read in Marlowe's translation. It looks too as if it may have been intended as a puff, designed to remind audiences that Shakespeare had also written a play called *Julius Caesar*. The passage has been rightly stigmatized as irrelevant and the analogy which it presents is a very dubious one. The murder of Hamlet's father is, at this stage, the only circumstance comparable to the assassination of Caesar, and a man's ghost can scarcely be the precursor to his own death. The syntax is uncertain, and there is palpable confusion in the lines:

> As starres with traines of fier, and dewes of blood
> Disasters in the sunne.

Punctuation is inadequate, and the last five lines, like parts of the Shakespearian addition to *Sir Thomas More*, ramble on without a single comma. The compositor may have been to blame, but the general impression is of a tentative draft which the dramatist himself abandoned.

Much the same conditions apply to Hamlet's somewhat diffuse discourse at I.iv.18-38.[22] Pointing is defective and the writing is sometimes slipshod. The repetition of 'us' (lines 18-19) is ungainly, but less so than that of 'our' in three consecutive lines (20-2). There are several admirable lines and phrases, but also one or two that are flabby or otiose: 'east and west' (17), 'Swinish phrase' (19), 'as pure as grace' (33), and the parenthesis at 26:

> (Since nature cannot choose his origin)

is obscure and superfluous. The antecedent to 'his' is obviously 'men' in line 23 (followed by 'them' ... 'their' ... 'they'), so that a false quantity results. The same thing happens a few lines later when 'these men' (30) is followed by 'His vertues' (33.) At 36, 'particular fault', though reasonably remote from 'particular men' (23), sounds nevertheless clumsily

---

[21] Q1 suggests that the passage had been deleted, though fragments of it appear in both that text and the *Brudermord*. The possibility that abridgement involved some rewriting is considered below, p. 191.

[22] The view that the passage was cut in order not to give offence to King James's Danish consort is demolished by Greg in a trenchant note (*op. cit.*, p. 332).

repetitive. The speech ends with the notorious 'dram of eale' which has produced a plethora of fantastic emendations.[23] The simplest explanation of this crux is that the sentence is unfinished, the implication being that Shakespeare lapsed into incoherence and gave up the struggle. He must have realised that this lengthy meditation, whatever its rhetorical merits, was going some way towards turning his hero into a sententious bore.

The Osric section (V.ii.110-50, 162-3) differs from the foregoing since it cannot reasonably be regarded as a tentative draft. But the Q2 stage-direction preceding line 84, *'Enter a Courtier'*, suggests that Shakespeare had no very clear plan.[24] The portrayal of Osric, though not inconsistent, is variable, and the whole episode falls into three sections. In the first (84-110) and last (151-89) he is foolish and affected but makes his meaning clear in language that is not unduly extravagant. In the middle section (110-50) his speech is excessively flowery and provokes parody that is even more fantastic from Hamlet and, subsequently, Horatio (at 162-3). Hence, it may be argued that Shakespeare found himself lured into an elaborate Jonsonian burlesque of affectate Court language but, prompted no doubt by the realisation that one Polonius was enough, soon reverted to his original scheme.

For the rest, there is reason to suppose that Q2 preserves at least one afterthought, inserted in the foul papers in the form of an unperfected draft. This is the Queen's account of the accidental drowning of Ophelia (IV.vii.167-84) which is at variance with the several references to her suicide in V.i.[25] Whether this led to the deletion of Horatio's lines at I.iv.75-8:

> The very place puts toyes of desperation
> Without more motiue, into euery braine
> That lookes so many fadoms to the sea
> And heares it rore beneath.

is not clear. These seem pointless except as a preparation for the suicide

---

[23] The various attempts to explain the passage as it stands are no more convincing than the emendations.

[24] The Q1 reporter evidently saw Osric as a *'Bragart Gentleman'* (see stage-direction), but was unable to recall his name. Neither could the compiler of the *Brudermord*, who dubs him Phantasmo. Possibly the part made little impression at the time. The Osric type had already been over-exploited, even by Shakespeare.

[25] J. M. Nosworthy, 'The Death of Ophelia', *Shakespeare Quarterly*, XV, pp. 345-8.

of some character or other, and Ophelia, in the event, proves to be the only candidate.[26]

All in all it would appear that it was a variable and extraordinarily difficult set of foul papers that found its way to Roberts's printing-shop. It goes without saying that such a manuscript could never have been put to playhouse use and it is reasonable to conclude that, upon receipt of it, the book-holder promptly arranged for the preparation of a fair copy. In view of the formal correspondence between Q1 and the Folio, it is also legitimate to suppose that this transcript omitted all passages peculiar to Q2 except perhaps the perplexing section at IV.iv.9-66. And if such was the case, it means that some one hundred and seventy lines that are included in the text of every modern edition were, in all probability, never spoken on the stage during Shakespeare's lifetime.

V

It will be evident that the foregoing analyses of Q1 and Q2, though they incorporate several modifications and independent judgments, are not essentially at variance with received opinion. Such conformity does not extend to the Folio which remains problematic and has produced a wide diversity of interpretations. It is generally agreed that somewhere behind the text lies the authority of an independent manuscript, though the use made of that manuscript is much disputed, and that many of its variant readings, some of which are preposterous, are errors perpetrated by Jaggard's compositors. Beyond this all is controversy.

The modern approach to the Folio problems may be said to start with Dover Wilson's *The Manuscript of Shakespeare's 'Hamlet' and the Problems of its Transmission* (1934). Wilson's conclusion, which has gained wide but not universal acceptance, is that the Folio was printed from a transcript of the official prompt-book and that the hazards of transcription render it less authoritative than Q2, printed from Shakespeare's foul papers. In 1951, Dr. Alice Walker denied the use of manuscript copy and argued, from a formidable array of verbal errors, mistakes of punctuation and abnormal spellings common to both texts, that the Folio was in fact printed from a copy of Q2 which had been collated with a manuscript, which she took to be the prompt-book transcript postulated by Wilson, and marked accordingly.[27] This view

[26] In the *Brudermord* she throws herself from a high hill, and this may be what happened in the *Ur-Hamlet*. If so, it is not unlikely that Shakespeare originally intended to follow suit but changed his plans.

[27] *op. cit.*, and *Textual Problems of the First Folio*, pp. 121-37.

was skilfully and strenuously challenged in 1955 by Harold Jenkins, who maintained that numerous divergences in erroneous readings, stage-directions and speech-headings, punctuation and orthography are conclusive for manuscript copy.[28] At the same time, he conceded that some use must have been made of a copy of Q2 and suggested that 'either the scribe who made a transcript for the printer (Dover Wilson's scribe C) or someone in the printing-house itself made reference to the quarto'.[29]

And so it came about that Greg, probably for the first and only time in his life, was reduced to something bordering on confusion. His original position was that the Folio is 'substantive in its own right'[30] but, following Dr. Walker's demonstrations, he admitted that 'the evidence for the Folio having been printed from Q2 amounts to something not far short of proof'.[31] Thereafter, he acknowledged the strength of Jenkins's case and declared that 'the absence of any general typographical resemblance between the Quarto and Folio texts is a difficulty in the way of Dr. Walker's thoroughgoing theories in the case of other plays besides *Hamlet*".[32] These contradictions, since he was confronted, at very short notice, with two opposed but extremely well-argued cases, need occasion neither surprise nor censure, and they do not in any way detract from what can only be termed a masterly survey of the whole *Hamlet* problem. Perhaps the most significant development in Greg's later handling of the play is the sceptical attitude now adopted towards Wilson's hypothetical transcript of the prompt-book. His initial proposition in relation to the Folio runs thus:

> If Q2 was printed from Shakespeare's foul papers and the Folio was not printed from Q2, it would seem likely that the Folio was printed from, or at least had behind it, the official prompt-book, and this view has indeed been widely accepted, though the evidence in its favour is not altogether clear.[33]

Then, following a brief but penetrating analysis, he observes: 'On the whole it seems to be a rather queer prompt-book, if prompt-book it is, that lies behind the Folio'.[34] It may be remarked that these are doubts which Jenkins now shares.[35]

[28] 'The Relation Between the Second Quarto and the Folio Text of *Hamlet*', *Studies in Bibliography*, vii, pp. 69-83.

[29] *op. cit.*, p. 83.  [30] *The Editorial Problem in Shakespeare*, p. xix (note).
[31] *The Shakespeare First Folio*, p. 329.  [32] *ibid.*, p. 333 (note).
[33] *ibid.*, p. 316.  [34] *ibid.*, p. 323.
[35] 'Playhouse Interpolations in the Folio Text of *Hamlet*', *Studies in Bibliography*, xiii, p. 47 (note)

It will be convenient to return to this question of the prompt-book later and to concentrate, for the present, on the other main problem. It may be said at the outset that both Dr. Walker and Jenkins evidently have a good deal of right on their side, and it should be possible to suggest a *tertium quid*. Jenkins, in the present writer's opinion, establishes that manuscript copy was used, but seriously underestimates the impact of Q2 on the Folio and sets too much store by the claim that 'no clear typographical links between Q2 and the Folio have been discovered'.[36] On the other hand, Dr. Walker, as Jenkins protests, fails to take into account a number of serious Folio divergences which are unlikely to have been entered even in a collated Q2, and the kind of marked copy that she envisages, though not open to the same practical objections as her collated Q1, does not quite fit the circumstances. We may, with these reservations in mind, turn to consider the evidence, firstly for Folio dependence on Q2, and secondly for its dependence on a manuscript.

## Common Errors

Dr. Walker claims fourteen readings in Q2 and the Folio as common errors. Jenkins casts reasonable doubt on a number of these, but his attempts to explain away the remainder are not wholly convincing. The notorious line (I.iii.74):

> Are of a most select and generous cheff (chiefe Q1, 2) in that,

is scarcely disposed of by the suggestion that it is 'possible that the three texts agree because their readings are the right ones, though we do not understand what Shakespeare meant'.[37] Nor does the argument that 'designe' (for 'designd': I.i.94), 'Paiocke' (III.ii.295), 'somnet' (III.iii.18) and 'Villaines' (for 'villanies': V.ii.29) were independent misreadings of Shakespeare's handwriting by Q2 compositors and the Folio MS. scribe carry much conviction. In fact 'somnet' (Folio 'Sonnet') also occurs in Q2, with a different compositor, at I.iv.70, and this points not to common error but to anomalous spelling. It is conceivable that Shakespeare, reputedly careless with minims, intended 'sommet' but actually wrote 'somnet' in both places, and that the Q2 compositors mechanically set up what stood before them in the foul papers. But the anomaly is not simply one of minim confusion, for both vowels are abnormal.

---

[36] 'The Relation Between the Second Quarto and the Folio Text of *Hamlet*', *Studies in Bibliography*, vii, p. 75.

[37] *ibid.*, p. 71.

One cannot suppose that all three peculiarities would normally survive transcription, especially as the meaning is perfectly clear. Nor is it likely that the Folio compositor C would have perverted 'somnet' to 'Sonnet' at I.iv.70. if he had been setting from manuscript. The later 'somnet' in the Folio occurs in one of B's stints. It would be strange indeed if Shakespeare's extraordinary spelling passed through the hands of one scribe (or, on Wilson's reckoning, two) and four compositors without any one of them attempting at least partial normalisation.[38]

The variant at I.iv.70 opens up the further interesting possibility that if in fact Q2 was used at the Folio stage, its errors may, on occasion, have given rise to different errors. Something of the kind may be suspected at III.ii.30-1 where compositor B converted Q2 'the gate of Christian, Pagan, nor man' into 'the gate of Christian, Pagan or Norman'. The change may not be a happy one but at least it shews that B was shrewd enough to realise that Q2 does not ring true. It has to be admitted that if we are looking for a phrase that runs trippingly on the tongue, it is only in Q1, 'the gate of Christian, Pagan/Nor Turke', that we find it. This reading perhaps merits more consideration that it appears to have received. The reporter, as the Lucianus actor, was involved in the scene and gives a reasonably good account of the relevant part of Hamlet's speech.[39]

The conclusion, then, is that the Folio contains errors which it almost certainly derived from Q2. It is possible that they are less numerous than Dr. Walker claims, but that is beside the point. Three or four clear examples, widely distributed, are sufficient for the needs.

*Orthography*

Dr. Walker concentrates on anomalous spellings, of which she detects about two dozen. Jenkins argues that seven of these are not anomalous at all and that seven more are dubious, but concedes 'Pollax' (I.i.63), 'ranck' (I.iii.73), 'ore-teamed' (II.ii.531), 'dosen' (II.ii.566), 'fixion' (II.ii.578) and 'how' (for 'hoa': V.ii.322). These he accepts, along with other common features, as evidence that 'the scribe who made a transcript for the printer (Dover Wilson's scribe C)' made occasional reference to Q2.

No critic appears to have given much consideration to the general

---

[38] Confusion may, of course, have arisen through the use of marks of nunnation.

[39] The speeches are placed in the wrong order in Q1 but, verbally, the reporting is quite good. The remainder of the speech following the phrase under discussion is almost word-perfect.

orthographical pattern of the Folio, though this is relevant. There are, throughout the whole play, constant examples of agreement between Q2 and the Folio, sometimes in close propinquity. A selection of these clusters will serve as illustration:

I.v.59-90      *custome; *alwayes; *Violl (Q1, 2: viall); leaperous (Q1, 2 leaprous); sodaine; wholsome; Vnhouzzled (Q2: Vnhuzled); vnnaneld (Q2: vnanueld); Luxury; Matine; *neere; *vneffectuall.

I.v.150-91      *selleridge (Q1, 2: Sellerige); *Pioner; heereafter; *Anticke; *encombred (Q1, 2: incombred); *doubtfull; spight.
(Note: at 156 'Hic & vbique' is typographically identical in all three texts, save that Q2 has a comma after 'Hic'.)

II.i.61-4      Brothell; falshood; wisedome; windlesses; assaies.

II.ii.495-519      whiffe; fals; Milkie; Newtrall; A ro wsed (Q2: A rowsed); Fallies (Q2: follies for 'fellies'); boule.

III.ii.1-32      liue (for 'lief'); Cryer; Ayre; Smoothnesse; Sute; Mirrour; tardie; greeue; Theater.

III.iv.83-9      mutine; Vertue; Proclaime; Ardure.

IV.i.33-7      Ho; ioyne; ayde; drag'd (Q2: dreg'd); Chappell.

IV.v.77-96      sorrowes; Battaliaes (Q2: battalians); vnwholsome; meere; Keepes; Beggard (Q2: beggerd).

IV.vii.62-196      exployt; demy-Natur'd; farre; Brooch, sodaine, comming ore; doo't; Cataplasme; solemne; Challice; liberall Shepheards; boughes; Clambring, chaunted; Pul'd (Q2: Puld); custome.

V.i.272-322      sence; blew (for 'blue'); wandring; Spleenatiue; Theame (291, though the Folio reads Theme, Q2 theame at 289); summe; Woo't; Sindging; meere Madnesse; Cuplet (Q2: cuplets).

V.ii.255-414      stirre; Honor; voyce; president (for 'precedent'); foile (266, though the Folio reads Foyles, Q2 foiles at 264); rub; Carowses; Springde; Loe; venome; adiew; volly; ore-crowes; strooke (Q2: strook); Carnall; accidentall; Falne; hast (for 'haste').

One or two of these spellings might, perhaps, be classed as anomalous and there is a sprinkling of unusual ones. It might, therefore, be argued that these derived from the foul papers and survived both print and transcription were it not for the fact that a number of those from Act I (marked above with asterisks) were plainly transmitted to the Folio via Q2, from Q1, which was printed from a reporter's manuscript. Other examples from the first act will serve to confirm this:

I.i.23      Fantasie; 43 Scholler; 45 harrowes (Q2: horrowes, Q1: horrors); 63 Pollax; 90 Moity (Q2: moitie); 134 vp-hoorded (Q1: hoorded).

I.ii.147      shooes.

I.iii.73      ranck (Q1: rancke).

THE GENERAL TEXTUAL PROBLEMS

I.iv.9    *wassels* (Q2: *wassell*, Q1: *wassel*); 10 *Renish* (Q2: *Rennish*, Q1: *renish*); 48 *Sepulcher;* 52 *compleat* (Q1: *compleate*); 73 *Soueraignty* (Q1, 2: *soueraigntie*).

I.v.41    *Propheticke* (Q1: *prophetike*); 129 *busines.*

Identical spellings of the kind listed above are frequent and so obvious that a complete tabulation would be merely tedious and space-consuming. Most of the examples given are, of course, quite ordinary Elizabethan spellings of quite ordinary words, but the fact that each of them was susceptible of wide orthographical variation must be allowed for. Thus, to take what may seem the weakest example cited, there is at least an even chance that, at V.ii.299, compositor B, who elsewhere has such spellings as 'Buzze', 'begge', 'Gibbe', 'killes', 'Kinne' and 'Drumme', would have set up 'rubbe', had not his choice been determined by the Q2 spelling.[40]

Correspondences involving accepted variant spellings cannot, in themselves, be reasonably held to prove anything, but their ancillary weight is considerable. They occur frequently and are uniformly distributed. They often fall into groups. Those groups occasionally include anomalous or unusual spellings which are also scattered throughout the play. Such a combination of circumstances is unlikely to be fortuitous. The fact that in the first act so many of these correspondences can be traced to Q1 eliminates the possibility of manuscript origin, and there is no reason to suppose that what holds for one act is not operative for the other four. The obvious explanation is that most, if not all, of them represent mechanical reproduction of Q2 spellings by the Folio compositors. If so, the use made of Q2 must have been considerable.

### Capitalisation

The evidence provided by orthography is corroborated by the Folio use of capitals. If the three Hand D pages of *Sir Thomas More* faithfully reflect Shakespeare's normal habits, the majuscules which Heminge and Condell received in his papers must have been almost as scarce as the blots. It may therefore be assumed, in the present state of knowledge, that all but a handful of the capitals which appear in Q2 were compositorial in origin, though no clearly defined policy is apparent. In the Folio, capitalisation is florid but systematic, covering designation of rank and kinship (though 'daughter' is inconsistent) and the names of

---

[40] Admittedly B also has 'rub' (as Q2) at III.i.65, but the whole of that section (the 'To be or not to be' speech) rests substantially on Q2, See below pp. 158-160.

animals, birds, flowers, heavenly bodies and so forth. In addition there are many arbitrary capitals, so that the Folio, as a whole, comes fairly near to later seventeenth-century practice.

Correspondences between Q2 and the Folio, which are multitudinous, must clearly be treated with the utmost caution. Few, if any, of them can be termed anomalous, but there are occasions when the Folio use of both capitals and lower-case letters seems rather out of character and may therefore have been a legacy from Q2. The following agreements in capitalisation (Folio forms are given and variant spellings are ignored) are more or less unexpected:

| | |
|---|---|
| I.i.107 | *Romage;* 167 *Easterne.* |
| iv.48 | *Sepulcher* (also in Q1). |
| v.59 | *Orchard* (also in Q1); 72 *Lazar-like.* |
| II.ii.159 | *Center;* 161 *Lobby;* 479 *Geulles;* 529 *Bisson.* |
| III.ii.272 | *Garden.* |
| iv.53 | *Picture;* 67 *Moore.* |
| IV.iii.46 | *Barke;* 62 *Cicatrice;* 66 *Letters.* |
| vii.96 | *Iemme;* 161 *Challice;* 167, 176 *Brooke;* 171 *Shepheards.* |
| V.i.98 | *Chaplesse;* 234 *Lome;* 235 *Beere-barrell;* 304 *Akers.* |
| ii.13 | *Cabin;* 24 *Axe;* 42 *Comma;* 66 *Angle.* |

It would be idle to pretend that this list carries much conviction as a whole, but some of the later examples are curious. Jaggard's compositors did not, as a general rule, use capitals for domestic and commonplace things (brook, shepherds, loam, acres, cabin, axe), and 'Chaplesse' contrasts oddly with 'chopfalne' (both texts) at V.i.212.

The occasions when the Folio unexpectedly retains lower-case forms, as in Q2, are numerous and, since here, too, exaggerated claims must be avoided, the reader may well be spared an exhaustive list of words that might have been capitalised if the Folio compositors had followed their normal conventions. It will suffice to remark that for Acts I–III the relevant sections are (approximately) as follows:

I.ii.94-5; 106-8; 129-59: iv.8-9; v.21; 126-32.
II. i.1-48; 77-100: ii.400-568 (intermittently).
III. i.10-46; 52-4; 63-8: ii.85-6; 203-7; 349; 379: iii.11-23; 36-42; 56-62; 79-80: iv.32-88.

As with capitals, so with lower-case usages, the most striking examples occur in the last quarter of the play and, as this section as a whole seems decisive, tabulation is desirable:

IV.iii.46–70  *mother; homage.*
  vii.62–91  *exployt; practice; accident; forgery of shapes and trickes.*
   141–63  *contagion; conuenience . . . time and meanes; drift . . . performance; wager . . . commings (Q2: cunnings); bowts; stuck; purpose.*
   167–84  *leaues . . . streame; boughes; sliuer; creature; garments.*
V.i.2   *saluation.*
  ii.1–25  *mutines; rashnesse; sea-gowne; royall knavery; command.*
   38–67  *amities; debatement; bearers; shriuing time; th'impression; changeling; insinuation; passe; points; opposites; th'election; coozenage; conscience.*
  198–243  *tune . . . time; habite . . . encounter; collection; opinions; tryalls; wager; practice; gain-giuing; readinesse; presence; distraction; nature honour, and exception.*
  259–66  *reconcilement; president; place; foile (266: but Folio Foyles, Q2 foiles at 265, 270).*
  363–98  *volly; spirit; th'election; occurrents; quarry; hauocke; proud death; feast; shoote; th'abilitie; command'ment; question.*

It is not, of course, suggested that all these words were necessarily candidates for capitalisation in the Folio, but the admission, by all compositors, of so many lower-case forms is curious. We may wonder why compositor B set 'question' at V.ii.383 but 'Question' at III.i.56 and III.ii.48, and why convention should have been ignored in 'saluation' and the vocative 'proud death'. In fact, compositor B's work, especially in V.ii.373–97, is astoundingly at variance with his normal practice. In these two dozen lines, while his punctuation differs from that of Q2, there are one or two suggestive orthographical correspondences. But he adds only two capitals ('Cell' and 'Inventors') to those of Q2 ('Princes', 'England', 'Polake'), which are, of course, insignificant, and misses ten or more other chances. The result is that the Folio, at this point, looks wholly uncharacteristic. One would never suppose, on purely typographical grounds, that Fortinbras's lines.

> His quarry cries on hauocke. Oh proud death,
> What feast is toward in thine eternal Cell.
> That thou so many Princes, at a shoote,
> So bloodily hast strooke.

were set by the same hand, as, for example, II.ii.604–8:

> But I am Pigeon-Liuer'd, and lacke Gall
> To make Oppression bitter, or ere this,
> I should haue fatted all the Region Kites

With this Slaues Offall, bloudy: a Bawdy villaine,
Remorselesse, Treacherous, Letcherous, kindles villaine!

It is relevant to add that there are no capitals in the Q2 setting of this second passage. In fact, the whole soliloquy, II.ii.575-634, contains more than sixty capitals (apart from 'Hecuba' and 'Iohn a-dreames') in the Folio. In Q2 it has precisely five.

There are, finally, a few interesting cases of transposed capitals:

| | |
|---|---|
| I.v.38 | Q2: *noble Youth;* F: *Noble youth.* |
| 151-2 | Q2: *Sellerige . . . oath;* F: *selleredge . . . Oath.* |
| II.ii.383 | Q2: *Picture in little;* F: *picture in Little.* |
| V.ii.231 | Q2: *prouidence . . . Sparrowe;* F: *Prouidence . . . sparrow.* |
| 283 | Q2: *cup an Vnice;* F: *Cup an union.* |
| 347 | Q2: *sergeant Death;* F: *Sergeant death.*[41] |

The fact that two or three compositors were involved means little, as the process is an intelligible one, at least in relation to mechanical setting from printed copy. It is doubtful whether such transpositions would have arisen if the compositors, at these points, had been setting from manuscript.

The main question to be asked is: why did both B and E, in the latter section of the Folio, lapse so frequently into lower-case usages contrary to their normal practice? There is no reason to suppose that a manuscript, whatever conventions it followed, would normally be accountable for this, and least of all, perhaps, the transcript by scribe C—if such a thing ever existed—since there is an even chance that, by 1620-3, a professional scribe would have been as lavish in his use of capitals as the Folio compositors themselves normally were.[42] In the last analysis, the irregularities in the Folio can be best explained as having arisen from hasty and perfunctory use of Q2.

*Punctuation*

Dr. Walker cites three plausible cases (I.ii.17; II.ii.420; III.i.60-4) where the Folio either followed the pointing of Q2 or was led astray by it. To these may be added the brackets, common to both texts, at I.i.85;

(For so this side of our knowne world esteem'd him)

[41] This list does not claim to be complete.
[42] Ralph Crane is a case in point, though he certainly had nothing to do with *Hamlet*.

and I.i.88:

> Did forfeite (with his life) all those his Lands.

## Stage-directions

Dr. Walker offers a handful of stage-directions common to both texts: I.i.18; I.ii.1; I.v.149; III.ii.238; III.iii.26; IV.i.33; V.ii.342. Jenkins adds I.i.1; II.ii.169; IV.v.96; V.i.1, but questions whether any such correspondences are decisive. Such doubt is reasonable since a copyist is liable to be less vigilant with stage-directions, especially with those of the *Exit Fran.* kind (I.i.18), than with dialogue. Even so, two of Jenkins's own examples and one of Dr. Walker's strongly suggest Folio derivation from Q2:

IV.v.96     *A Noise within.* (set to the right of, and in line with the text).

V.i.1.     *Enter two Clownes.* (with regular use of the speech-heading *Other* for the second of them).

V.ii.360     *Enter Osricke.*

The first of these is unquestionably a typographical link. The two clowns, with their loose speech-headings, were evidently so designated in the foul papers but one would expect more precision in a transcript, especially if it served as a prompt-book. No intelligent scribe (or book-keeper) is likely to have failed to recognise that the first clown is in fact a sexton, as the character himself reveals at line 177. Since Osric brings news of Fortinbras's arrival, his entry at V.ii.360 is perfectly in order, but there is no indication in either text that he had left the stage after the duel. The omission of an *Exit* around line 320 must therefore be a common error.[43]

There is, then, a considerable body of evidence of various kinds to support the view that the Folio made extensive use of Q2. All the categories dealt with above are amply represented in Act I, and many of the examples found there are manifest legacies from Q1 which cannot, therefore, be referred to any manuscript except, perhaps, to that furnished by the actor-reporter. Apparent Q1 survivals persist throughout the play but these have been deliberately excluded from the present argument simply because opinions differ about the extent to which Roberts's compositors relied on that text. Even when these are ignored, the Folio, throughout Acts II and III and the early scenes of Act IV,

---

[43] The position is far from clear. Osric speaks line 316 and Laertes replies at 317. Hamlet orders the door to be locked at 321 and this should preclude the possibility of an exit, and, presumably, of Osric's entry at 360.

continually gives the impression of being something of a palimpsest of Q2. From some point near the middle of Act IV to the end of the play, as examples in almost every category have shewn, there is a markedly greater degree of reliance on the Quarto. This is in accordance with Dr. Walker's convincing argument that composition was lagging behind press-work. Of the Folio pp. 277-80 (V.i.1.—V.ii.213) she observes:

> The pages are very carelessly set and are characterised by careless typographical and verbal errors as well as closeness to the spelling of Q2. The number of apostrophes (necessary and superfluous) and of parentheses suggests B's hand.[44]

This, irrespective of which compositor was involved, seems applicable to Act V as a whole.

The main arguments for supposing that the Folio was set up from manuscript are presented by Jenkins in an admirably lucid and penetrating analysis[45] which may here be outlined and briefly discussed.

### Erroneous readings

Jenkins lists a number of nonsensical Folio readings which are unlikely to have been the errors of a compositor working from printed copy and are even less likely to have been inserted in that copy by a corrector. Naturally he makes much of the fact that the Folio 'inobled' (three times) for Q2 'mobled' (twice) testifies to misreading of manuscript copy. It could, of course, be argued that compositor B, confronted with an unfamiliar word, assumed error in Q2 and made his own fatuous emendation, but 'mobled' is not the only unusual word in the Pyrrhus speeches. Doubtless he found 'totall Gules' just as baffling, but there is little evidence of the emender's zeal behind the Folio 'to take Guelles'. Reference to independent authority is virtually attested, moreover, by the Folio correction 'Bisson Rheume', for one questions whether compositor B would have grasped the significance of Q2 'Bison rehume' without guidance of some kind. Jenkins's other examples, all of which are persuasive, will be discussed later.

### Stage-directions and Speech-headings

Jenkins remarks that, in the matter of stage-directions, 'the most

---

[44] *Textual Problems of the First Folio*, p. 130. Hinman has since shewn that these pages were set by compositor E, but this does not invalidate Dr. Walker's general argument.

[45] *op. cit.*, pp. 76-82.

obvious thing that emerges from a comparison of Q2 and the Folio is the remarkable non-conformity of the two texts' and proceeds to shew that certain variations are completely pointless.

I.ii.159    Q2  *Enter Horatio, Marcellus and Bernardo.*
           F    *Enter, Horatio, Barnard, and Marcellus.*
II.ii.221   Q2  *Enter Guyldersterne, and Rosencraus.*
           F    *Enter Rosincran and Guildensterne.*
III.ii.52   Q2  *Enter Polonius, Guyldensterne & Rosencraus.*
           F    *Enter Polonius, Rosincrance, and Guildensterne.*

These transpositions are certainly peculiar, but Jenkins does not allow for the possibility that a marginal directive to transpose *u* to *n* in Rosencrantz marked in Q2 was misinterpreted as an instruction to reverse the order of the names. Discrepancies in speech-headings are more difficult to account for. Where Q2 normally has *Pol.* for Polonius and *Ros.* for Rosencrantz, compositors A and C invariably use *Polon.* and both B and C favour *Rosin.* Jenkins also notes that, though both texts have *Mar.* for Marcellus, the Folio provides a single instance of *Marcell.* at I.v.148. One hesitates to attribute these uneconomical changes to two or three harassed compositors. On the other hand, it is not easy to see why they should have been made by a transcriber.

The dumb-show can also be included in this category. Its Folio variants may well have been entered in a copy of Q2, but, if so, the collator must have worked mechanically since several of the changes are pointless. A moment's reflection would have told him that nothing was to be gained by substituting 'the King's eares' for 'the sleeper's eares', or 'Exits' for 'leaues him'. Equally pointless is the change from 'an other man' to 'a Fellow', and it may be doubted whether, around 1621-3, a collator would have adhered to either of these loose designations when he was at liberty to substitute 'poisoner' or even, as in Q1, 'Lucianus'. But such considerations are irrelevant. The Q2 version, with its staccato phrasing, its imprecision and omission of significant detail, and its fanfare of trumpets must certainly represent Shakespeare's original conception, which was left standing in the foul papers. One would swear that it was a recollection of Lady Anne's reception of the advances of Gloster in *Richard III* that led him to set down '*shee seemes harsh awhile*'. The adjective, with its implication of 'damnable faces', does not seem particularly appropriate. The Folio version, in contrast, had clearly been edited by the book-keeper, who substituted 'Hoboyes' for 'Trumpets', presumably as better fitting the occasion, the explicit and theatrical 'Exits' for 'leaues him' (which might be taken as implying that she merely takes a turn about the stage), and 'some two or three Mutes' for 'some three or foure', doubtless in accordance with the company's resources. The change from 'harsh' to 'loath and vnwilling' makes for better dumb-show, with less of Lady Anne about it, as does that from 'condole' to 'lament'. The alteration of 'an other man' to 'a Fellow' is something of a mystery unless the word was intended in its pejorative sense to indicate that, even in dumb-show, the Hyperion to a satyr contrast was to be given due emphasis. Be that as it may, the Folio version of the dumb-show as a whole would seem to be substantive in its own right.

*Punctuation*

Jenkins observes that the punctuation of certain parts of the Folio, notably the 'What a piece of work is a man' speech, is radically different from that of Q2 and cannot have derived from that text. He finds that of eleven parentheses in Q2 only two are retained in the Folio, and this, in view of compositor B's addiction to brackets, is striking. Yet more significant are the ten cases which he cites where 'the Folio has been led into wrong, or at least inferior, punctuation precisely through not following Q2'. This cannot, of course, be taken to mean that the Folio, on these occasions, reproduces the punctuation of the manuscript. What it does suggest, however, is that the manuscript itself was scantily pointed.

*Orthography*

There are striking differences between Q2 and the Folio in their spelling of proper names—notably Rosencrantz, Guildenstern, Fortinbras and Gertrude—and not a single significant coincidence. This, in conjunction with the fact that the Folio spellings are consistent throughout, irrespective of compositor, is held by Jenkins to be conclusive for manuscript copy. There is certainly much reason in this, but the very consistency of the Folio usage may point to regularisation at some indeterminate period. It is not impossible that they were systematically marked in Q2 by a conscientious collator, especially as a number of them are really corrections. The three principal names appear in Q2 almost invariably as 'Gertrard', 'Rosencraus' and 'Guyldensterne' (twice as 'Guyldersterne').[46]

[46] It is pertinent to remark that, throughout Act I, Q2, despite its extensive use of Q1, has its own consistent forms for proper-names which appear in Q1 as *Ofelia, Leartes, Fortenbrasse, Elsenoure, Voltemar* and, of course, *Corambis*. What was possible for the one text must obviously have been possible for the other.

It is difficult, as Jenkins remarks, to argue from general divergences of spelling, but those passages which, for one reason or another, can confidently be held to have been set up from Q2 invariably retain a fair number of its spellings, and it may, with caution, be urged that orthographical differences spread over passages of reasonable length elsewhere argue for manuscript setting. The Voltemar episode (II.ii-58-80) provides a particularly good example. The Folio version contains no spellings that necessarily link it with Q2. Divergences in commonplace words include 'Suppresse' (Q2: 'supresse'), 'Nephewes' (Q2: 'Nephews'), 'Highnesse' (Q2: 'highnes'), 'Sicknesse' (Q2: sickness'), 'falsely' (Q2: 'falsly'), 'Vnkle' (Q2: 'Vncle'), 'Soldiers' (Q2: 'souldiers'), 'intreaty' (Q2: 'entreatie), 'shewne' (Q2: 'shone'). These are not significant in themselves, but several of the changes are trivial and unnecessary so that one may doubt whether compositor B would have troubled to make them and whether, in any case, he would have substituted the less for the more usual form ('Frends', 'Vnkle', 'intreaty') had he been working from Q2. But it is quite clear that he was not. Reliance on some other copy is attested at the outset by the amended stage-direction: '*Enter Polonius, Voltumand, and Cornelius*', which replaces Q2 '*Enter Embassadors*',[47] and the spelling '*Voltumand*' for Q2 '*Voltemand*' is symptomatic. Thus, the Folio prints 'Norwey' (three times) for Q2 '*Norway*', '*Poleak*' (twice) for 'Pollacke', and '*Fortinbras*' for '*Fortenbrasse*'. We may, if we wish, contend that the one personal name is an error and the other a regularisation, but what is quite inconceivable is that compositor B, if he had been setting from Q2, would have substituted the archaic forms 'Norwey' and 'Poleak' for the more normal ones.[48] Even more inexplicable would be his alteration of Q2 'enterprise' to 'Entreprize', a spelling which hints at etymological knowledge that one would hardly suppose B to have possessed.

The evidence, then, is conclusive for manuscript setting of some twenty or more consecutive lines at this point. There appear to be no other examples of comparable length, apart, of course, from two passages (II.ii.244-78, 352-79) which do not figure in Q2, but on countless occasions in the Folio, for the space of two or three lines or so,

---

[47] Polonius enters at line 40, but the dialogue makes it clear that he leaves the stage for a moment, at line 53, though no exit is marked in Q2 and the Folio. The Folio amendment at line 58 is quite necessary.

[48] The forms in the Folio *Macbeth* are '*Norway*' and 'Norweyan', but these occur only in compositor A settings.

there is a perceptible deviation from Q2 practice, and this suggests that all such passages were set from manuscript. It follows that, if Jenkins is correct in his diagnosis of erroneous readings and faulty punctuation, all the examples which he cites must belong to this category. It is, therefore, instructive to find that, in almost every case, the general orthographical pattern of the adjacent lines has no necessary connexion with that of Q2. Even more striking, perhaps, is the fact that, in every one of the eighteen passages, the apparent reliance on the manuscript coincides with one or more capital errors in Q2 which the Folio corrects. As these correspondences are important, the relevant details may be tabulated. The Folio errors cited by Jenkins are given under location references, with Q2 readings in brackets. In the third column the variants, preceded by line reference, are set out in the same order.

| Erroneous readings | Spelling in relation to Q2 | Folio corrections of Q2 errors |
|---|---|---|
| II.ii.525 ff. inobled (mobled) | Different (521-43) | 525. O who (a woe); 527. Inobled Queene is good (lacking); 528 flame (flames); 529. Bisson (Bison), Rheume (rehume). |
| II.ii.580 warm'd (wand) | Similar (576-92) | 580. his (the); 581. in's (in his). |
| III.i.48 surge (sugar) | Different (28-54) cf. 55-90, which resembles Q2 | 46. lonelinesse (lowlines); 49. Deletes too(?). |
| III.i.99 then perfume left (their perfume lost) | Indeterminate | 97. I (you); 99. the (these). |
| IV.iii.7 neere (neuer) | Different (5-11) | 7. Folio should have corrected smooth and euen which is hypermetrical and tautologous. |
| IV.vii.143 I but dipt (that but dippe) | Mainly unlike (128-49) | 141. for that purpose (for purpose). |
| IV.vii.156 commings (cunnings) | Mainly unlike (150-63) | 155. should (did); 163. how sweet Queene (but stay, what noyse?) (?) |
| IV.vii.183 buy (lay) | Conflated? (see below) | 178. tunes (laudes); 184. is she (she is) |

*Erroneous Punctuation*

| | | |
|---|---|---|
| I.ii.202 | Different (199-212) | 200. *at all points* (*at poynt*). |
| I.iii.8-10 | Dubious (1-10) | 3. *Conuoy is* (*conuay, in*); |
| | Like Q2 (12-38) | 6. *fauours* (*fauour*). |
| I.iv.56 | Different (52-63) | 49. *enurn'd* (*interr'd*); 58. Ghost beckens Hamlet (Beck-ins). |
| II.i.41 | Different (37-49) | 38. *warrant* (*wit*); 39. *sulleyes* (*sallies*); 40. *i'th* (*with*). |
| II.ii.145-6 | Different (139-55) | 142. *Precepts* (*prescripts*); 143. *his* (*her*); 146. *repulsed* (*repell'd*); 148. *Watch* (*wath*). |
| IV.iii.24-6 | Different (20-30) | Folio omits three lines (28-30), evidently because a correction was taken for a deletion (see below). |
| IV.v.112 | Similar | 112. *the* (*this*). |
| IV.vii.45-6 | Mainly unlike (36-51) | 42. Exit Messenger (lacking); 48. *and more strange* (lacking); 49. *Hamlet* (lacking); 50. delete King; 51. *Or* (*and*). |
| IV.vii.58-9 | Dubious (56-61) | 55. *aduise* (*deuise*); 63. *checking* (*the King*); Metrical irregularities and some Folio deletions. |
| IV.vii.101-3 | Indeterminate | 99. *especialle* (*especiall*)?; 101b-103a deleted? |

Thus, of the eighteen passages cited by Jenkins as evidence for manuscript copy, at least eleven depart from the orthographical pattern of Q2, in some cases with perceptible suddenness, while only two preserve the spellings of that text, and of these, IV.v.112 seems the most dubious of·Jenkins's examples. This argues powerfully that manuscript copy was in fact used, and the manifest need for correction of Q2 readings in every single passage explains why.

This survey of the evidence has been undeniably lengthy, but the issue is an important one. The conclusion to which we are led, unless we are prepared to reject either Dr. Walker's arguments or Jenkins's out of mere prejudice, is that the Folio was based on both Q2 and a manuscript. In view of the general character of the evidence the possibility that the actual copy for the Folio was a transcript which alternated spasmodically between quarto and manuscript is something that can be ruled out, and the only explanation that is left to us is that

Jaggard's compositors worked simultaneously from both copies. This may seem to verge on the fantastic, but the process envisaged is, of course, not essentially different from that which Roberts's compositors evidently followed when setting up Q2. That such a method would have been laborious and confusing can scarcely be denied, but the Folio *Hamlet* is, after all, a laboured and confused text.

The first thing that may be cited in support of such a hypothesis is the general impression, which is that the Folio throughout reveals close affinities with Q2 but with constant divergences that argue reference to a second source. This impression, in its broad outlines, is well exemplified in that part of II.ii which covers the Pyrrhus material and Hamlet's soliloquy and yields the following analysis:

> *Manuscript settings:* 473-92; 520-60; 599-611.
> Q2    settings:    493-519;    561-98;    612-34.

This, however, merely isolates the main source of copy for each section, and frequent reference to the ancillary copy must obviously be allowed for. If the compositors were committed to the method suggested here, it was not through mere caprice but was dictated solely by the need to correct the errors of the one copy in the light of the other. Hence, what we have to reckon with is the compositor's eye (almost certainly in a fine frenzy rolling) glancing from quarto to manuscript, from manuscript to quarto, and occasionally bodying forth the shapes of things unknown—of which B's notorious 'kinde Life-rend'ring Politician' at IV.v.143 is a choice example. The result would inevitably be a series of rapid alternations, and this is precisely what the Folio text appears to offer. The 'To be or not to be' (III.i.56-91) soliloquy may serve as an illustration.

There can be no doubt that Q2 was the primary copy for this soliloquy. The general orthographical correspondence is very close, and there are several notable spelling links—'outragious', ('Heart)-ake', 'dispriz'd' (Q2: 'despiz'd'), 'Borne', 'Puzels' (Q2: 'puzzels'), 'loose' (for 'lose'), 'Nimph' and 'Orizons'. Much the same holds for punctuation. Dr. Walker has pointed out that both texts concur in omitting necessary commas—'to sleepe ∧ No more' and 'To dye ∧ to sleepe'— and there is throughout a marked similarity in the placing of punctuation marks. The occasional replacement of a comma by a colon is in accordance with the heavier pointing normally found in the Folio and is not necessarily significant. In setting from Q2 compositor B had, verbally, a very straightforward task. He had to make good the omission of 'of vs all' at line 83 and to normalise two spellings— 'quietas' and 'hiew'. It is questionable whether he was called upon to amend any erroneous readings, though not all editors have been satisfied with 'despiz'd' in line 72 and 'pitch' in line 86. Even so, the single need for supplementation would have involved reference to the manuscript and, since the Q2 punctuation does little to clarify the sense of a quite difficult speech, it is reasonable to suppose that B occasionally glanced at the manuscript, hoping for the guidance which he sometimes received.

The outcome is interesting. Lines 56-62 were set directly from Q2. Spelling and punctuation are practically identical and the one or two variants are insignificant. At 63, however, B evidently consulted the manuscript, possibly because he was not satisfied with the Q2 pointing. At any rate, he amended the punctuation and in the process set up a couple of manuscript spellings:

Q2: That flesh is heire to; tis a consumation.

F: That Flesh is heyre too? 'Tis a consummation.

He then reverted to Q2 for lines 63-7, where again there is general agreement, even in defective pointing, and no variation of any consequence, but in 68 realised the inadequacy of Q2's comma after 'pause'. Hence, in lines 67-8, we again find amended punctuation and altered spelling:

Q2: When we haue shuffled off this mortall coyle
Must giue vs pause, there's the respect . . .

F: When we haue shufflel'd off this mortall coile,
Must giue vs pawse. There's the respect . . .

Here, it may be noted, 'shufflel'd' is the kind of portmanteau error that could arise through B turning from one copy to the other, setting 'shuffle-' from Q2 but tacking on to it the ending of a manuscript spelling 'shuffel'd'.[49] Spelling and punctuation confirm dependence on Q2 for lines 68-74, but B was now less attentive, printing 'poore' for 'proude' in line 71 and being misled by the z of 'despiz'd' into setting up 'dispriz'd'. At 75 'quietas' (in Roman type) doubtless puzzled him and led him back to the manuscript, so that 75-6 are divergent in orthography and pointing and a superfluous adjective creeps in:

[49] The -el for -le spelling is apparently one deriving from the foul papers. Cf. 'metteld' (II.ii.593), 'puzzels' (III.i.80).

Q2:  When he himselfe might his quietas make
      With a bare bodkin; who would fardels beare,

F:    When he himselfe might his *Quietus* make
      With a bare Bodkin? Who would these Fardles beare.

The rest of the soliloquy (77-90) was evidently set up from Q2 and B once again misread his copy at 86 and 87. Apparently he turned to the manuscript only for the supplement in line 83 and the mark of interrogation which replaces Q2's inadequate comma in line 89.

This may be to consider too curiously and too fancifully, but the fact remains that, when the two texts cease to be almost identical, the divergences are striking ones, and it is certainly odd that B should have substituted 'heyre too' and 'pawse', both of which have an archaic air, for the virtually standardised spellings of Q2. It is curious, too, that spelling and punctuation go hand in hand, and that linked with them is the need for correction or, at least, enlightenment. This last consideration may not carry much weight when based on one or two divergences in a single speech, but, as has already been shewn, every reference to the manuscript posited by Jenkins coincides with palpable errors in Q2. And this, it may be remarked, holds for the Folio in its entirety.

Jaggard's preference for printed copy is generally admitted, and, if the procedure here suggested is the correct one, there can be little doubt that the Folio compositors worked as far as possible from Q2, which may be termed the main copy, but with constant reference to the manuscript. But it is clear that the Quarto itself must have differed in one important respect from those used for other Folio texts, namely in bearing correction-marks instead of the corrections themselves. It may be granted that amended readings might occasionally have been interlined or entered in the margin, but the general character of the Folio text does not suggest that this was done to any considerable extent. It is highly questionable whether such a method would have produced the curious conflation that informs, for instance, the Queen's 'Willow' speech at IV.vii.167 foll., where close adherence to Q2 alternates with manuscript spellings and the absurd misreading 'buy'.

The markings, whatever shape they took,[50] were presumably comprehensive, as the consistency of the Folio speech-headings and

[50] Johnson's practice, in the copy of Warburton's Shakespeare which he used for the *Dictionary*, was to underline the relevant word and enter a mark in the margin. This would have sufficed for Jaggard's copy of Q2.

spelling of proper names implies, but there are grounds for believing that they were more than once misinterpreted by Jaggard's compositors. One case in point may be 'or Norman' at III.ii.30-1, where B, confident that he had diagnosed the error, did not trouble to check the manuscript. A directive at IV.ii.19 evidently resulted in imperfect consultation. Q2 'apple' must clearly have been marked for amendment. Accordingly B referred to the manuscript, recovered the correct reading 'Ape' and straightway reverted to Q2, oblivious to the fact that he had made no more than a half-correction. The variant readings at this point are illuminating. Q2 prints:

> he keepes them like an apple in the corner of his iaw, first mouth'd to be last swallowed,

and the Folio:

> He keepes them like an Ape in the corner of his iaw, first mouth'd to be last swallowed.

Both readings have had their adherents, though no one appears to have explained the extraordinary gastronomical process whereby Claudius swallowed either apples, apes, officers or sponges. What B failed to recover from the manuscript was obviously the supplement preserved, perhaps imperfectly, in Q1:

> For hee doth keep you as an Ape doth nuttes,
> In the corner of his Iaw, first mouthes you,
> Then swallowes you.

It may be noted that the Folio reversion to Q2 in the second clause, attested by the -'d in 'mouth'd' but -ed in 'swallowed', also results in a reading which does not quite ring true. Emendation to 'to be at last swallowed' seems possible.

A different misinterpretation of a correction mark occurs at IV.iii.28-30, where the Folio omits three lines that appear in Q2:

*King.* Alas, alas.
*Ham.* A man may fish with the worme that hath eate of a
    King, & eate of the fish that hath fedde of that worme.

But, as Q1 shews, the required reading is '. . . a King, & a Beggar eate . . .' Presumably, B misread a mark of correction as one of deletion and, again disdaining to consult the manuscript, made bad worse.

Errors arising from conflation of copy may be fairly numerous. Seemingly pointless repetition of words and phrases is a marked feature of the Folio and Jenkins has argued persuasively that many of these were playhouse interpolations.[51] When such repetition is corroborated by Q1, with its vestige of playhouse authority, this explanation must inevitably hold. When, however, it is exclusive to the Folio it is reasonable to assume that duplication arose through the compositor switching from one copy to the other. At I.v.107, the Folio prints:

> My Tables, my Tables; meet it is I set it downe.

Jenkins observes that the repetition, which is not in Q1, 'deepens the impression of uncontrollable emotion only at some metrical expense', but the implication that it represents one of Burbage's additions to his part seems a dubious one since the emotion is not so much deepened as changed.[52] Conflation of copy affords at least a reasonable explanation here, as also in the confused passage about Yorick's skull at V.i.198-9:

> This same Scull Sir, this same Scull sir, was *Yoricks* Scull, the Kings Iester.

The repetition here may be an actor's interpolation, but if so, it is not clear what effect it was expected to achieve.

Perhaps the most remarkable example of copy conflation occurs at V.ii.43:

> And many such like Assis of great charge.

Compositor E had, of course, to correct the corrupt Q2 reading:

> And many such like, as sir of great charge.

but the hybrid spelling that he produced can hardly have been that of the manuscript, which must certainly have read either 'Ases', or, assuming the need to make the pun obvious, 'Asses'.[53] Similar conflation has already been noted in 'shufflel'd' at III.i.67.

### vi

There is no point in further pursuing the implications of double copy. The hypothesis, relating to both Q2 and the Folio, is one which may or

---

[51] 'Playhouse Interpolations in the Folio Text of *Hamlet*', *Studies in Bibliography*, xiii, pp. 31-47.

[52] One might suggest that Q2 implies, 'Quickly, my tables . . .' whereas the impression given by the Folio repetition is, 'My tables! Now where on earth are my tables? . . .'

[53] The conflation seems more typical of compositor B, to whom (*pace* Hinman) I am inclined to allocate the setting of p. 279b.

may not prove acceptable to future editors of the play but in no way affects the eclecticism which is now recognised as editorially inevitable. It would be rash, in the present state of knowledge, to claim that Q2, in the light of these findings, can no longer be regarded as the chief authority, yet extreme vigilance is obviously called for with a text based on a difficult manuscript and checked against something as dubious as Q1. If, as suggested here, the Folio was set from Q2 but was consistently amended in the light of an authoritative manuscript, it should, theoretically, provide the better text. Possibly it does, though this is something that we may hesitate to assume. Jaggard's compositors were perfunctory and high-handed at the best of times and if, as seems certain, their work on *Hamlet* was hurried, it is scarcely possible to set limits to their capacity for error.

The main task that remains is that of defining the manuscript that was used, in whatever way, at the Folio stage. That it was a prompt-book of sorts may be taken for granted, but modern criticism has generally lent too attentive an ear to assumptions that are tenuous in other respects. The notion that Q2 preserves the play as originally performed and that the Folio manuscript represents an abridgement, aiming either to shorten an excessively long play or to remove passages that may have given offence to James I or his consort, is one that may conveniently be dispensed with. The reduction in bulk which the Folio actually achieves is practically negligible, while the omitted passages, most of which seem perfectly harmless anyway, cannot possibly be accounted more offensive than others which the Folio retains. It is likely, too, that the transcript prepared by Wilson's scribe C is mythical rather than hypothetical. If such a transcript was prepared expressly for the use of the printers, as both Wilson and Jenkins appear to think, it is very curious indeed that they should have made such extensive use of Q2. Dr. Walker naturally demurs from such a conclusion but, in arguing that the transcript was made because the prompt-book needed renewal, she heaps conjecture on conjecture. To claim that the Folio manuscript was a kind of prompt-book is one thing. To claim that it was the book of the play as it was normally performed at the Globe Theatre is quite another matter.

eleven

# Hamlet

## The Occasion and the Folio Text

i

It is strange, in view of the endless controversies which have been provoked by practically every aspect of *Hamlet*, that so little attention has been given to the kind of audience for which it may originally have been intended. It seems that critics in general have been content to accept the play as a perfectly regular contribution to the Globe Theatre repertoire and, in the light of its enormous and enduring popular appeal, they can scarcely be blamed. Nevertheless, there are reasonable grounds for believing that *Hamlet* was originally conceived in relation, if not to a special occasion, at least to a special audience. It is possible, in this respect, to draw a rough analogy between it and *Troilus and Cressida*. Both begin by posing a problem, the one in respect of performance, the other of length, and in both cases the assumption that Shakespeare was writing for a particular occasion disposes of the initial problem and affords a ready explanation of many of the other peculiarities and problems.

It has already been argued that the Q2 text, which runs to nearly four thousand lines, did not serve as the basis for any actual performance, but there can be little doubt that the Folio, which to all intents and purposes is merely Q2 topped and tailed, represents a stage version, and quite certainly the original one. But the the Folio *Hamlet* runs to approximately 3,700 lines, and that figure alone must surely establish that the extant authentic versions cannot have been intended for the Globe. *Hamlet* is, in fact, the longest play in the canon by several hundred lines, and it is not without significance that the play which runs it a very poor second, *Troilus and Cressida*, was itself a *pièce d'occasion* which never reached the public theatre, whose normal requirements apparently amounted to something between 2,700 and 3,300 lines.

The arithmetic, moreover, does not tell the whole story, for *Hamlet* is one of the most time-consuming of plays. The soliloquies, meditations and sententiae all impose their own relaxed tempo. The various actions, notably the dumb-show, the fight in the graveyard and the final duel have also to be taken into account, together with the stage-business attaching to the inner-play, the march of Fortinbras's army, the Ghost's martial stalk and so forth. *Hamlet* in its entirety has become something of a fetish in the modern theatre, but the conditions applicable to audiences familiar with the whole of the plot and most of the dialogue have no bearing on those which prevailed in Shakespeare's own theatre. There is really no escape from the conclusion that he intended a very large proportion of the dialogue of *Hamlet* to be delivered deliberately and impressively, or, if not, the less Shakespeare he. All in all, the Folio text envisaged as the basis of an afternoon performance at the Globe in late November, with light thickening somewhere towards the middle of Act IV, does not constitute a convincing picture, and full representations during summer must be judged possible rather than probable. The Globe audience, we may assume, was usually given value for money, and there is no reason for supposing that bonuses were either given or expected. Hence, it is surely taxing credulity over-far to assume that Shakespeare wrote *Hamlet* in its received form expressly for his public theatre, knowing full well that some five hundred or more lines would have to be cut.

It would be manifestly absurd to suggest that *Hamlet*, like *Troilus and Cressida*, contains a substantial body of material that can be adjudged unsuitable for the average Globe audience, but one or two passages raise certain doubts. Hamlet's conversations with the Players, with their commendation of the play that was caviar to the general, their denunciation of bombast, clownage and dumb-shows, and their contempt for the groundlings and barren spectators are hardly the kind of thing that would normally have been admitted in a play addressed to an audience of which those very groundlings constituted a considerable and quite vocal element. The rather lengthy advice that Ophelia receives from both Polonius and Laertes might be called in question. So could certain of Hamlet's soliloquies and meditations. These, it might be urged, accord better with private than with public performance. The important point, however, is not that *Hamlet* contains a few passages that might be accounted (perhaps wrongly) unsuitable for use at the Globe but that it offers a great deal that is superfluous to workaday needs. It may safely be reckoned that the Globe audience's expectations would have been amply satisfied by a straightforward presentation of

Hamlet's revenge, informed by the economy, structural dexterity, action, suspense and sensations that had already been so admirably exercised in *Romeo and Juliet* and *Julius Caesar*. The things which would not have been expected, at least in their existing extended form, include the advice, soliloquies and meditations already mentioned, most of the conversation with the Players, together with the Pyrrhus speeches, and either the dumb-show or the inner-play. If Shakespeare, at the outset, had chosen to present a basic *Hamlet* the result could in fact have been one of the shortest plays in the canon. It is pertinent to remark that Belleforest, though diffuse and digressive, tells rather more of the adventures of Hamlet within the compass of fifty pages, and there is no warrant for assuming that the *Ur-Hamlet* was by any means a long play. *The Spanish Tragedy*, which is not without relevance, affords a most impressive demonstration of just how much incident can be packed into three thousand lines.

It is not, of course, suggested that supererogatory material of the kind specified was inadmissible in a play designed for the Elizabethan public theatre or that the Folio version, with, perhaps, one or two tactful alterations, would have been anything but acceptable to the average Globe audience. But that is not the point. What we have to consider, over and above the inordinate length of the play, is whether Shakespeare, whose approach to his public, though infinitely artistic, was, at the same time, forthright and unencumbered, would deliberately have treated it, on this one occasion, to quite such a comprehensive display of windlasses and assays of bias. In *Hamlet* it is Shakespeare rather than the Prince who is the procrastinator. At all points the play pauses to consider curiously, and this is a feature for which the most plausible explanation would seem to be that it was originally designed for spectators who were themselves disposed to consider curiously and had time in which to do so. *Hamlet* abounds in superfluities, but they are superfluous only in relation to the two-hour traffic of the public stage. No one who has studied the play to any purpose is likely to have remained unaware that every incident, however seemingly digressive, makes its own subtle and distinctive contribution to the leading motives of plot, character and motivation. But this intricate and masterly exposition must assuredly have been intended for a more leisured occasion than any that the Globe could provide.

That there was, in fact, more than one such occasion between the completion of the play in or about 1601 and 1603 is attested by the title-page of Q1 which claims to present the play 'As it hath beene diuerse times acted by his Highnesse seruants in the Cittie of London: as also in the two Vniuersities of Cambridge and Oxford, and else-where'. In view of the disreputable character of the Q1 text, the claim is, in one respect, an impudent one, but there seems no reason to doubt its basic veracity. Whether 'the Cittie of London' is to be taken literally is a moot point. Greg thought that it is not, and remarks that 'the only performances were presumably at the Globe, which was in South-wark'.[1] This, however, ignores the possibility of private representa-tions. It is highly unlikely that *Hamlet* figured in the normal repertoire of either the Blackfriars or St. Paul's theatres during this period, but it may have been used elsewhere in connexion with honourable occasions. There was a week of plays and feasting at Hunsdon House, the home of the Lord Chamberlain, in March 1600,[2] and on December 29th, 1601, Elizabeth dined there and subsequently attended a perform-ance at Blackfriars which was presumably given by Shakespeare's company.[3] These require mention merely as an indication that there were opportunities for a performance of *Hamlet* within the City itself. There is nothing to suggest that it was in fact performed on either of these occasions and certainly no reason for supposing that it was expressly written for one of them. On the other hand, this initial claim on the title-page cannot very well be held to refer to Globe perform-ances, and these, since there must already have been several by 1603, may be covered by the uninformative 'else-where'. Fortunately the University performances are more positive.

ii

The precise date of *Hamlet* remains unsettled, but modern critical opinion is almost unanimous in its acceptance of either 1600 or 1601, and these two dates may be taken as establishing the probable range. It is clear, on the evidence of II.ii.341-79, that this was the period when the fame of the Boys' companies temporarily eclipsed that of the Lord Chamberlain's men, who, apparently, found themselves forced to travel. Records of provincial tours between 1597 and 1603 are unfor-tunately scanty. Chambers cites only a payment to 'the players' at Oxford in 1599-1600, and one of thirty shillings 'to three companies of players', also at Oxford, in 1600-1.[4] It is not possible to prove that any of these companies was the Lord Chamberlain's, still less that *Hamlet*

---

[1] *The Shakespeare First Folio*, p. 307.
[2] E. K. Chambers, *William Shakespeare*, II, p. 322.
[3] *ibid.*, p. 327.　　　　[4] *ibid.*, pp. 323, 327.

was one of the plays performed, but there seems little reason to doubt that these entries cover, at some point, the Oxford performance referred to on the title-page of Q1.

The Cambridge performance may belong to 1602–3 when Shakespeare's company embarked on an extended provincial tour, but the dates for their appearances in East Anglia are rather late in relation to the publication of Q1. It is apparent, however, that a visit by the company was fresh in the mind of the author of *The Return from Parnassus*, which was presented at St. John's College, Cambridge, in late 1601 or early 1602. This topical entertainment includes impersonations of Burbage and Kempe, and if these two had actually visited Cambridge, the date of their visit can be fixed with reasonable precision. Kempe appears to have left the Chamberlain's company in 1599 and to have set off on a prolonged continental tour, from which he returned in September 1601. By the winter of 1602 he had thrown in his lot with the Earl of Worcester's men, but Chambers was doubtless correct in claiming that, immediately following his return, he rejoined the Chamberlain's for a spell.[5] The visit to Cambridge must therefore have taken place some time between his return on September 2nd, 1601, and the presentation of the *Parnassus* play around Christmas of that year.

In view of his close links with Cambridge, some significance attaches to Gabriel Harvey's autograph note in his copy of Speght's 1598 edition of Chaucer:

The Earle of Essex much commendes Albions England: and not vnworthily for diuerse notable pageants, before, & in the Chronicle. Sum Inglish, & other Histories nowhere more sensibly described, or more inwardly discouered. The Lord Mountioy makes the like account of Daniels peece of the Chronicle, touching the Vsurpation of Henrie of Bullingbrooke. which in deede is a fine, sententious, & politique peece of Poetrie: as proffitable, as pleasurable. The younger sort takes much delight in Shakespeares Venus, & Adonis: but his Lucrece, & his tragedie of Hamlet, Prince of Denmarke, haue it in them, to please the wiser sort. Or such poets: or better: or none.

>Vilia miretur vulgus: mihi flavus Apollo
>Pocula Castaliae plena ministret aquae:

quoth Sir Edward Dier, betwene iest, & earnest. Whose written deuises farr excell most of the sonets, and cantos in print. His Amaryllis, & Sir Walter Raleighs Cynthia, how fine and sweet inuentions? Excellent matter of

5 *The Elizabethan Stage*, II, pp. 207–8.

emulation for Spencer, Constable, France, Watson, Daniel, Warner, Chapman, Siluester, Shakespeare, & the rest of owr florishing metricians.[6]

The date of this note has been much disputed, but it is now generally agreed that it must have been written before Essex's execution in February 1601. The *terminus a quo* is, of course, 1598, but so early a date is unacceptable in view of the reference to *Hamlet*, which cannot, in the light of other evidence, be placed earlier than 1600. The suggestion that Harvey was alluding to the *Ur-Hamlet* cannot be taken seriously, since there is no reason for believing that Shakespeare wrote it, or that it had anything in it 'to please the wiser sort'.[7]

The point immediately relevant is that Harvey's knowledge of *Hamlet* must have been based on a performance, since the note is evidently earlier than either quarto and since there is little likelihood that he had had the opportunity to read the play in manuscript. It is inherently probable that he was among those present when *Hamlet* was given at Cambridge, and the tone of the note suggests that it reflects university opinion. Harvey's was the small world of the out-and-out pedant, and it is reasonable to surmise that his 'younger sort' and 'wiser sort' were practically synonymous with undergraduates and Fellows. The distinction drawn may have been a general one; it was certainly a Cambridge one. In the second *Parnassus* play, Gullio proclaims that he will

> worshipp sweet Mr Shakespeare, and to honoure him will lay
> his *Venus and Adonis* vnder my pillowe.
>> *1 Return from Parnassus*, 1201-3.[8]

while, in the last part of the trilogy, Iudicio speaks for both the younger and the wiser sort:

> Who loues not *Adons* loue, or *Lucrece* rape?
> His sweeter verse contaynes hart robbing lines,
> Could but a grauer subiect him content,
> Without loues foolish lazy languishment.
>> *2 Return from Parnassus*, 301-4.

There is a further link with the last *Parnassus* play which suggests that the note may reflect Cambridge opinion. Harvey includes his friend

---

[6] G. C. Moore Smith, *Gabriel Harvey's Marginalia*, pp. 232-3.
[7] For a general survey of critical opinion see E. A. Honigmann, 'The Date of *Hamlet*', *Shakespeare Survey* 9, pp. 24-6.
[8] *The Three Parnassus Plays*, ed. J. B. Leishman. All references are to this edition.

MSP

Spenser, who died in January 1599, and Thomas Watson, who died in 1592, among 'owr florishing metricians', though he must obviously have known that both of them were dead. But 'florishing', as critics have pointed out, refers to their works and not to the men themselves, and both are among the poets cited in 2 The Return from Parnassus, 202-45. It is mildly surprising to find, in both note and play, that Watson's insipid verse was still current eight years or so after his death, and odd, perhaps, that Henry Constable should be given such prominence in both lists. But the names in the Parnassus play were drawn from Bodenham's Belvedere, which appeared in 1600 and evidently became popular with undergraduates. It may, with caution, be urged that Harvey's comment was prompted by the impact of this book upon 'the younger sort'. Certainly the sub-title of Bodenham's anthology, The Garden of the Muses, affords as good an explanation as any for that fact that Spenser and Watson are spoken of as 'florishing metricians'.[9] If this surmise is correct, the backward dating limit for Harvey's note must obviously be 1600—the year in which Belvedere was published.

Clearly this evidence is insufficient to support far-reaching conclusions and its main value lies in the fact that it goes some way towards corroborating the claim of the Q1 title-page that Hamlet had been performed 'in the two Vniuersities of Cambridge and Oxford', and admits the view that these performances were given in 1600 or 1601. The Burbage-Kempe episode in 2 The Return from Parnassus might seem to argue for the latter date, but too much reliance cannot be placed on it. It is likely that Kempe, despite his dereliction, was still thought of in relation to the company with which he had acquired his fame, and even if the Chamberlain's men, with Kempe among them, were at Cambridge late in 1601, the possibility of other visits, during his absence, cannot be ruled out. The Parnassus play may in fact argue against, rather than for, a performance of Hamlet late in 1601, since it makes no allusion to a play that must surely have made a profound impression. And it is safe to affirm that the anonymous playwright who deplored Shakespeare's failure to handle graver subjects than 'loues foolish lazy languishment' can have known little or nothing of the new and penetrating tragedy which had in it that 'to please the wiser sort'.

What the Q1 title-page, supported by other evidence, establishes is that Hamlet had been played in both universities before 1603 and possibly as early as 1600, and at this point the distinction between town and

[9] 'Flourish' from O. F. florir (Mod. F. fleurir), ultimately from Lat. flos.

> For he was likely, had he beene put on
> To haue prou'd most royally.

But within the context of the play such qualities, through the drift of circumstance, are seldom revealed. He is Prince of Denmark in little more than name, and though Laertes may allege that

> on his choyce depends
> The sanctity and health of the whole State.

what we are shewn is a man in whom the obligation to revenge has almost completely usurped the purposes and qualities of an heir apparent. There is not that consistent and developing pattern of a prince who is destined to the succession that we find in the portrayal of Hal in the *Henry IV* plays, and that, maybe, because Hamlet is a different kind of prince. Heir apparent is in fact a misnomer, since the Danish crown is elective. His hopes have already been thwarted by his uncle, and there comes a time when the people cry that Laertes shall be king. Moreover, Claudius, whose stratagems can scarcely miscarry, is determined that his nephew shall not live to succeed him, and at no point in the play does kingship stand within the prospect of Hamlet's belief. Court, battlefield, council chamber and all the other parts and trappings of sovereignty are something that he has put behind him for ever.

Ophelia is wrong in one particular, for the scholar's mind is never overthrown. Hamlet's eagerness to go back to Wittenberg is made clear at the outset and is prompted by the impulse to secede from a world that he does not understand and return to one that he does. The implicit distinction is between a society that is free and responsive to 'the rights of our fellowship' and one which is nothing but a prison, even to a man who could be bounded in a nutshell and count himself a king of infinite space. The Denmark which has readily received Claudius as its king, and accepts the drunkenness and general corruption which he brings with him, lies outside Hamlet's experience and scale of values, and the breakdown of the family order, which leaves him with an uncle-father and an aunt-mother, perplexes and disgusts him. After the Ghost's disclosures, there is, of course, no possibility of retreat and as he becomes more and more benetted round with villanies, so he is forced to renounce, one after another, even those hopes which had survived. What he does not surrender are the habits, the disciplines and the values of the scholar from Wittenberg.

Hamlet's university associations are impressed on the audience from the outset. In I.ii, there is first his impatience to go back to school, followed by reluctant compliance with his mother's request, and later his encounter with Horatio, which brings yet more talk of Wittenberg. With Shakespeare, as with Marlowe, first impressions are important ones, and, in his initial presentation of Hamlet, he could scarcely have made his intentions more obvious. In I.v, the hero's response to the Ghost's injunctions, in which he renounces

> all triuiall fond Records,
> All sawes of Bookes, all formes, all presures past,
> That youth and obseruation coppied there,

and sets all down in his tables, is, as Elze noted long ago, precisely that of a thinker and a scholar. Again it is the scholar who, in II.ii, enters 'reading on a Booke', claimed by Warburton, on the strength of the section quoted at line 199 foll., to have been a copy of Juvenal.[13] The symbolic force of this entry is considerable. Literacy is not a prerequisite of the Shakespearian tragic hero, and we do not associate Othello, Lear, Macbeth, Antony or Coriolanus with the pursuit of learning. The tragedies, save for Timon's rather ostentatious patronage of the poet and painter, have little reference to literature and the arts. Books, as a general rule, serve a specific purpose. They are the tools of Prospero's trade. Brutus and Imogen indulge in a little bed-time reading. But Hamlet comes in 'reading on a Booke', simply, it would seem, because he is a scholar who loves reading for its own sake. The importance of this circumstance must not be exaggerated, but it is reasonable to assume that, for an Elizabethan audience, it carried a certain recognisable significance.

Immediately following this comes the meeting with Rosencrantz and Guildenstern, and since this is, in effect, a reunion of Wittenberg students its implications are obvious enough, as indeed is the tone of the whole section. Even so, one passage peculiar to the Folio (lines 244-76) was evidently added in order to strengthen the impression. It may be accounted a reasonably representative example of undergraduate crosstalk, outwardly light-hearted and even flippant, but with its roots set deep in speculative philosophy. And it is Hamlet the scholar who

[13] Beatrice White in 'Hamlet's Reading' (Neuphilologische Mitteilungen, LXV (1964), pp. 92-4) shews that the play owes other debts to Juvenal, and that certain of its themes and allusions may be referred back to Cicero's Tusculan Disputations. This strengthens the claims already advanced by T. W. Baldwin in William Shakespeare's Small Latine and Lesse Greeke and amply supports the present thesis that Shakespeare was concerned to depict Hamlet as a scholar who would have been recognisably such to an academic audience.

rounds off the section with a schoolman's meditation on man's status in the universe.

Again, it is Hamlet the student who converses with the Players and requests one of them to speak a speech from the play that 'was neuer Acted: or if it was, not aboue once'. The excerpt from '*Æneas* Tale to *Dido*' is something that, on *prima facie* grounds, might confidently be designated university drama. It is widely held to be a parody of part of Aeneas's long speech in *Dido, Queen of Carthage* (II.i.121-288), and this strengthens the university link. *Dido* was clearly written while Marlowe was still at Cambridge and was presumably performed there by the Children of the Chapel Royal, who toured East Anglia in the early summer of 1587. The title-page of the 1594 Quarto refers to a performance by the Children but there is no clear evidence that the play ever passed into general currency, and it may well have been '*Cauiarie* to the Generall'.[14] There can be little doubt that, when *Hamlet* was performed at the universities, the audiences immediately recognised the dramatic genre of the Pyrrhus speeches and accordingly accepted Hamlet as a person whose taste had been conditioned by that genre. It is also conceivable that the spectators at Cambridge viewed the whole section as a tribute to their most gifted playwright.

The great soliloquy which ends the second act is notable, among other things, for Hamlet's proclaimed uncertainty about the veracity of the Ghost's revelations. Something of this has already appeared in earlier scenes, and the doubts continue into III.ii, until Claudius's guilt is established by his behaviour during the Play-scene. Wilson, who has shewn that Hamlet's attitude is strikingly at variance with the normal Elizabethan convention, which accepted ghosts as reliable witnesses, attributes this scepticism to an academic training.[15] There is force in his contention that

> Horatio and Hamlet are students, so that their views will naturally be highly sophisticated by reading. Moreover, they are scholars of a university renowned for a particular school of theology. They have been studying together at the university of Wittenberg, Luther's university, the very cradle of the Reformation.[16]

[14] Many critics hold that the *Dido and Aeneas* given by the Admiral's Men on January 8th, 1598, was Marlowe's play, but the subject was doubtless handled by other dramatists. *Dido, Queen of Carthage*, was unquestionably intended for performance by a company of boy actors and its suitability for use by an adult company is dubious.

[15] *What Happens in 'Hamlet'*, pp. 66 foll.      [16] *ibid.*, pp. 67-8.

Wilson perhaps goes too far in claiming that Lutheran doctrine informs the play as a whole, but there can be little doubt that both Hamlet and Horatio, in their different ways, respond to the Ghost as students of that time, whether of Wittenberg, Oxford or Cambridge, might have been expected to respond. It goes without saying that the full implications of those responses would have been more readily comprehended by an audience that was itself academic than by the heterogeneous company that normally frequented the Globe.

It is, of course, Shakespeare himself who tells us that Hamlet is a student, and the foregoing illustrations aim merely to suggest that he consciously sought to bring this home to his audience by presenting what may be termed a series of specifically student reactions both to persons and to situations. When, about half way through the play, Hamlet turns to Polonius with

> Now my Lord, you plaid once i'th'Vniuersity, you say?

Shakespeare has made his point. There is nothing in what follows that seems directly allusive, though Hamlet's skill in fencing may, with caution, be accounted an attribute of the typical Wittenberg student. Such details are, however, less ponderable than the general character-pattern which Shakespeare imposes on his hero.

Hamlet is essentially the idealised pattern of a student who lives by reading and thought and who tests all situations in the light of reason and accumulated knowledge. He is, within Shakespeare's terms of reference, a philosopher in his own right, for, although we may hesitate to apply such a term to a man whose 'philosophy' is compounded from a few scraps of Montaigne and Lavater, these are nevertheless powerfully symbolic. Hamlet mistrusts intuition and seeks for proof in accordance with the principles of logic. He delights in verbal skirmishes, in disputation and enquiry. No other Shakespearian character asks so many questions, and his distinctive catechistic methods are strikingly revealed in his enquiry about the Ghost (I.ii.-190-244), in his quizzing of Rosencrantz and Guildenstern (II.ii.227-379) and in the Graveyard colloquy (V.i.126-235), all of which follow the accepted pattern of academic disputation. Another conspicuous feature is his interest in the arts, and particularly his manifest love of drama—a form which, in the decade preceding *Hamlet*, had owed so much to Lyly, Marlowe, Greene and other university men—and in all forms he reveals the scholar's search for perfection and truth.

Hamlet's general character range embraces a series of antitheses which have often brought consternation to the critics. He can pass unconstrainedly, even abruptly, from sublime meditation to displays of bawdy which exceed those of any other Shakespearian tragic hero. His gentleness alternates with savagery in word and deed. His extreme courtesy towards some characters contrasts strongly with his extraordinary rudeness towards others, and sympathy goes hand in hand with cynicism. These are not necessarily contradictions which furnish problems for the commentator and raw material for the psychologist, though they might be so regarded if the hero were a courtier, a general or in fact almost anything but what he is. The point is that these antitheses in Hamlet's character result from the rigid application of his ideals of value, truth and justice. He is rude only to those who merit rudeness, and savage only with those who seek his overthrow. He can discourse on speculative philosophy with Horatio and exchange bawdy pleasantries with Rosencrantz and Guildenstern. In short, he conducts himself like any reputable undergraduate. The student of today who is equally at home in library or public bar, who expounds metaphysics in one breath and recounts bawdy stories in the next, and who lives in peace and charity with his neighbours but half-kills his opponents on the playing-field provides a sufficiently apt analogy, and one which cannot easily be drawn from any other stratum of society. There is, therefore, some justification for believing that Shakespeare, having, by explicit statement, defined Hamlet as a student, sought, and achieved, verisimilitude in general portrayal of character. Certainly, if we accept Hamlet as the idealised pattern of an undergraduate, we also accept a norm which eliminates many of the so-called character problems. The familiar tags—mental instability, indecision, procrastination, melancholy, manic-depression—yield before what may be termed the consistent inconsistency of a particular character type, and this, in turn, goes some way towards explaining the hero's apparent sexual immaturity and the delays resulting from his preoccupation with absolute proof and perfect revenge.[17]

It is legitimate to infer that an Elizabethan play which converted its central character into an idealised student and which, by and large,

[17] The central dilemma is that of the naturally contemplative man, hitherto the inhabitant of a closed and congenial society, who is suddenly exposed to an alien world and confronted with an ineluctable and terrifying course of action. It is not suggested that any responsible critic has ever thought otherwise, but it may fairly be alleged that too little attention has been given to the specific background of Hamlet's contemplation.

presented a recognisable pattern of university society, even to the extent of admitting Polonius to the company, was designed in the first place for an academic audience, and the whole tone of the play amply supports this view. It has already been seen that, characterisation apart, there is much that seems to have a palpable design on such an audience. University plays and the academic methods of disputation are given fair prominence, and Shakespeare's extraordinarily rich and varied display of rhetoric would not have passed unnoticed at either Oxford or Cambridge. Above all there is the fact that *Hamlet* is such an intensely philosophical play. The power of contemplation, which ranges from Hamlet's own grave and penetrating discoveries down to the saws and moral instances of Polonius and the homespun philosophy of the Gravediggers, informs many of the characters. Claudius, the one primary male character who has no academic connexions, is yet a contemplative villain whose cast of mind can be well illustrated by comparison with Edmund in *King Lear*. Edmund invokes a particular doctrine as his justification for a particular course of action, whereas Claudius, whose deeds and conscience remain oddly at variance, offers no such justification. The philosophy which underlies his advice to Hamlet in I.ii.87-117 and his remarks to Laertes in IV.vii.111-14:

> Not that I thinke you did not loue your Father.
> But that I know Loue is begun by Time;
> And that I see in passages of proofe,
> Time qualifies the sparke and fire of it.[18]

has little bearing on his own motives and actions. What it signifies is that Claudius, scoundrel though he may be, is a meditative man who has worked out for himself a view of life, even though it may not be our view. The distinction that may be drawn is that Edmund's is an applied philosophy, Claudius's a pure one, which is not at all the kind of thing that might be expected of a tragic villain.

If we reason the needs we can hardly escape from the conclusion that Claudius's reflections, which have little direct bearing on either plot or character, are superfluous to the basic requirements, and this applies to other characters, even to Hamlet himself. Nor are these reflective passages the only expendable matter. The information about the boy actors, the Pyrrhus speeches, Hamlet's advice to the Players, to take only a few instances, are all acts of supererogation when judged strictly

[18] Q2 extends the meditation to fourteen lines but the abridged Folio version is sufficient for the needs.

in relation to the essential needs of a tragedy written expressly for a popular audience. This is not to imply any disparagement of Shakespeare's public at the Globe, for whom he wrote plays of comparable stature. *Othello*, presumably a Globe play, offers an effective norm of comparison. It is direct and passionate and contains scarcely a line that is not demonstrably material to the functions of poetic drama. *Hamlet*, in comparison, appears digressive and amorphous, and such appearances are not wholly deceptive if the two authentic texts are thought of in terms of Globe theatre needs. On the other hand, the moment we envisage *Hamlet* as something expressly written for leisured presentation before a scholarly and contemplative audience, we concede Shakespeare's right to consider curiously in an ampler context and come eventually to recognise the mastery of his design.

The basic facts are that, in 1600 or 1601, Shakespeare wrote the tragedy of *Hamlet*, and that, by 1603, the play had been presented at both universities. These are sufficient in themselves to establish an even chance that the play was composed with these academic occasions in view. The abnormal length and leisurely tempo of the play, together with a number of general peculiarities, virtually eliminate the possibility that it was originally intended for the Globe and provide elementary grounds for non-committal postulation of a private occasion. Since the play, in Shakespeare's hands, is made to centre upon what are, in effect, the activities of a group of students, which includes the hero, and since much of the incidental matter directly pertains to the habits, interests and commitments of students, it seems wholly reasonable to claim that *Hamlet* was first set down in compliance with grand commissions or earnest conjurations from one or both of the universities. To this may be added the rider, to which it will be necessary to return in the next chapter, that Shakespeare, from the first, went to some pains to insure that his academic tragedy would be readily adaptable to the needs of the popular stage.

Conversely, it might be argued that the original *Hamlet* was a Globe play of average length which the dramatist subsequently augmented for performance at the Universities. This hardly calls for consideration. The student-hero and the scholarly and philosophical horizons are the pith and marrow of the play and it is inconceivable that they were not present from the outset. Moreover, unless the accumulated wisdom of all reputable bibliographical critics is fantastically wide of the target, Q2, which includes practically the sum total of this academic matter, is a document which reveals Shakespeare in the actual process of composition and, except on the unverifiable assumption that he was the author of the *Ur-Hamlet*, there are no grounds of any kind for supposing that he ever penned two radically different versions of this or any other play.

iv

This hypothesis has considerable bearing on the transmission of the play. Taken in conjunction with certain conclusions reached in the previous chapter, it furnishes the probability that Q2 and the Folio represent two stages, presumably the penultimate and the final, in the history of the occasional play. In terms of what happened in 1600 or 1601, it may be assumed that the dramatist delivered an extremely difficult set of foul papers to the company and that these were handed over to a scribe. Prior to transcription, however, Shakespeare deleted several passages, but made one or two additions, which the Folio preserves and Q2 omits. The chief of these, II.ii.244-76 and II.ii.352-79, are readily intelligible as afterthoughts, especially in relation to university performances. The first converts Hamlet's meeting with Rosencrantz and Guildenstern into a representative academic skirmish which utilises the principles of disputation and alternates, student-like, between profundity and facetiousness, thus serving to clarify the status of the participants. The second passage, which relates to the activities of the Boys' companies and the stage-quarrel augments a topical allusion. In Q2 all we are told is that the inhibition of the City tragedians comes by the means of the late innovation, though exactly what the innovation was remains obscure. The Folio addition provides a full and up-to-date explanation of their wanderings and, by implication, those of Shakespeare's own company.

This transcript, which was unquestionably the basis, either directly or indirectly, of the Folio text doubtless served as prompt-copy for the performances at Oxford and Cambridge, and would also have been used on later occasions, if there were any, when a presentation of *Hamlet* in its original form was called for. If so, it can hardly have served also as the official Globe prompt-book. The extreme length of both Q2 and the Folio makes it quite necessary to assume that an abridged version, which reduced the original by about five hundred lines and which may have incorporated some actual revision, was prepared for use in the public theatres. It cannot, of course, be asserted that Shakespeare himself was responsible for this revision, though it seems unlikely that he would have entrusted the work to anyone else, and few inferences can confidently be drawn. It is reasonable to suppose that, once the necessary alterations had been made, a further transcript, which became the official prompt-book, was made and that no trace of this has survived, except, perhaps, among the recollections of the Q1 reporter.

Once it is allowed that the Globe prompt-book was an abridged version of the original tragedy, the late transcript by scribe C, postulated by Wilson, melts into thin air. It is generally held that prompt-books needed renewing from time to time, but, in the case of *Hamlet*, this would clearly have applied only to that used at the Globe. There is certainly no reason for believing that the original full-length transcript was so frequently put to theatrical use that a second copy had to be made round about 1620. Nor would a document prepared for stage purposes at that date have been likely to retain matter relating to the Boy actors and the long-forgotten stage-quarrel. The alternative suggestion is that the hypothetical late transcript was prepared expressly as Folio copy, but this, too, is invalidated by Dr. Walker's demonstration that Jaggard's compositors made extensive use of Q2. If they had been presented with a new, well-penned and authoritative manuscript they would naturally have used it as their sole copy and would certainly not have saddled themselves with the complicated process of consultation of which the Folio offers ample testimony.

It follows, then, that the manuscript which found its way into Jaggard's printing-house, and served as a corrective to Q2, may well have been the 1600 or 1601 transcript itself. The case must rest mainly on the ground that no subsequent copy of that particular version was ever likely to have been required. That the Folio version, as such, was in existence before 1603 is established by Q1, which, in the matter of omissions and additions, corroborates the Folio in every detail, except possibly for IV.iv.9-66. Jenkins has argued persuasively that the Folio preserves a number of playhouse interpolations, seemingly made with Shakespeare's acquiescence,[19] and since many of these are also found in Q1, it is clear that they must have been inserted before 1603. The obvious inference is that such minor concessions to the actors, like the additions to the dialogue, were made when the play was under rehearsal —that is, at a time when Shakespeare was open to suggestion. Less certainty attaches to the stage-directions peculiar to the Folio. Greg, whose opinion in such matters carries very great weight, lists eighteen additional directions and observes that they 'are often of a kind typical

[19] 'Playhouse Interpolations in the Folio Text of *Hamlet*' *Studies in Bibliography*, xiii, pp. 31-47.

rather of the author than the book-keeper',[20] but this scarcely warrants his assumption that most of them stood in the foul papers which, for reasons already stated, cannot be regarded as a perfected draft. It is at least equally probable that Shakespeare inserted them in the scribal fair copy and, if so, it is reasonable to suppose that this, too, was done at the original rehearsal stage as the directions are, after all, strictly necessary to the business of production.

From this it would appear that the manuscript which lies behind the Folio text had virtually achieved its final form before the play was actually presented, though other evidence points to revision after 1606, when the Act of Abuses came into force. A few of the Q2 profanities are altered in the Folio, but the purging was done very perfunctorily, so that several quite strong asseverations, for instance 'Gods bodykins' at II.ii.554 and 'Oh God, your onely Iiggemaker' at III.ii.132, were left standing. It is tempting to link this casual expurgation with the half-hearted attempt in the Folio to divide the play into acts and scenes, which does not extend beyond II.ii. Both features must have figured in the Folio manuscript, but it is not easy to see what purpose they served. One possibility is that sometime between 1606 and 1623 a desultory attempt was made to convert the manuscript into a prompt-book. Another is that partial editing was carried out in anticipation of publication. Neither explanation is really satisfactory but that hardly appears to matter. It is clear that whatever was contemplated was quickly abandoned and the results, such as they were, seem to have no bearing on the main textual problems.

Despite the unfortunate lack of firm evidence, it is possible to rest the case on several propositions. Firstly, if a transcript had been prepared in or around 1620, either as a replacement of the prompt-book or specifically as copy for the Folio, it would almost certainly have been fully divided into acts and scenes and have been consistent in its expurgation. Secondly, if a prompt-book, it would probably have omitted matter such as that relating to the stage-quarrel, which had served the turn in 1601 but would have become quite meaningless after the lapse of twenty years. Finally, unless the Folio version was in fact the same as that habitually performed at the Globe, there is no conceivable reason for believing that a second transcript was ever needed. In any case, all such requirements could have been met simply by amending a copy of the Good Quarto.

The conclusion to which we are led is that the Folio text reflects

[20] *The Shakespeare First Folio*, p. 318.

Heminge and Condell's concern to present their friend's plays 'absolute in their numbers, as he conceiued them'. It would appear, in the light of Dr. Walker's demonstration, that Jaggard's intention was to print, as far as possible, from Q2, but evidently this was not acceptable to Shakespeare's executors, possibly because they were aware of the manifold errors of that text, and possibly because they knew that it represented a version of *Hamlet* that had never been used in actual performance. The choice before them was to supply Jaggard either with the shortened Globe version or with the 'first Originall' as it had been performed at the universities, and it is unlikely that they had any difficulty in reaching their decision. Accordingly, the original transcript, which had probably lain unused for years, was turned in to the printing-shop, where it was duly collated with the Q2 copy, and setting-up proceeded in accordance with the methods defined in the previous chapter.

twelve

# *Hamlet*

## The Globe Version and the First Quarto

The claim that both Q2 and the Folio represent two narrowly separated stages in the creation of a private and occasional *Hamlet* carries with it the quite necessary assumption that there was also a Globe version. Whatever may have been Shakespeare's original purpose in writing *Hamlet*, it would be merely foolish to suppose that he was anything but aware, from the very start, that a tragedy which centred on a revenge story, incorporated ghost, fight, duel, madness, dumb-show and inner-play, and left the stage littered with the dead and dying contained all the ingredients of popularity. It is likely, therefore, that while he was penning the one version he was planning the other. The later plays shew that he was adept at such things. *Macbeth*, though specifically designed to entertain, interest and flatter King James, was nevertheless executed, and presumably conceived, in a form wholly acceptable to a popular audience, and we know, from Simon Forman's testimony, that it was in fact performed at the Globe. We also know, again from Forman, that *The Winter's Tale* and probably *Cymbeline* were presented at the same theatre at a time when they were comparatively new plays, though both were evidently written with the newly acquired Blackfriars theatre in mind. It has already been remarked that the Folio *Hamlet* could quite easily have been yet another of these dual-purpose plays but for its excessive length.

It is quite clear that Shakespeare's tragedy, in some form or other, soon achieved popular success. The title-page of Q1, irrespective of the conclusions already drawn from it, stands as evidence for a wide diversity of performances, and Anthony Scoloker's commendation of *Diaphantus* in 1604 as a work that 'should please all, like Prince *Hamlet*' is conclusive for the contemporary reputation of Shakespeare's play. So, too, is the reference a year later in *Ratseis Ghost*, which makes special mention of the part of Hamlet and thereby suggests that this was already recognised as one of the classic roles. Further proof, if any is needed, may be found in the fact that, following *Hamlet*, the revenge genre took on a new lease of life.

It would be absurd to suppose that all this was the outcome of a handful of private performances of the Folio text, and the obvious inference is that it was the version presented at the Globe which won the play its enduring popularity. That version, it has been claimed, cannot have been far in excess of three thousand lines, and there seems little reason to doubt Shakespeare's own responsibility for the adaptation. The main purpose of such an adaptation would, of course, have been to reduce the original play by upwards of five hundred lines, but it would be incautious to assume that an author, as distinct from a book-keeper, would merely proceed to make a series of cuts until the requisite total had been reached. The task of abridgement, viewed in the light of the present hypothesis, must have been a delicate one, since the shorter version was intended for performance by precisely the same body of actors as had presented the longer one, and if there is one cardinal principle that can be invoked it is that no form of revision liable to result in theatrical confusion may be assumed.

There remains the question whether Q1, obscured though it is by the reporter's memorial aberrations, may conceivably be held to have derived from the postulated abridgement. The possibility is one which critics in general appear to have ignored, and they can scarcely be blamed, since remarkably few of the conclusions that can be drawn from Q1 are unambiguous in their application. The two or three sections of tolerable blank-verse peculiar to this text are a case in point. It would be wholly reasonable to claim that these passages, which effectively reduce quite substantial portions of the Folio, are substitutions made by Shakespeare or another in the Globe abridgement. On the other hand, Duthie makes out a plausible case for believing them to be merely the reporter's substitutions for sections which he was wholly unable to remember, though he concedes that one particular alteration 'may have appeared in a previous stage-version of the Q2 text'.[1] He rests his case on a most impressive demonstration that the passages in question are a mosaic of recollections drawn both from *Hamlet* and from other plays and accordingly stigmatises them as un-Shakespearian. Against this it may be argued that no one was more likely to echo Shakespeare than Shakespeare himself, and that he would

[1] *op. cit.*, p. 273.

almost certainly have done precisely this if he was refashioning the
original play. If it is thereupon protested that Shakespeare is unlikely to
have written such pedestrian verse the obvious rejoinder is that these
passages reproduce not what the author wrote, but what the reporter
more or less supposed him to have written. And that, if we bear in mind
the Q1 version of, say, the 'To be, or not to be' soliloquy or Gertrude's
Willow-speech, opens up gloomy and indeterminate possibilities.

Greg corrects and modifies certain of Duthie's conclusions, and
argues firmly that 'Q1 represents correctly a report of the genuine text
obtained for acting in the country by a company that had no right to
it'[2]—a contention whose immediate relevance to Q1 itself no responsible critic is likely to dispute. He allows, rather more positively than
Duthie, that the sections unique to Q1 may have been derived from an
authorised stage adaptation, but does not actually affirm that that
adaptation was the version prepared for the Globe theatre. Since,
however, he maintains, no less firmly, that the Folio version cannot
have been 'habitually acted in its entirety', it is clear that, in his own
mind, he regarded the authorised adaptation and the Globe version as
one and the same thing. No one familiar with Greg's normal methods
could suppose him to have envisaged a multiplicity of versions.

If, as seems probable, there were two official versions of *Hamlet*, the
one for private presentation and the other for public, there are
reasonable *prima facie* grounds for believing that Q1 derived from the
latter. In other words, there is, theoretically, a greater likelihood that
the pirate's report stemmed from his participation in several performances of the abridgement and not from the original, which, by 1603,
may have been used on no more than a couple of occasions. Unfortunately, things could have been quite different in practice. The report
may in fact rest simply on the Oxford and Cambridge performances,
and the memorisation process belongs, in any case, at least as much to
rehearsal as to stage presentation. Even more discouraging is the
reflection that, if the pirate had acted in both versions, there is every
likelihood that what lies behind Q1 is a conflated text.

If the Bad Quarto of *Hamlet* belonged to the same class of reported
text as, say, the 1597 Quarto of *Richard III* or the 1608 Quarto of *King
Lear*, it could stand as something little short of absolute proof. Unfortunately it is not in that category, and the extraordinarily variable
quality of its reporting renders it a difficult text to classify. The largest
assumption that we are entitled to make, in the present state of know-

[2] *op. cit.*, p. 306.

ledge, is that the responsible agent sustained successively the roles of Marcellus, Lucianus and a Court supernumerary, and the present writer has elsewhere attempted to demonstrate that, on this basis, there is a consistent degree of accuracy in the Q1 presentation of the reporter's own speeches, of dialogue in which he was directly involved, of his main cues, and, in the second half of the play, of dialogue accompanied by memorable action in which he himself may well have been a mute participant.[3] This is credible so far as it goes, but it still leaves a vast proportion of the text unaccounted for, and it is here that problems arise. It does not surprise one to find that substantial sections of the remainder are fantastically chaotic, since this is a sufficiently common feature of reported texts, but the chaos is by no means widespread, and there is a fair quantity of tolerable paraphrase. It is when we are confronted by pieces of remarkably accurate reporting in scenes which evidently did not involve the reporter that light begins to thicken. Thus in Q1, I.iii begins with six lines of what are apparently loose paraphrase of 1-35, reports 36-8 accurately, reverts to a rather better paraphrase of 39-54, gives a remarkably good account of 55-81, despite omission of some half-dozen lines, and apparently ends with further loose para-phrase. Marcellus, it may be noted, leaves the stage at the end of I.ii and returns at the beginning of I.iv. It is curious, therefore, that he should have had such lively recollections of Polonius's speech, which occurs in the middle of a scene which did not concern him and of which he should, in theory, have retained little more than a uniformly hazy impression. What may have happened in practice will be con-sidered later.

Elsewhere there are striking moments of accuracy. The dialogue between Hamlet and the Ghost in I.v is quite well reported in Q1. Admittedly Marcellus would have been lurking in a corner of the stage throughout the scene, but he is not directly implicated, and the dialogue itself is complex. Polonius's speech at II.ii.40-9 contains several verbal inaccuracies, but does little real violence to the original. The amazing thing is not that the pirate should have remembered the lines imperfectly, but that he should have remembered them at all. The reporting of III.i is curiously spasmodic. Following the invincible chaos of the 'To be, or not to be' soliloquy, come a dozen lines of poor reporting which are succeeded by surprisingly good versions of lines 103-15 and 122-54, after which the scene tails off miserably. The

[3] 'Hamlet and the Player who could not Keep Counsel', Shakespeare Survey 3, pp. 74-82.

reporter's ability to recall, even sporadically, the subtleties of the Nunnery passages is quite surprising, especially when viewed in relation to his breakdown earlier in the scene. It may be remarked that, in the actual performance, he was probably in the tiring-house making himself ready for the part of Lucianus at this point. There is little that calls for comment in the last two acts, though the reporting of V.i.1-237 is, from time to time, far better than the complexity of the original would lead us to expect.

Clearly it is impossible to lay down any hard-and-fast rules about the reporter's memorial processes, but it would seem that he had lucid intervals in quite unexpected places, and that due allowance should be made for this. When, therefore, we find substantial omissions in Q1, the possibility that they testify to abridgement in the underlying version must be admitted, along with the customary explanation that they were due to failure of memory. Similarly, we need to assume a more guarded attitude towards Duthie's interpretation of what he terms un-Shakespearian passages of blank verse. If Shakespeare, in the interests of abridgement, rewrote certain parts of the play, these sections of Q1 could well represent memorial reconstructions, of indeterminate quality, of what he wrote.

The general principle which emerges is that Q1 may, in an overall way, be a more reliable text that has usually been supposed. But the problem admits of no satisfactory solution. If, as Duthie and others have assumed, Q1 derives from the full original version, whether that be Q2 or the Folio, it reproduces about 58 per cent of the content of that version. If, on the other hand, its basis was an official abridgement of c. 3,000 lines, it must be reckoned to preserve, however, imperfectly, something like 70 per cent. This, for an ordinary Bad Quarto, is so high a figure that its acceptance would undeniably confer a fair measure of respectability on Q1, and would certainly justify the view that the reporter, however erratic in matters of detail, had little difficulty in recovering the general pattern of his original.[4]

What confronts us in the final analysis is a logical circle. Before we can assume a reasonable reliability in Q1, we have to assume that that text derived from an abridgement, but before we can assume that abridgement, we have to assume a certain reliability. It follows, therefore, that any further deductions will necessarily be highly tentative, but even so it is desirable that the enquiry should be pursued since

---

[4] The really bad reported Quartos appear to reproduce about 50 per cent of the originals, but allowance has to be made for deliberate abridgement.

every variation peculiar to Q1, unless it can be confidently reckoned an aberration on the part of the reporter, is open to other interpretations, including that of revision.

ii

The problematic scene in which Fortinbras and his army march over the stage (IV.iv) is a useful point of departure. In Q2 this runs to sixty-six lines of dialogue and soliloquy, but the Folio preserves only the first eight lines and so reduces the scene to little more than an action:

*Enter Fortinbras with an Armie.*
*For.* Go Captaine, from me greet the Danish King,
Tell him that by his license, *Fortinbras*
Claimes the conueyance of a promis'd March
Ouer his Kingdome. You know the Rendeuous:
If that his Maiesty would ought with vs,
We shall expresse our dutie in his eye,
And let him know so.
*Cap.* I will doo't, my Lord.
*For.* Go safely on.       *Exit.*

The corresponding scene in Q1 is identical in scope:

*Enter Fortenbrasse, Drumme and Souldiers.*
*Fort.* Captaine, from vs goe greete
The king of Denmarke:
Tell him that *Fortenbrasse* nephew to old *Norway*,
Craues a free passe and conduct ouer his land,
According to the Articles agreed on:
You know our Randevous, goe march away.    *exeunt all.*
(sig G4v)

Such agreement suggests that the eight-line dialogue was all that was ever used on the stage, and that the additional fifty-eight lines in Q2 belong to the category of discarded material discussed in an earlier chapter. Critics have, however, pointed out that not only did the Q1 reporter incorporate a line peculiar to Q2:

The Nephew to old *Norway*, *Fortenbrasse*. (IV.iv.14)

but that the purveyor of *Der Bestrafte Brudermord* similarly recalled:

ô from this time forth,
My thoughts be bloody, or be nothing worth. (IV.iv.65-6)

in the assurance which he makes Hamlet give to Horatio that:

von dieser Stund an will ich darnach treten, wo ich den König allein finde, ihm
das Leben zu nehmen.

This, if trusted home, would seem to establish that the complete Q2
scene was used in the earliest performances but was reduced to Folio
length some time before 1603. The implication is that Q1 conflates the
two versions.

Such a conclusion rests rather heavily on the testimony of *Der
Bestrafte Brudermord*, which proves, on examination, to be more apparent than real. The two passages occur at different points in the play, the
one belongs to a soliloquy and the other to ordinary dialogue, and the
fact that both relate to Hamlet's intention of killing Claudius obviously
carries little weight since that is after all the principal motive throughout the play. The alleged verbal parallel 'from this time forth' and
'von dieser Stund an' cannot be taken seriously. The slightly melodramatic German phrase is a seventeenth-century commonplace,
and would scarcely be distinctive at any period. Moreover, 'Stund'
is not the same as 'time' and 'an', which adheres to the set formula
'von Stund an', is unacceptable as a rendering of 'forth'. The fact that
both phrases mean 'henceforth' can hardly be held to constitute a valid
parallel.

The Q1 line must therefore be judged entirely on its own merits, and
since it is clear that the reporter's concern was to recover a mere eight
lines, which he did more or less successfully, the possibility of contamination seems remote. Had he been familiar with the fifty-eight
additional lines of the Q2 version, the odds are that he would have
reproduced them in some form or other. Certainly he would not have
been deterred by yet another soliloquy.

The question is whether the phrase 'nephew to old *Norway*' is not
better explained as a small but necessary revision made in the Globe
version. The political background of *Hamlet* is somewhat sketchy at the
best, and though it is true that the relationship has been stated at
I.ii.28, 'Norway, Vncle of young *Fortinbras*', that is not the kind of
detail that the average spectator would be likely to recall after the
passing of three whole acts devoted to people who are far more interesting than Fortinbras. It is not unreasonable to surmise that the Folio
version of Fortinbras's first appearance was found to fall short of the
needs, so that Shakespeare, in adapting the play for the public theatre,
added a helpful reminder.

There is a notorious addition in Q1 at III.ii.50:

And then you haue some agen, that keepes one sute
Of ieasts, as a man is knowne by one sute of
Apparell, and Gentlemen quotes his ieasts downe
In their tables, before they come to the play, as thus:
Cannot you stay till I eate my porrige? and, you owe me
A quarters wages: and, my coate wants a cullison:
And, your beere is sowre: and, blabbering with his lips,
And thus keeping in his cinkapase of ieasts,
When, God knows, the warme Clowne cannot make a iest
Vnlesse by chance, as the blinde man catcheth a hare:
Maisters tell him of it. (sig. F2r-F2v)

Critics have rightly ignored the possibility of fabrication by the reporter, and the generally held view is that the passage is an actor's gag. It looks to be the kind of topical gibe that would have gone down well with certain sections of the Globe audience, but very few critics, apart from Furnivall and Brinsley Nicholson, have been willing to allow that Shakespeare himself may have been responsible for the passage—at least in its original form.

As it stands in Q1 the passage undeniably looks like a piece of gagging, and like nothing else. But the same would hold, under similar conditions, for such remarkable Q1 performances as, for instance,

Look you now, here is your husband,
With a face like *Vulcan*.
A looke fit for a murder and a rape,
A dull dead hanging looke, and a hell-bred eie,
To affright children and amaze the world:
And this same haue you left to change with this. (sig. G2v)

and it may well be that appearances are deceptive. The one thing that is absolutely certain is that the crudeness of the addition is due, in no small degree, to the reporter, whose memory evidently let him down badly. The offending clown had a stock of five jokes (a cinquepace): yet, although these were familiar in men's mouths as household words, the reporter was able to recover only four of them. Two of these have been traced by Wilson to *Tarlton's Jest-Book*, but if they are correctly presented in that text, it would seem that the Q1 reporter got them wrong.[5] The whole point of one of them is that the beer was not sour, but small! Defects of this character are tantamount to proof that what Q1 preserves is a mere travesty of an original which may have been

[5] 'The Copy for *Hamlet* 1603, etc.', *3 Library*, IX, pp. 240-1.

an actor's gag but may equally well have been an authentic addition.
Furnivall's characteristic question: 'whose but Shakespeare's is the
"cinkapase of ieasts", etc.?'[6] merits consideration. One would judge
that such a phrase was not beyond the scope of Jonson or Webster or
even Marston, but that is irrelevant. The point is that it is striking,
sophisticated and literary, and therefore suggestive of a writer rather
than an actor—even when, as in this case, the actor was presumably
Burbage. Once we appreciate this, certain other phrases in the passage—
'one sute Of ieasts', 'the warme Clowne', 'as the blinde man catcheth a
hare'—appear in a new light. They are pitched rather above ordinary
prose level and have even a touch of distinction. It is pertinent to remark
also that the whole passage is skilfully worked in. It has the air of
following quite naturally from Hamlet's other complaints about
excessive clownage; it constitutes a legitimate development of those
complaints; and it ends with a formula, 'Maisters tell him of it', which
accords with others that occur elsewhere in the advice to the Players:
'Pray you auoid it', 'O reforme it altogether'. Even 'Maisters' has a
Shakespearian ring, for it is the form of address used by Hamlet when
the Players arrive at Elsinore in II.ii.

It is important that the passage should be related to the attendant
circumstances. If an actor interpolated a dozen lines of gag precisely at
that point where Hamlet has just denounced the clown who speaks
more than is set down for him, it can only have been either because he
was extraordinarily imperceptive or because he was deliberately intent
on baiting Shakespeare. But the passage is wholly intelligible as a
Shakespearian addition. There can be little doubt that Hamlet's advice
to the Players expresses its author's own deeply felt convictions, and
no one would question the earnestness of the denunciation of intrusive
clowning as it is presented in Q2 and the Folio. It is not unreasonable,
therefore, to surmise that when he came to prepare a version of the
Globe he decided to develop his point with specific illustration. It may
have been, as some critics have supposed, that his motive was to settle a
score with Kempe, but the predilections of his audience together with
his recognition of the need to set out his grievance fully and unequi-
vocally would provide a sufficient explanation for the expanded passage.

iii

The theory of revision unquestionably points to one possible way of
resolving the problems attaching to these two passages, and it will

[6] 'Hamlet 1603' (Griggs Facsimile), p. vii.

therefore be convenient, at this point, to consider certain other Q1 peculiarities, which, like the foregoing, may conceivably serve as evidence for revision, though not, as yet, for abridgement. These are all casual variants in the bibliographical sense, though two of them have opened the door to controversy which is anything but casual.

(a) *Marcellus's Lines* (I.i.40 foll.: Q1 sig. B1v-B2r)

It is generally held that the Q1 reporter was the actor who had played Marcellus and the evidence is virtually conclusive, since Marcellus's speeches are almost identical in all three texts. There are, however, several small divergences, of which the following may be noted:

I.i.40    Breake off your talke, see where it comes againe.
          F.(Q2):    Peace, breake thee of:
                     Looke where it comes againe.

I.i.53    Tis gone and makes no answer.
          F.(Q2):    'Tis gone, and will not answer.

I.i.66    With Marshall stalke he passed through our watch.
          F.(Q2):    With Martiall stalke, hath he gone by our Watch.

We cannot, of course, rule out the possibility that these Q1 variants are compositors' errors, though of a somewhat unusual kind. It is possible too, that Marcellus was not word-perfect, or that he had deliberately tampered with his part. As evidence for revision the variants do not amount to much, but all three are, in a sense, improvements. In the first 'your talke' applies to both Bernardo and Horatio and seems more satisfactory than the 'breake thee of' which applies only to the former character. The Q2 and Folio 'will not' in line 53 comes perilously near to nonsense. If the Ghost has gone, obviously it will not answer. In line 66 'he passed through' is more graphic and more precise than 'hath he gone by'. It suggests that the freedom of movement traditionally ascribed to ghosts, coupled with their ability to surmount all resistance. A different and more impressive action is implied.

There is a case, albeit a slender one, for regarding all three variants as Shakespeare's afterthoughts. Certainly the variant at I.i.66 does not look like an actor's substitution.

(b) *Corambis and other Names* (I.ii.1 foll.)

Polonius appears as 'Corambis' in Q1 and as 'Corambus' in *Der Bestrafte Brudermord*, while his companion, Reynaldo, becomes

'Montano' in Q1. The change has not been adequately explained, but Greg's view may be cited:

> The most plausible suggestion respecting the change of names, though it is not altogether satisfactory, is that Corambus and Montano were those borne by the characters in the early *Hamlet* and that they were there, or had at least become on the stage, recognisable caricatures of Lord Burghley and one of his followers; that Shakespeare, rewriting the play soon after Burghley's death in 1598, thought it more decent to alter them to Polonius and Reynaldo; but that the reporter reverted to the traditional names as more generally familiar.[7]

This rests on several very large assumptions. There are no grounds for supposing that the old counsellor was named Corambus in the *Ur-Hamlet*, or that he ever carried any reference to Burleigh, or that the reporter would have been likely to substitute the names that may (or may not) have figured in a play which he may (or may not) have known. It has, in fact, been far too readily assumed that Corambis and Montano were the original names; Polonius and Reynaldo, the substitutions. Yet the latter names demonstrably belong to the foul papers of *c.* 1600, while the former ones appear to derive from a stage-version of *c.* 1601-3 and, so far as we know, from no other source. It is significant that somewhere roughly between the staging of *Hamlet* and the publication of Q1, the name of 'Corambus' appeared in *All's Well that Ends Well*, and that of 'Montano' in *Othello*. And it was Shakespeare, not a reporter and not the author of the *Ur-Hamlet*, who was using them.

This problem of nomenclature extends to other characters. In II.ii and elsewhere, Q1 has 'Voltemar' for Folio 'Voltemand'. Rosencrantz and Guildenstern are invariably 'Rossencraft' and 'Gilderstone'. In III.ii the Player-King is 'Albertus', instead of Gonzago, and his territory is 'guyana', not Vienna. This last variant is manifestly corrupt, and may be a printer's misreading of 'Vienna', but it could equally well be a perversion of either 'Genoa' or 'Guienne'.[8] The other Q1 forms are certainly not compositorial and must be assigned to the reporter. It is evident that he was unable to recollect the names of certain minor characters since Bernardo, Francisco and Osric are all

---

[7] *The Shakespeare First Folio*, p. 330 (Note B).

[8] Some critics hold that 'Guiana' was intended. Topical allusions to the New World were not uncommon, but Guiana could scarcely have been represented as ruled by a Duke whose story had been often writ in choice Italian.

anonymous in Q1, and this might lead us to suppose that he had half-forgotten Rosencrantz, Guildenstern and Voltemand, and had wholly forgotten Gonzago. Such an assumption is scarcely warranted. At II.ii.562, Q1 refers to the inner-play as 'the murder of *Gonsago*', so that the name was assuredly accessible to the reporter's consciousness. And if, as seems certain, he played Lucianus, Hamlet's lines at III.ii.248–53 were the cue for his entry. Hence there can be little doubt that 'Albertus' and 'guyana' (or whatever the form should be) were the names with which he was familiar.

The same applies, in greater or lesser degree, to the other names. Voltemand's speech at II.i.60–80 is accurately rendered in Q1 and Wilson's theory that the reporter had a copy of the part has won general acceptance. If it is correct, it affords a sufficient guarantee for the form 'Voltemar': if it is not, it imposes on us the alternative view that the Voltemand actor was implicated in the piracy, and that would furnish an even firmer guarantee. A not uncommon English contempt for outlandish names may have led the reporter to pervert those of Rosencrantz and Guildenstern to forms such as Dogberry or Mistress Quickly might have used, but this is hardly credible. The strangeness of both names is one of spelling rather than sound. They are spoken freely throughout the play, and the invariable linking of the two renders them memorable—or rather, unforgettable.

We are led inevitably to the conclusion that four or five of the names peculiar to Q1 were those known to the reporter through the stage version, and there is no reason why Corambis and Montano should not belong to the same category since the wholesale set of changes craves a single comprehensive explanation. It does no great violence to probability to suppose that Shakespeare himself made the changes when he adapted the play for performance at the Globe. It is possible that he thought it prudent to do so. The identification of Polonius with Burleigh may or may not be justified, but it is certain that the name signifies 'the Pole' and that his dramatic status is practically that of a plenipotentiary. We know, from the circumstances which led to the withdrawal of Marlowe's *Massacre at Paris* and later of Chapman's *Byron's Conspiracy*, that the representatives of foreign powers were sometimes moved to protest, and may wonder, therefore, whether the Polish ambassador would willingly have suffered the name 'Polonius' to be bandied about the public theatres, especially in relation to so contemptible a character. The same applies, perhaps, more forcibly, to Rosencrantz and Guildenstern, since these were the actual names of two highly placed Danish families. The other names appear to offer no grounds for speculation.

Briefly, the names that were eligible for use in private performances were presumably deemed inappropriate for public use and several of them were accordingly changed in such a way that they could not confuse the actors. Polonius, Reynaldo and, perhaps, Gonzago, evidently needed more radical treatment. If this is substantially correct, it means, of course, that 'Corambis' was substituted for 'Polonius', and not vice versa, though the Folio convention admits the possibility that the company subsequently reverted to the original names. This reversal of procedure may not appeal to every reader, but he should first consider whether his preference in the matter is not a purely sentimental one. The corroboration supplied by *Der Bestrafte Brudermord* cannot be disregarded, and there are, besides, various grounds for believing that Q1, though the earliest printed text, preserves the latest version known to us.

(c) *The Groundlings* (III.ii.11: Q1 sig. F2r)

In Q2 and the Folio Hamlet denounces the actor who will

> teare a Passion to tatters, to verie ragges, to split the eares of the Ground-lings: who (for the most part) are capeable of nothing, but inexplicable dumbe shewes, & noise.

This would have been all very well in Oxford and Cambridge but the effect that it would have produced at the Globe, where those same groundlings constituted an important and very vocal part of the audience, can be left to the imagination. For 'Groundlings', Q1 substitutes 'ignoraut' [*sic*] which is something that no self-respecting groundling would take as being applicable to himself. The change reflects that tactful attitude to the mob which applies to Marc Antony, Menenius Agrippa, Sir Thomas More, and, it pleases us to believe, Shakespeare himself. The possibility that the Q1 variant was due to the reporter is almost negligible. The word occurs in a longish passage of conspicuously accurate reporting. Nor does it seem likely that such a word as groundlings would have been forgotten in this context.

(d) *Laertes's Speech* (IV.viii.184-92: Q1: sig. H3v)

The Q1 rendering of Gertrude's Willow speech is one of the reporter's most disastrous efforts. Its almost total annihilation of sense and meter, combined with an inept recollection from *Twelfth Night*, testify to hopeless confusion. It would be foolish to place too much reliance on any Q1 reading at this point, but Laertes' response merits notice:

> So, she is drownde:
> Too much of water hast thou *Ofelia*,
> Therefore I will not drowne thee in my teares,
> Reuenge it is must yeeld this heart releefe,
> For woe begets woe, and griefe hangs on griefe.

The opening half-line, though doubtless inaccurate, *may* point to revision. The reading of Q2 is:

> Alas, then she is drownd.

and that of the Folio:

> Alas then, is she drown'd?

Neither of these inspires confidence. The Queen begins by telling Laertes that his sister is drowned. His improbable response:

> Drown'd! O where?

is doubtless a device for admitting the exquisite, but extra-dramatic, account of the drowning. Since that account is very full and quite explicit, it seems ridiculous that Laertes should ask, as in the Folio, whether she is drowned, or that he should offer the unintelligent comment preserved in Q2. It is, then, possible that behind the Q1 reading there lurks Shakespeare's subsequent attempt to amend one of 'those things, could not escape laughter'. The note of momentary stoical resignation implicit in 'So, she is drownde' seems relevant both to the immediate context and to Shakespearian practice on other such occasions.

The two lines which follow are palpably a travesty, but the concluding couplet looks like a genuine substitition designed to close the scene on a more melodramatic note.[9] We may be reluctant to ascribe it to

---

[9] It is widely held that the couplet was due to the reporter having recalled *The Spanish Tragedy*, II.v.39-41:

(*Isa.*) O wheres the author of this endles woe?
*Hier.* To know the author were some ease of grefe,
For in reuenge my hart would fine reliefe.

This is possible, but the collocation 'woe-revenge-heart-grief' is not a very distinctive one. In any case, Shakespeare was quite capable of echoing Kyd.

Shakespeare, but the fact remains that it conforms to a rhetorical
pattern that he frequently used in other plays: cf.:

> Haste still paies haste, and leasure, answers leasure;
> Like doth quit like, and *Measure* still for *Measure*.
>
> *Measure for Measure*, V.i.415-6

> Away, and mock the time with fairest show,
> False Face must hide what the false Heart doth know.
>
> *Macbeth*, I.vii,81-2

> Gods benyson go with you, and with those
> That would make good of bad, and Friends of Foes.
>
> *ibid.*, II.iv.40-1

> Cowards father Cowards, & Base things Syre Bace:
> Nature hath Meale, and Bran, Contempt, and Grace.
>
> *Cymbeline*, IV.ii.25-6

(e) *Hamlet's Age* (V.i.154 foll.: Q1: sig. I1r)

Hamlet's age has provoked much barren controversy. In Q2 and the
Folio, the Gravedigger claims to have taken up his job 'that day that
our last King *Hamlet* o'recame *Fortinbras*', and adds that it was 'the very
day, that young *Hamlet* was borne'. At line 167 he says that he has been
sexton for thirty years. The obvious deduction that Hamlet is thirty is
unacceptable since he is consistently represented as a very young man.[10]
It is likely that Shakespeare, whose regard for mathematics is invariably
slighter than that of his commentators, gave little thought to the matter.
The revelations in I.v do not, in any case, tally too satisfactorily with
I.i.60-1, where Horatio identifies the Ghost by

> the very Armour he had on,
> When (he) th'Ambitious Norwey combatted.

If, as this implies, Horatio was himself present at the battle (fought on
the day of Hamlet's birth), his own age would be at least forty-five—
that is, if we base our calculations on V.i,—whereas it is perfectly
obvious that Shakespeare intended the two men to be roughly coeval.

The conclusions that Q1 allows us to draw are quite different. There
is no reference to the Gravedigger having been at his trade for thirty
years, and all that we have to go upon is the statement that Yorick's
skull 'hath bin here this dozen yeare', as against twenty-three in Q2 and

[10] Another obvious deduction is that Hamlet and 'young Fortinbras' are of
roughly the same age!

the Folio. Since the implication in Q2 and the Folio is that Hamlet was seven when Yorick died, the 'dozen yeare' would make him nineteen at the time of the play. This is consistent with our general impression.

The Q1 report of V.i has its lucid intervals, but the overall quality does not inspire confidence. As far as figures are concerned, the reporter recalls correctly the 'eight yeare, or nine yeare' at lines 182-3, but at 150 he converts 'three yeares' into 'seauen yeares' and, at 204, 'a thousand times' into 'a hundred times'. His 'dozen yeare' may therefore be no more than a memorial substitution, though it is not easy to see why he should have forgotten a number as specific as 'three & twenty'. Memorial error, one would judge, would have been more likely if the original reading had been something like 'two dozen' or 'a score'. The possibility that the inconsistency was brought home to Shakespeare, who made the necessary adjustment in the Globe version, is admissible, though it cannot be regarded as compelling.

<h4 align="center">iv</h4>

The foregoing scraps of evidence, though individually vulnerable, have cumulative weight and warrant the view that the play underwent at least casual revision, perhaps by the author. They do not, however, testify to abridgement and one of them, ironically enough, could be taken as evidence for augmentation. It has already been hinted that the case for abridgement is likely to rest heavily upon those sections exclusive to Q1 which Duthie stigmatises as un-Shakespearian, but our judgment on these must depend largely on the conclusions that can be drawn from two other passages.

(a) *I.iii.1-136* (Q1: sig. C1v-C2v)

This scene, which involves Ophelia, Laertes and Polonius, abounds in good advice and moral instances, and it goes without saying that, if cuts were made, it is here that we might expect them. The Q1 version runs to seventy lines, thus reducing Q2 and the Folio by one half, but is coherent and business-like, despite the inevitable crop of memorial errors. The general impression, for the greater part, is that it may well have derived from a quite competent abridgement. There is little that suggests rewriting, as distinct from cutting, and the semblance of revision at the end of the scene is probably an improvisation by the reporter.

Greg, in a note on the Marcellus theory, offers some important and relevant comments:

OSP

It is, however, not free from difficulties. Marcellus is on the stage in I.iib and I.iv and we should therefore have expected him to know the beginning and end of I.iii rather than the middle; yet it is the middle portion, between Polonius and Laertes, that is well reported, whereas the opening and closing portions, between Laertes and Ophelia and between Ophelia and Polonius, are little more than paraphrase.[11]

The middle section (lines 55-81) is, to all intents and purposes, identical with Q2 and the Folio save for three omissions, at 59-60, 68-9 and 75-7. It seems unlikely that these were due to forgetfulness. For one thing, the reporter's memory was obviously serving him very well indeed at this point, and for another, the whole speech remains perfectly coherent, shewing no sign of the dislocation that loss of memory usually entails. The only acceptable alternative is to suppose that the Q1 report was based on a version in which three small but discreet cuts had been made.

This assumption clearly has a bearing on the adjacent portions. Greg's term, 'little more than a paraphrase', is accurate but misleading. Q1 reduces the first section from 54 lines to 22, gets off to an accurate start:

> My necessaries are inbarkt.

and then, by substituting 'I must aboord', conveys the main information attaching to lines 1b-4. The five lines that follow give the gist of lines 5-35, and what they surrender—Laertes's florid rhetoric and his views on princely conduct—is matter that is strictly superfluous to dramatic need, though it is very much in character. There is, however, a degree of character revelation in Q1, since the reporter proceeds to a correct rendering of three lines of *sententiae* (36-8). The speech ends with two lines:

> Belieu't *Ofelia*, therefore keepe a loofe
> Lest that he trip thy honor and thy fame.

which perhaps convey Laertes' meaning more directly than do the corresponding lines in the authentic texts. Ophelia's retort affords the only clear-cut example of bad reporting in this section. It is a loose paraphrase of Q2 and the Folio, with the customary errors, omissions, substitutions, and metrical irregularity. It certainly lacks the efficiency of the speeches which precede it in Q1 and it is worth noting that the reporter, compelled for the moment to improvise, extends the seven lines of his original into nine.

[11] *The Shakespeare First Folio*, p. 302 (Note B).

The closing section is similarly variable. Lines 82-100 are reproduced with commendable accuracy save for lapses at 91-3 and 97-8. Lines 100-14 are omitted and this is presumably a memorial loss since relics of them intrude into the 'Springes to catch Woodcocks' speech, which Q1 reduces to five lines of patchwork. Following this Ophelia speaks the line:

I shall obay my lord in all I may.

which differs from Q2 and the Folio yet has a faintly Shakespearian ring. The scene is thereupon brought to an end thus:

Cor. *Ofelia*, receiue none of his letters,
"For louers lines are snares to intrap the heart;
"Refuse his tokens, both of them are keyes
To vnlocke Chastitie vnto Desire:
Come in *Ofelia*, such men often proue,
"Great in their wordes, but little in their loue.
*Ofel*. I will my lord.                              *exeunt.*

These lines suggest a dubious report of matter different from that of Q2 and the Folio, but the couplet, which is taken over from *Twelfth Night*, II.iv.119-21, raises an awkward problem. If Marcellus was the reporter, he must surely have remembered the lines immediately preceding his own entry at the beginning of I.iv. This argues that what Q1 preserves is an authentic piece of revision—a supposition which the added *sententiae* could very well support since they are wholly in character. The question is whether Shakespeare, as the presumed reviser, would have been likely to echo a couple of lines from another play.

The scene as a whole emerges as a report by an actor who forgot at least fifteen lines and produced a garbled version of about twenty. The worst lapses occur towards the end of the scene, precisely at the point where Marcellus would be thinking more about his impending entry than about exactly what was being spoken on the stage. His partial report of the first hundred lines of Q2 and the Folio is consistent in its verbal accuracy. There are some fairly substantial omissions, but these are all of material that can be reckoned expendable, and the text remains coherent. On balance it seems probable that the reporter omitted the passages in question not because he had forgotten them, but because they had been excluded from the stage version with which he was most familiar. It is reasonable, therefore, to assume that these apparent cuts, together with accompanying deviations and, rather dubiously, the closing lines, point to revision and abridgement of the Folio version for use at the Globe. The closing couplet, though far from conclusive, admits the possibility that Shakespeare himself was the reviser—and there is, of course, no earthly reason for assuming that he was not. Comparison between Q1 and the authentic texts suggests that the postulated abridgement was carefully planned and executed. Polonius's advice to Laertes, though slightly reduced, surrenders none of its qualities as an actor's show-piece. Nor does Ophelia appear to suffer any diminution—except at the hands of the reporter. Revision in both cases appears to defer to actors who had already played the parts in the original version, and there is no sign of amendments liable to cause confusion. There is a notable curb only on Laertes' verbosity, but his part is a small one, so that any competent actor could have taken the changes in his stride.

(b) *III.ii.165-238.* (Q1: sig. F3r-F3v)

The Q1 version of the Inner-play differs considerably from that common to Q2 and the Folio. It alters King and Queen to Duke and Duchess in both stage-direction and speech-headings, but it is unlikely that this was intended as a correction. It is true that Gonzago is termed Duke, but Lucianus is described as 'nephew to the King' in all texts, and, in any case, Q1 retains '*the King and the Queene*' in the dumb-show. The alteration was doubtless intended to distinguish the inner-play characters from Claudius and Gertrude—a distinction which is not made clear in Q2 and the Folio.

Much more significant is the fact that the dialogue between these two characters, which runs to about seventy lines in the authentic texts, is reduced to thirty in Q1. Lines 165-89 are replaced by fourteen quite different ones. Thereafter there is almost complete agreement, save that Q1 omits 191-2, 198-221 and 226-31. The possibility that the reporter had forgotten all but a few stray couplets can be ruled out. In the first place, he almost certainly participated in the inner-play, and, in the second, his rendering of the adjacent dialogue, which is complex, is far too accurate to admit the supposition that he was unable to recover a sequence of rhyming couplets. There seems, therefore, to be no escape from the conclusion that Q1 preserves an authorised replacement whose only perceptible function was to shorten the episode—which it does to the extent of forty lines,

This section is even more eligible for abridgement than I.iii. The original, which is clearly a burlesque of earlier Senecan tragedy, is deliberately prolix, as witness the opening speech which consumes six lines in saying, 'We have been married for thirty years.' The Q1 version dispenses with the verbosity joke, but remains a parody of the Senecan vein, as such clichés as 'whilome', 'kill my heart' and 'when ended is my date' testify. One or two faint echoes of the original suggest author-revision, but as neither version is written in Shakespeare's normal style, absolute proof is not possible. It may be noted, however, that the collocation of 'weakely' and 'pipes' in association with 'musicke' recalls the 'weake piping time of Peace' with its 'lasciuious pleasing of a Lute' in the opening speech of the Senecan *Richard III*, which, like the *Hamlet* passage, also has lines beginning with 'And now' and 'And therefore'. As evidence this does not amount to much, but it cannot be entirely disregarded.

### V

It remains to consider what Greg terms 'the four outstanding differences' between Q1 and the other texts. These comprise the altered placing of the Nunnery scene, a scene in which Horatio tells Gertrude of Hamlet's return to Denmark, a section in the Closet scene in which Gertrude protests her innocence, and an allegedly different account of the circumstances of Hamlet's escape on the voyage to England. Duthie's analysis of these is a remarkable *tour-de-force*, but the conclusions that he draws are hard to reconcile with the present hypothesis. This is inevitable since he is non-committal on the subject of abridgement, admitting that he can find no evidence either way but that 'nothing would surprise me less than that a fairly drastic stage abridgement of *Hamlet* was made, legitimately or otherwise, for provincial performance',[12] and firm in his belief that the passages of blank verse peculiar to Q1 were composed by the reporter in order to make good his memorial losses.

Duthie's main thesis, that Q1 was based on a report by the actor who had played Marcellus and, possibly, other minor roles, and that the memorial reconstruction often resulted in a tissue of reminiscences of other parts of the play, and of other plays to boot, is supported by a demonstration so comprehensive that it has, quite rightly, won general acceptance. His claim that some of these reminiscences were drawn, deliberately or involuntarily, from the *Ur-Hamlet* is less easy to accept since it presupposes that the reporter had acted in a play of which, in

[12] *op. cit.*, p. 272.

any case, we know practically nothing, and an array of parallels drawn from Kyd is neither here nor there.[13] A fuller recognition of the implications of the Q1 inner-play might have enabled Duthie to indulge his obvious predilection for abridgement, but the main weakness here lies in the assumption, shared by later critics, that abridgement itself was determined solely by the needs of provincial performance. The *Hamlet* presented at Bath or Norwich may assuredly have been a shortened form of the version normally used at the Globe, but that version must itself have been a reduction of the excessively long original play preserved in the Folio.

The Q1 blank-verse passages pose a number of problems. Earlier critics assumed either that they were relics of Shakespeare's original draft, or that they were incorporated from the *Ur-Hamlet*, or that they were supplied by a hack-poet in order to give coherence to a defective report. Duthie successfully refutes these views but, as has already been hinted, the alternative which he provides is not free from difficulty. If the reporter had some skill, however meagre, in the turning of blank verse, it seems incredible that he should have used it so spasmodically, especially if, as Duthie further supposes, his work 'was revised and to some extent amplified by himself or by a second agent (perhaps an actor too).'[14] On the other hand, if we assume, for the sake of argument, that these passages had been supplied by Shakespeare himself in the course of revision, we are led to two conclusions, neither of which is intrinsically vulnerable: (1) that the echoes of *Hamlet* and other plays arose because the dramatist was refashioning existing material and because they were in any case part and parcel of the Shakespearian manner; (2) that what Shakespeare wrote suffered, in greater or lesser degree, at the hands of the reporter, who, in consequence, may have been responsible for some, but not all, of the reminiscences. Such an

---

[13] The catalogue of parallels, based on the findings of Widgery, Sarrazin, Boas and Robertson, which Duthie gives (pp. 181-4) is less impressive than it looks. Some of the parallels are tenuous, some relate to the old *Jeronymo*, which is not Kyd's, and some depend on Elizabethan commonplaces. Moreover, various interpretations are possible. Thus Hamlet's protest to Laertes in Q1, 'I neuer gaue you cause', may be a recollection (by the reporter) of *The Spanish Tragedy*, III. xiv. 148:

> *Hieronimo*, I neuer gaue you cause.

But it may equally well be an anticipation (by Shakespeare) of Michael Cassio's

> Deere Generall, I neuer gaue you cause.

[14] *op. cit.*, p. 273.

assumption is clearly not unwarrantable. The trouble is that it imposes the need to make distinctions which are almost too subtle for the intellect.

We may now turn to consider the variant passages.

## (a) *The Nunnery Scene* (Q1 : sig. D4v-E2r)

The Q1 version represents a running together of II.ii.159-70 and III.i.56-169, so that immediately after Polonius's formulation of his plan for testing Hamlet, comes the 'To be, or not to be' soliloquy, followed by the rejection of Ophelia. Thereafter, Q1 reverts to a version of II.ii.171-III.i.55. The same sequence occurs in *Der Bestrafte Brudermord*, and it is generally accepted that the change is deliberate. There seems no reason for dissenting from Greg's summing-up:

> The object may have been to simplify the action—perhaps also to avoid the characteristic Shakespearian oversight whereby at II.i.101 and 117 Polonius bids Ophelia accompany him to the King and yet arrives alone at II.ii.40.

The change, as Duthie shews, produced its own crop of inconsistencies, but these were probably inevitable. The alteration may belong to the postulated Globe revision, but it is not clear that it contributed very much to the abridgement. It was certainly carefully planned and the adjustment of dialogue to accommodate the altered sequence is skilful. Several lines were added to allow the Nunnery scene to lead directly on to the baiting of Polonius.

> *King.* Loue? No, no, that's not the cause,                *Enter King and*
> Some deeper thing it is that troubles him.                *Corambis.*
> *Cor.* Wel, something it is: my Lord, content you a while,
> I will my selfe goe feele him: let me worke,
> Ile try him euery way: see where he comes,
> Send you those Gentlemen, let me alone
> To finde the depth of this, away, be gone.        *exit King.*

Duthie assigns these lines to the reporter-versifier on the ground that many of the phrases echo other parts of the play. Thus 'cause' is applied to Hamlet's supposed madness at II.ii.49, 101, III.i.6, and III.ii.338. Claudius's 'troubles him' echoes 'this troubles me' at I.ii.224, and Corambis's 'something it is' links with III.i.172, 'there's something in his soule.' The phrase 'content you a while' anticipates IV.v.210:

> Be you content to lend your patience to vs.

which Q1 converts into:

> Content you good Leartes for a time.

Again, 'let me worke' echoes 'I went round to work' at II.ii.139, 'Ile
try him euery way' uses 'try' in the same sense as II.ii.159, 'Send
you those Gentlemen' recalls 'bring these gentlemen where *Hamlet*
is' at II.ii.37, 'let me alone to finde the depth of this' relates to
III.i.190-1:

> Let his Queene Mother all alone intreat him
> To shew his Greefes.

and III.i.193-4:

> If she finde him not,
> To England send him.

Finally, 'away' echoes 'Away I do beseech you, both away' at II.ii.169.
  This is all very possible but, as Duthie admits, the echoes are sometimes very faint, and they seem, singly and collectively, altogether too
commonplace to allow any clear inference to be drawn. It would be
more to the point if a parallel to Corambis's distinctive 'I will my
selfe goe feele him' could be found, though even this would not settle
the issue. The fact that, in the authentic texts, 'cause' is used four times
in connexion with Hamlet's madness suggests that a fifth such usage
could as well be Shakespeare's as the reporter's, but it would be futile
to drive evidence of this kind any further. Briefly, the whole passage
points to deliberate and quite skilful revision and the case for ascribing
this to Shakespeare himself is at least as strong as the case against. If he
was the reviser, he must certainly have written a link for Corambis
(Polonius), and the lines in Q1 would be, at best, a defective report of
that link. There is no evidence of abridgement, though the alteration
may conceivably have permitted small economies in the adjacent
dialogue.

(b) *The Change in Gertrude's Attitude* (Q1: sig. G3r-G3v)

  The Queen's innocence is something which Q2 and the Folio allow
us to assume, but it is never explicitly stated. In Q1 she both protests her
innocence:

> Alas, it is the weaknesse of thy braine,
> Which makes thy tongue to blazon thy hearts griefe:
> But as I haue a soule, I sweare by heauen,
> I neuer knew of this most horride murder:
> But Hamlet, this is onely fantasie,
> And for my loue forget these idle fits.

and her readiness to further Hamlets' revenge:

> (*Ham.*) And mother, but assist mee in reuenge,
> And in his death your infamy shall die.
> *Queene. Hamlet*, I vow by that maiesty,
> That knowes our thoughts, and lookes into our hearts,
> I will conceale, consent, and doe my best,
> What stratagem soe're thou shalt deuise.

Q1, in these particulars, closely resembles Belleforest's portrayal of the Queen, and the resemblance is reinforced by one or two close verbal parallels. The last two lines have an obvious connexion with *The Spanish Tragedy*, IV.i.46-50:

> *Bel. Hieronimo*, I will consent, conceale,
> And ought that may effect for thine auaile,
> Ioyne with thee to reuenge *Horatioes death*.
> *Hier.* On then; whatsoeuer I deuise,
> Let me entreat you, grace my practises.

These features have been held, quite understandably, to prove that the Q1 lines derived not directly from Belleforest, but from the *Ur-Hamlet*. Duthie agrees with this in principle, but dissociates the last two lines from the early *Hamlet* play and regards them as the reporter's confused recollection of *The Spanish Tragedy* itself. Against this, it has to be allowed that many of the plays written around 1590 echo one another to an alarming degree. *Arden of Feversham*, for example, contains lines which have very close parallels in Kyd and in Marlowe's *Edward the Second* and *Massacre at Paris*, and it is almost unnecessary to remark that such parallels are frequent in the *Henry VI* plays. Hence, though it is mere conjecture that Kyd's lines established a formula which was subsequently invoked in the *Ur-Hamlet* either by Kyd himself or by an imitator, no one familiar with the drama of the period is likely to dismiss it as wholly improbable.

All in all, it seems certain that the Q1 lines were prompted by recollections of the *Ur-Hamlet*, and the question is whether this came about by accident or design. Duthie's contention, that the reporter, finding himself hopelessly at a loss, produced an imbroglio of Shakespearian and pre-Shakespearian matter is one that cannot lightly be set aside, especially as the Closet scene is wretchedly reported throughout. At the same time, no theory of author-revision would presume that the play which served as the main source of Shakespeare's original *Hamlet* was completely ignored when it came to revision. On the contrary, since Q2 and the Folio deviate from Belleforest, and, by implication, from the *Ur-Hamlet*, there is a reasonable case for believing that Shakespeare may have reverted to the earlier and more familiar pattern when he prepared the Globe version. Much obviously depends on whether the lines under discussion can justifiably be regarded as a garbled version of an authoritative replacement, and this can be more profitably discussed when the remaining differences have been considered.

(c) *Horatio and the Queen* (Q1: sig. H2v-H3r)

The short scene between Horatio and the Queen, peculiar to Q1, stands in lieu of IV.vi of the authentic texts:

> *Enter Horatio and the Queene.*
> *Hor.* Madame, your sonne is safe arriv'de in *Denmarke*,
> This letter I euen now receiv'd of him,
> Whereas he writes how he escap't the danger,
> And subtle treason that the king had plotted,
> Being crossed by the contention of the windes,
> He found the Packet sent to the king of *England*,
> Wherein he saw himselfe betray'd to death,
> As at his next conuersion with your grace,
> He will relate the circumstance at full.
> *Queene.* Then I perceiue there's treason in his lookes
> That seem'd to sugar o're his villanie:
> But I will soothe and please him for a time,
> For murderous mindes are always jealous,
> But know not you *Horatio* where he is?
> *Hor,* Yes Madame, and he hath appoynted me
> To meete him on the east side of the Cittie
> To morrow morning.
> *Queene.* O faile not, good *Horatio*, and withall, commend me
> A mothers care to him, bid him a while
> Be wary of his presence, lest that he
> Faile in that he goes about.
> *Hor.* Madam, neuer make doubt of that:
> I thinke by this the news be come to court:
> He is arriv'de, obserue the king, and you shall
> Quickely finde, *Hamlet* being here,
> Things fell not to his minde.
> *Queene* But what became of *Gilderstone* and *Roffencraft*?
> *Hor.* He being set ashore, they went for *England*,
> And in the Packet there writ down that doome

To be perform'd on them poynted for him:
And by great chance he had his fathers Seale,
So all was done without discouerie.
   *Queene* Thankes be to heauen for blessing of the prince,
*Horatio* once againe I take my leaue,
With thowsand mothers blessings to my sonne.
*Horat.* Madam adue.

Duthie's elaborate analysis of this scene is a model of subtlety and ingenuity, but his findings do not carry conviction. He holds that the reporter was himself the author of the blank verse, that the metrical breakdown which occurs towards the middle of the scene arises because 'the structure of the reporter-versifier's work has been destroyed by an interpolation made in the course of a revision of his verse', that such revision was the work of a second agent, and that the compositor was misled by the several interpolations.[15] This is heaping conjecture upon conjecture with a vengeance and leads us back once more to the question: why should so much attention have been lavished upon a relatively unimportant episode when so many necessary questions of the play went unconsidered? And is it really credible that a reviser who, at this point, busied himself with the adjustment of the reporter's personal pronouns, could have allowed

> For in that dreame of death, when wee awake,
> And borne before an euerlasting Iudge,
> From whence no passenger euer retur'nd,

and similar absurdities to pass unchecked?

Duthie's case for the reporter-versifier rests on evidence similar to that applied to (a), but he now makes both reporter and reviser indebted to recollections of passages which appear elsewhere in the play. Two of the alleged echoes, 'sugar o're', recalling III.i.48, and 'obserue the king', recalling II.ii.600 and III.ii.78, are reasonably convincing, but once again too much weight is accorded to isolated words so commonplace that they could have been used by any Elizabethan in any context. If Horatio addresses the Queen as 'Madame', it is surely because that is the normal convention and not because the reporter unconsciously recalled the use of the form by Ophelia at III.i.42 and by Polonius at II.ii.86 and 96.

There is no need to pursue this point since most of these echoes, real or illusory, could equally well figure in specifically reported matter.

[15] *op. cit.*, p. 156.

The general impression left by the whole scene is that it had once
known better days and that the report is defective. This view affords a
simpler explanation of the metrical dislocation, which is perhaps more
widespread than Duthie allows. If such a line as

> As at his next conuersion with your grace,

is regular, it is thanks to the compositor, who should have set 'conversation', The meter of

> For murderous mindes are always jealous

depends on the last word having retained the three-syllable pronunciation that was current in 1590 but seems to have disappeared by 1600.
Elsewhere the meter, though not demonstrably defective, gives an
impression of insecurity such as we often find in the reported sections of
blank verse.

Two other matters in this scene call for consideration. Horatio
speaks of meeting Hamlet 'on the east side of the Cittie', yet Elsinore
is never represented as a city in the authentic texts. On the contrary, the
impression given in II.ii, when the actors arrive at Court, is that the city
is some distance away, though at this point Shakespeare was probably
thinking of London rather than of Elsinore or even Copenhagen. The
salient point, however, is that this reference to 'the east side of the
Cittie' can only have arisen through error. It is unlikely that Shakespeare himself would have introduced such an incongruity, but equally
unlikely that the reporter would have done so if he had actually composed the scene. The obvious course is to interpret it as one of those
unconsidered and ludicrous trifles that so often found their way into
memorial reports.

The other notable feature of this scene is the line:

> Being crossed by the contention of the windes.

There is nothing corresponding to this in Q2 or the Folio, yet the line
unquestionably stood in the version underlying *Der Bestrafte Brudermord*, which, at the corresponding point, has:

> Nun begab es sich, dass wir eines Tages contrairen
> Wind hatten.

This raises its own particular set of problems, but also affords corroboration, for we may at least proceed, without prejudice, on the assumption
that Q1 and the *Brudermord* derived from a common source at this

point. And that source may well have been authoritative. The essential fact is that in a scene which, presumably through bad reporting, is thoroughly pedestrian there yet survives this one admirable line which will stand up to the severest scrutiny. That it is beyond the conscious scope of the supposed reporter-versifier goes without saying. The more positive consideration is that a line which is quite worthy of Shakespeare is also typical of him. The idea of 'commotion in the winds' recurs again and again, especially in the tragedies, and there are several passages in *King Lear* which have fairly close affinities with the Q1 line.[16] The clearest example occurs in *Hamlet* itself, at IV.i.7-8:

> Mad as the Seas, and winde, when both contend
> Which is the Mightier.

It might be argued that the line peculiar to Q1 is simply a dim recollection of this passage, but if so, how did the same unconscious echo find its way into the *Brudermord*?

### (d) *Hamlet's Voyage (ibid.)*

Duthie originally claimed that the scene just discussed gives a confused account of Hamlet's escape which has points in common with both the authentic texts and the *Brudermord*. His conclusions, which lead back to the *Ur-Hamlet*, need not be set out here as Greg has demonstrated that the Q1 account is quite consistent with Q2 and the Folio, save for the 'contention of the windes', which, he thinks, 'the *Brudermord* may well have borrowed from the provincial version while going elsewhere for its main narrative.'[17]

One thing that emerges with reasonable certainty is that the scene unique to Q1 was inserted in the interests of abridgement. Horatio's brief account of the circumstances of Hamlet's escape and return permits the omission of IV.vi, in which the sailors deliver Hamlet's letter to Horatio, and V.ii.1-81, where Hamlet gives his friend an unnecessarily long account of the whole adventure. This allows the play to be shortened by about one hundred lines. The scene itself obviously constitutes a revision, and, as Greg observes, 'the action is somewhat simplified, and the change obviates the awkwardness of delaying the account of Hamlet's adventures till after the Graveyard scene.'[18] The

[16] Cf. *King Lear*, III.i.4-5 (Contending . . . wind . . . sea) and 11 (to-end-fro-conflicting wind and rain); II.iv.6 (contentious storm) and IV.vii.32-4 (warring winds . . . cross).

[17] *The Shakespeare First Folio*, p. 305.    [18] *ibid.*, p. 303.

revision process appears, in so far as it concerns the changed portrayal
of Gertrude, to relate back to some point in III.iv. The vile condition of
the whole of the Closet scene in Q1 renders speculation hazardous, but
the report of IV.i suggests that there may have been some change in
presentation since Gertrude tells Claudius:

> Whenas he came, I first bespake him faire,
> But then he throwes and tosses me about,
> As one forgetting that I was his mother.

There is no suggestion of physical violence in Q2 or the Folio. It is
possible that in this respect the Globe performances made some concession to the groundlings.

One purpose of the revision in both sections was evidently to alter
the character of the Queen. It is not easy to see why Shakespeare or
anyone else should have gone to the trouble of making a change that is
dramatically pointless. Gertrude may affirm her innocence and
promise, with apparent enthusiasm, that she will assist Hamlet in any
stratagem that he may devise, but in the event she assists in nothing
because nothing further is devised. The initiative, after the Prayer scene,
lies entirely with Claudius, and Hamlet's ultimate vengeance is
achieved more by luck than judgment. Dramatic expediency may
therefore be ruled out, and the only alternative explanation would seem
to be that the change was prompted by censorship or the anticipation
of censorship. Even if Anne of Denmark had not already become
Queen of England, it was obvious that she would almost certainly do
so, and it was therefore politic that any Queen of Denmark represented
on the English stage should be more sinned against than sinning. In the
Folio version, which, it has here been suggested, was used only for
private performance, Gertrude's innocence is never actually established.
She gives no indication of siding with Hamlet, nor is it clear that she
even believes that Claudius had murdered her husband. Her behaviour
after the Closet scene argues very strongly that she does not, since her
attitude to Claudius remains outwardly unchanged and the only
stratagems that she consents to are those of his devising. It is reasonable
to surmise that the Master of Revels demanded that she should assume
a more positive and militant virtue before he finally granted a licence
for public performance. If so, the relevant revision may, of course, have
been later than the postulated abridgement, though it is unnecessary to
assume that it was.

## vi

The evidence presented in the foregoing sections, though variable in kind and quality, seems nevertheless to justify the conclusion that Q1 is throughout a memorial reconstruction of an official abridgement of the Folio version, with cuts, amendments and replacements for which Shakespeare was himself responsible. Absolute proof is impossible, but there is really very little room for doubt. Once we grant that the Folio text must have been far too long for normal use, an official abridgement for use at the Globe becomes a necessary assumption. If it were apparent that the abridgement, with its complement of revision, was made some years after the play's first appearance, it would be hazardous to press Shakespeare's claim, though, in theory, it would remain the strongest one up to at least 1612. Fortunately we can rest assured that there were no long intervals. It is clear that Q1 appeared probably two, and certainly not more than three, years after the completion of the play, and it is instructive to consider just what those two or three years entailed. *Hamlet* was prepared and rehearsed, it was played at Oxford and Cambridge, it was performed at the Globe in an abridged version, a memorial reconstruction of that version was made and used by a group of strolling players in the provinces, was subsequently sold by them to the stationers, and duly appeared in print sometime between May 19th, 1603, and the end of that year.[19] The Globe abridgement can therefore be assigned to 1602 at the latest, but it is much more likely that it followed fast upon the performances of the Folio version in 1601. There is really not the slightest reason for supposing that Shakespeare would have handed the delicate task of abridgement over to some other member of the company.

There the matter may rest. It would not be an unduly difficult undertaking to reconstruct a credible approximation to the Globe version since there are obvious deductions to be drawn from the Folio, from Q1 and, with certain reservations, from *Der Bestrafte Brudermord*. But the result would be of purely academic interest. Heminge and Condell were evidently concerned to preserve the fullest theatrical version of their friend's play and we should be grateful for that decision.

---

[19] The entry to Roberts in the Stationers' Register on July 26th, 1602, is presumably irrelevant since Q1 was evidently issued in contravention of it.

# Conclusion

Many attempts have been made to resolve the problems presented by the four plays discussed in this book, but remarkably few of the resultant proposals are anything more than partial or speculative. This, in view of the limited available knowledge, is inevitable, and we may do well to remind ourselves of the words uttered by that most judicious of Shakespearians, F. P. Wilson:

> That many printed books of that age have been lost I do not believe, but that many plays have been lost is certain. So serious are the losses that the historian of Elizabethan drama—especially of our drama in the sixteenth century, before the habit of reading plays had become popular—must often feel himself to be in the position of a man fitting together a jigsaw, most of the pieces of which are missing. Some sort of picture emerges, but is it the true picture?[1]

Against this verdict there is no appeal, and it would therefore be idle to claim that many of the conclusions which this book proffers are ultimately verifiable. Certain of them are revolutionary, and it may be cheerfully acknowledged that there is much here that runs counter to that kind of received opinion whose basis is all too often the blind acceptance of a tradition of conjecture. The claim which the present enquiry justifies is that, with the guidance afforded by recognition of the occasional character of these plays, we find that certain pieces of the puzzle fit together after all and that the picture which emerges, though unfamiliar, is unified, comprehensive and intelligible.

In support of this claim, it will not be amiss to specify those problematic aspects which orthodox criticism has never wholly accounted for. *Macbeth* has sections, not quite compatible with the rest of the play, which are written in a style demonstrably used by Shakespeare elsewhere, and the Folio text points to a highly spectacular conception which sets the play apart from all its fellow tragedies except the late and unfinished *Timon of Athens*. *Troilus and Cressida* poses controversial problems of classification and the Folio divergences, though slight, are distinctive and must be susceptible of logical interpretation. *The Merry*

[1] 'Shakespeare's Reading', *Shakespeare Survey*, 3, p. 16.

*Wives of Windsor*, by general consent, necessitates the postulation of a lost source play of analogous character, and Porter's comedy must obviously have claims at least as strong as those of any play hitherto proposed. The preservation, in the 1602 Quarto, of a longish section of competent but demonstrably non-Shakespearian dialogue raises problems whose solution cannot readily be attempted in terms of normal actor-reporting. *Hamlet*, in its authoritative versions, is a play of incredible length. There is no escape from this, nor from the fact that a considerable proportion of its dialogue would have held little meaning or appeal for an Elizabethan popular audience as distinct from a sophisticated one. And again we are confronted with a debased quarto which has intermittent vestiges of seeming authority that sort oddly with the efforts of the actor-reporter. The weakness of existing theories is that they almost invariably turn a blind eye to the crucial inner-play section of Q1.

Since the present book offers solutions to these problems, it is not unduly presumptuous to affirm that the picture which emerges is a fuller one than existed before. And it is one that carries with it the important corollary that Shakespeare acted as his own reviser. The notion that his manuscripts, once they had been delivered to the theatre, were, from time to time, chopped and changed by a diversity of book-holders and hack-poets is one that editorial expediency has often invoked and often inflated, though it will scarcely abide the test of common sense. His relations with his company from 1594 onwards were notably intimate and it is merely reasonable to suppose that all questions relating to the production of his own plays were referred to him, so that even the book-holder's intrusions may have been comparatively rare. There is, of course, specific reference to author-revision on the title-pages of *Love's Labour's Lost* (Q1: 1598), *1 Henry IV* (Q2: 1599) and *Richard III* (Q3: 1602 et al.), but internal evidence for the alleged correction or augmentation is wanting. It would seem, nevertheless, that the belief that Shakespeare made his own revisions was current among Elizabethan stationers, and such testimony may not be wholly insignificant. The acid test, however, is the qualitative one, and what has emerged from the foregoing investigations is a pattern of revision that is not merely credible but also extraordinarily skilful, with a dexterity that practically forbids the assumption that it could have been carried out by anyone but the dramatist himself. The transformation of *Macbeth*, whatever its aesthetic shortcomings, can only be regarded as a superlative craftsman's triumph over an extremely difficult assignment, and the conclusions drawn from the several versions of *Hamlet* lead, in the end, to an abridgement remarkable alike for its skill, its economy and its subtle assessment of audience appeal. *Troilus and Cressida* continues to perplex. There is no record of any Jacobean performance and attempts at revision to that end were evidently abandoned.[2] Yet those vestiges which have here been attributed to the Folio text may well constitute the most powerful testimony to Shakespeare's aptitude for revision. The Folio Prologue and apparently changed ending are small matters in themselves, but it can scarcely be denied that, on reflection, they will be found to go a long way towards reforming the tone and emphasis of a play that had formerly suited the occasion of hilarious comedy. In this connexion what did or did not happen during Shakespeare's lifetime is perhaps less relevant than the diametrically opposed interpretations offered by critics and producers in our own day.

It would be presumptuous to claim that an investigation whose primary concern is with transmission holds much that is of significance to those same critics and producers. Certain conclusions bearing on their problems and interests have, from time to time, emerged, and there is little that need be added here. On balance, it seems that *Troilus and Cressida* should be received and presented as comedy since the Quarto version, whatever the incidental superiority of individual Folio readings, is evidently that which was given, as comedy, at one of the Inns of Court, whereas the revised version was apparently an *ébauche*. At a time when stage presentation of hypothetical reconstructions is viewed more tolerantly than was formerly the case, it would doubtless be possible to offer something approximating to the Globe version of *Hamlet*, though it is questionable whether the result would justify the effort. The Folio text may, as here argued, preserve an 'occasional' version, but there is every justification for producers to retain that version, simply because all *Hamlet* audiences nowadays are sophisticated

---

[2] It is curious, as Bernard Harris reminds me, that there are no records relating to performance of any of the classical plays of Shakespeare's later period, and it may be that the non-performance of *Troilus and Cressida* has been too readily assumed. On the other hand, borrowings by Daniel and others (see Chapter I, p. 12) offer strong testimony that *Antony and Cleopatra* had been staged in or before 1607, while the case for *Coriolanus* may reasonably be held to rest on a perceptible echo in Jonson's *Epicœne*. There appears to be no such evidence to suggest a Jacobean performance of *Troilus and Cressida*, though the original Inn of Court presentation certainly impressed John Marston and the author of *Saint Marie Magdalens Conversion*.

and the needs of the groundlings no longer arise. The claim that *Hamlet* is substantially a play about university men admits a precept already anticipated in the practice of the late Nugent Monck, who observed:

> There is evidence in the text that Hamlet was meant to be played as a young undergraduate, and in our version at the Maddermarket Hamlet is always acted by someone young.[3]

Coleridge went straight to the heart of the matter when he defined Hamlet as 'a young man of fire and genius', and the portrayal suggested here distorts neither the prince nor the better sort of undergraduate.

*Macbeth* admits a firmer but more awkward dogmatism. Producers usually dispense with Hecate and her attendant embellishments and thereby achieve something that may not be markedly different from the play as originally presented. Yet this necessitates cutting what is already an abnormally short play, and, though professional reluctance to accept the full operatic and spectacular implications of the Folio text is understandable, it is questionable whether there is much justification for omitting material which, according to the present demonstration, is Shakespeare's own. The conclusion that the Folio preserves *Macbeth* as he liked it imposes certain aesthetic considerations which are decidedly uncomfortable. The play is nowadays quite justly ranked among Shakespeare's supreme achievements, but it is by no means clear that this has always been the case or that the dramatist himself apprehended the magnificence of his creation. Several of the earlier allusions, notably by Ben Jonson, are distinctly satirical or condemnatory, and the fact that Davenant's version supplanted the original until as late as 1744 speaks for itself. The Davenant 'improvements' in fact survived much longer in conflated texts, so that even Hazlitt quoted them under the impression that they were authentic. However reluctant we may be to accept Pope's notion of a Shakespeare who

> For gain, not glory, wing'd his roving flight,
> And grew immortal in his own despight.

we have no grounds for disputing its occasional truth, and it has obvious validity in relation to plays written at the royal command. If we accept, as we surely must, that the original purpose of *Macbeth* was to divert and flatter James I, what follows is the distinct likelihood of

[3] 'The Maddermarket Theatre and the Playing of Shakespeare', *Shakespeare Survey*, 12, p. 75.

achievement far outstripping intention, and of initial innocence yielding to later fashions and foibles. Many critical judgments that are valid in a later context must be accounted suspect in the earlier one, and our modern view of Macbeth as tragic hero cannot escape censure. The regicide and tyrant from whose evil sway the Stuarts, by implication, liberated Scotland is not likely to have engaged the sympathy or stirred the imagination of James, and Shakespeare's original conception may have been of a protagonist no better than Richard III in the earlier Tudor context. If so, we may do well to reflect on his claim to be regarded as one of what Charles Lamb termed 'the great criminal characters'. It is strange that that branch of Shakespeare criticism which concerns itself with 'problem-plays' should have failed to recognise that, hermeneutically, *Macbeth* is the most baffling of them all.

The present findings admit a firmer definition of editorial principles and it will suffice, since many of these have emerged sporadically, to offer here a summary in respect of each of the four plays.

## Macbeth

There is ample evidence for accepting the integrity of the play and none for doubting it. Shakespeare's sole responsibility, taken in conjunction with the evidence for a short original version and a barely augmented revised one, eliminates the likelihood of lost scenes and surrendered episodes. The view that Shakespeare, and not Middleton or another, had the rehandling of the play justifies the inference that the copy for the Folio was basically an augmented set of foul papers which had served as a prompt-book. The assumption that it was a transcript of this, though not impossible, is wholly unnecessary. A more optimistic view of the Folio text is admissible, and textual speculation may reasonably limit itself to the aberrations of Jaggard's compositors. These do not appear to be especially numerous.

## Troilus and Cressida

The Quarto preserves the play as it was actually performed, which the Folio does not, so that editorial acceptance of the Quarto version, *qua* version, seems inevitable. Whether the Folio Prologue should be incorporated or relegated to an appendix poses an awkward choice. Shakespeare evidently did not consider it indispensable, and it is hard to reconcile with an Inns of Court comedy. The Quarto contains numerous errors which the Folio corrects, but many Folio readings are themselves suspect in the light of what is known of Jaggard's compositors.

The group of variants exhibiting literal similarity is particularly difficult since it is sometimes quite impossible to decide whether it was Eld's compositor who was responsible for the misreading or Jaggard's. In such cases, the only course open to an editor is clearly to apply to the printed texts the principle laid down by Housman:

> The goodness of a MS. consists simply and solely in the goodness of the readings which it proffers; and our belief in its goodness, that is to say in the goodness of its readings, reposes simply and solely upon our judgment.[4]

## The Merry Wives of Windsor

Discussion of this play has been concerned with origins rather than transmission and it is, paradoxically, the examination of Crane's work on *The Witch* in relation to *Macbeth* which offers editorial guidance. It is clear that Crane, though an elegant scribe, was at times an extraordinarily perfunctory one. Carelessness, combined with strange orthography, occasionally results in misreadings which would have baffled any compositor, and one or two of these appear to have found their way into the Folio text. That he was, like many another scribe, occasionally guilty of sins of omission is a ready inference, and the Quarto of *The Merry Wives of Windsor* contains up to a dozen phrases or fragments which are lacking in the Folio but which seem to be required. The most curious example is at II.ii.2-3 where the Folio offers what, at first glance, seems to be the substitution:

> Why then the world's mine Oyster, which I, with sword will open.

for the Quarto's no less Shakespearian:

> I will retort the sum in equipage.

Greg quite rightly rejects this as evidence of literary revision, and comments: 'This phrase can only be worked into the Folio on the assumption of partly overlapping omissions in both texts.'[5] His concession that 'such coincidence may be thought unlikely' seems no longer necessary in the light of Crane's evident shortcomings.

Other Folio texts based on Crane's transcripts must obviously be viewed with suspicion. He was doubtless responsible for the sprinkling of apparent nonce-words which defy emendation, and there are often grounds for suspecting small omissions. This is likely to apply equally to clean texts such as *The Winter's Tale* and *The Tempest*

---

[4] *Iuvenalis Saturae*, p. xiv.                    [5] *The Shakespeare First Folio*, p. 335.

and to unsatisfactory ones such as *Measure for Measure*, which Johnson long ago recognised as darkened 'by distortion of phrase, or negligence of transcription', and *The Two Gentlemen of Verona*. There is, of course, nothing that an editor can do to make good the losses, but recognition of their probable origin will at least enable him to proceed unhampered by the heresies of successive revisions and collaboration.

### Hamlet

The Folio version must be accepted as theatrical and therefore authoritative, but there is manifest need for emendation. It is quite impossible to establish any hard-and-fast rules, but the present findings suggest that too much reliance may sometimes have been placed on Q2 and perhaps too little on Q1, which certainly emerges as a rather more reputable text than has hitherto been thought. The root problem lies in the fact that, although it is evident that sections of Q2 were set direct from Q1 and sections of the Folio direct from Q2, there exists no method whereby those sections can be satisfactorily defined, and even if they could numerous difficulties would remain. There can be little doubt that this kind of compositorial overlapping occurs, and its most disheartening implication is that complete agreement between the three texts is no guarantee of the correctness of any particular reading. Thus the accuracy of 'the sledded Pollax', though not in reasonable doubt, cannot be taken as proven simply because it is common to all three texts. Folio readings which concur with Q1 must, in theory, invalidate any variation occurring in Q2. Agreement between Q2 and the Folio does not necessarily discredit a Q1 variant, while agreement between Q1 and Q2 is no proof that the Folio is wrong.

Since the position could hardly be worse, something may depend on the acceptability of the thesis, presented earlier, that a copy of Q2 and a MS. were used concurrently for the setting of the Folio text. Though the procedure itself may have been promotive of error, the combination of authoritative manuscript and marked quarto means that Jaggard's compositors were working from highly reliable copy—that is unless we make the arbitrary assumption that the collator had scamped his job. This goes some way towards restoring confidence in the Folio text, whose manifest errors may, with comparatively few exceptions, have originated with Jaggard's compositors, and affords a basis for resolving difficulties, or, at least, for rationalising decisions. Thus, to take for example the notorious crux at I.ii.129, the fact that both quartos concur in reading 'sallied' carries little weight since Q2 was demonstrably dependent on Q1 at this point, whereas the Folio 'solid' is likely to have had the backing of both the manuscript and the marked quarto used as copy. The odds on it having been a sophistication introduced by compositor B, though not entirely eliminated, are greatly lengthened, and it is questionable whether any sneaking doubts should be allowed to linger since the Folio reading is an eminently satisfactory one. Assuredly there is no room for the kind of editorial ingenuity which rejects it in favour of a 'sullied' tortuously inferred from the Quarto readings. But here again the Housman principle is applicable, and, as one critic has observed, the usual procedure with sullied flesh is to wash it, not melt it.

The apparent use of double copy for *Hamlet* opens up certain other possibilities which may be mentioned, though they lie outside the scope of the present enquiry. One is that the combination of quarto and manuscript may have been followed in the setting of other disputed Folio texts, and it may, without prejudice, be remarked that such procedure might conceivably resolve the problems of *King Lear*. The other, equally tentative, is that, in the light of Hinman's conclusions about simultaneous type-setting, the possibility of double copy having been used in the printing of certain of the remaining plays merits consideration.[6] This is, of course, unlikely to apply to Folio texts based solely on manuscripts, of whatever kind, but when Jaggard's men were working entirely from printed copy it is obvious that they could as easily have had two quartos as one. If a single copy was used, it must certainly have been broken up, and it is permissible to wonder whether such fragmentation could be satisfactorily equated with the pattern which Hinman has established.

All in all there emerge two general conclusions which, though neither new nor challenging, have always rested on insufficient evidence. The occasional plays establish, as few of the others can, that Heminge and Condell were concerned to preserve the fullest available versions and accordingly disregarded the abridged *Hamlet*, the original and shorter *Macbeth* and even the original and more shapely *Troilus and Cressida*. Cognate with this, though depending partly on other evidence, is the conclusion that they did their best to insure that Jaggard was provided with accurate copy. Their good faith has sometimes been unnecessarily questioned, and there seems no longer any reason to doubt that they were sincere when they spoke of 'the office of their

[6] *The Printing and Proof-reading of the First Folio of Shakespeare*, passim.

care, and paine, to haue collected & publish'd them' or when they claimed that surreptitious copies were presented 'cur'd, and perfect of their limbes' and the rest 'absolute in their numbers, as he conceiued them'. The pity is that Jaggard and his compositors fell so far short of this counsel of perfection.

# appendix 1

# *Alternative Endings*

It has here been suggested that the Folio text of *Troilus and Cressida* provides an alternative ending for a revised version of the play which Shakespeare, in the event, did not trouble to complete. Surviving texts from the period suggest that this procedure was followed from time to time, and both *The Spanish Tragedy* and *Mucedorus* furnish clear-cut and familiar examples, though in neither was the second ending supplied by the author of the original play. Both plays were, of course, enormously popular over a long period, and the changed endings were doubtless part of a general process of renovation. The possibility that certain plays were fitted with alternative endings at the very outset, simply because their authors recognised that they would be subjected to varying stage conditions, does not appear to have engaged critical attention to any great extent, but seems interesting enough to justify a little guarded speculation.

## Timon of Athens

It is now generally accepted that the five-act tragedy of *Timon* was never completed, and the precise nature of the copy underlying the Folio text remains a mystery. Sections of manifestly roughed-out material alternate with perfected scenes which, to all appearances, had been carefully prepared for production. The possibility that these scenes, with the masque as the central point of interest, were assembled to provide a short entertainment at Court or elsewhere cannot be ruled out, especially as the music for the Masque of Amazons survives in B.M. Add. MS. 10444. More important, however, is the overall impression that *Timon*, with its generous provision for spectacle, was conceived, from the first, in terms of both the Blackfriars (and possibly the Court) and the Globe. The Globe version, if such a thing had ever materialised, would certainly have dispensed with some of the more elaborate devices and properties, and it is conceivable that an alternative ending would have been required. The final scenes in the Folio text are perplexing, but the redundant accounts of Timon's death and the preservation of two conflicting epitaphs, suggest conflation of alternative endings.

## Doctor Faustus

The Quarto of 1616, as Greg has demonstrated, preserves substantially the original play written by Marlowe and a collaborator. The impression conveyed at the end of V.ii, that the Devils carry Faustus off to Hell, body and soul, does not seem wholly consistent with V.iii, where the Scholars discover Faustus's mangled limbs, while their moral commentary seems to render the Epilogue, spoken by the Chorus, superfluous. Henslowe's inventory of stage-properties included a 'Hell mouth', and it is reasonable to conclude that this was used for all presentations of *Doctor Faustus* given at the Rose and Fortune theatres. On such occasions V.ii and the Epilogue would have sufficed. This implies that V.iii was supplied by Marlowe, or, his collaborator, for use when no such property was available—as, for instance, when the company was on tour.

## Sir Thomas More

Most of the problems raised by the several sets of additions to *Sir Thomas More* were resolved long ago by Greg in his monumental Malone Society reprint, though he was unable to suggest a possible location for the long addition in the hand of Henry Chettle. The possibility that this, in conjunction with the original body text, provides for an alternative ending appears never to have been given serious consideration. It is, therefore, worth recording that the late Una Ellis-Fermor, after seeing a performance of *Sir Thomas More*, expressed the conviction that the manuscript preserves three distinct endings. Unfortunately the letter in which she voiced this opinion did not go into detail, but the mere impressions of so able and sensitive a critic obviously command respect. If they were substantially correct, it follows that Mundy and his coadjutors were working to a double, or even triple, conception from the outset. This, in a play that apparently never reached the stage, is interesting and possibly significant. It may be remarked that *Sir Thomas More*, on this reckoning, opens up possibilities analogous to those claimed above for *Timon of Athens*.

# appendix 2

# *The Songs in* The Witch *and Ralph Crane*

The three songs which appear in Crane's transcript of *The Witch* have all survived in other versions, and the variants are relevant both to the editing of *Macbeth* and to the broader question of Crane's reliability. The texts are given here as they appear in *The Witch*. The following sigla are employed.

Dx.    Drexel MS. 4175.
1673.  *Macbeth* (Cademan's Quarto: 1673)
Dav.   *Macbeth* (Davenant's adaptation: Chetwin's edition 1674)
Bodl.  Bodleian MS. Mus b. 1. fol. 21

I

        Come away: Come away  ⎱in yᵉ aire.
        Heccat: Heccat, Come away ⎰
*Hec.*  I come, I come, I come, I come,
        with all the speed I may,
        with all the speed I may.
        wher's Stadlin?
                Heere  ⎱
        wher's Puckle ⎬in yᵉ aire
                heere  ⎰
10     And Hoppo too, and Hellwaine too ⎱in yᵉ aire
        we lack but you; we lack but you,  ⎰
        Come away, make up the count
*Hecc.* I will but noynt, and then I mount.
A Spirit  ⎫ There's one comes downe to fetch his dues ⎱aboue
like a Cat ⎬ a kisse, a Coll, a Sip of Blood         ⎰
descends  ⎭ and why thou staist so long
                          I muse, I muse.
        Since the Air's so sweet, and good.

    *Hec.*  oh art thou come
20               what newes: what newes?
        All goes still to our delight,
          Either come, or els
               Refuse: Refuse:
    *Hec.*  Now I am furnished for the Flight. . . .
25 *Hec. going up.*  { Now I goe, now I flie,
                { Malkin my sweete Spirit, and I.
        oh what a daintie pleasure 'tis
          to ride in the Aire
           when the Moone shines faire
    and sing, and dance, and toy, and kiss;
        Ouer Woods, high Rocks, and Mountaines,
    Ouer Seas, our Mistris Fountaines,
    Ouer Steepe Towres, and Turretts,
    we fly by night 'mongst troopes of Spiritts,
        No Ring of Bells, to our Eares sounds
        No howles of Woolues, no yelps of Hounds.
        No, not the noyse of waters-breache
        or Cannons throat, our height can reache.
        No Ring of Bells &c. } aboue

  2. *Come away*] ô *come away* Dx. *Oh come away*, 1673, Dav.
  6. *Stadlin*] *Stadling*, 1673, Dav.
10. *Hoppo*] *Hopper* 1673, Dav. *Hellwaine*] *helway* Dx., 1673, Dav.
11. *lack*] *want* 1673, Dav.
14. *Ther's . . . downe*] *heare comes one downe* Dx., Dav. *Here comes one, it . . .* 1673.
15. *Coll*] *cull* Dx., 1673, Dav.
18. *sweet*] *freshe* Dx.
21. *still*] *well* Dx., *fair* 1673, Dav.
25. *goe: now*] *goe, ô now* Dx., *go; now* 1673, *go and now* Dav.
27. *pleasure 'tis*] *pleasure is this* Dx., *Pleasure's this* 1673, Dav.
28. *ride*] *sail* 1673, Dav.
30. *and sing, and daunce*] *and (   ) and singe* Dx. *To sing, to toy* 1673, Dav.
32. *our Mistris*] *our* $\frac{cristall}{mistris}$ Dx., *Over misty* 1673. *and misty* Dav.
33. *Steepe*] *steeples* Dx., 1673, Dav.
36. *no yelps*] *nor yelps* Dx., 1673, Dav.
37. *not*] *nor* Dx., 1673, Dav.
38. *or*] *nor* Dx., 1673, Dav.

Notes
14. Read *heare* on dramatic grounds.

28. Read *ride*, though *sail* may indicate a change in presentation.
32. Read *our Mistris*. The later variants are possibly due to misunderstanding. The seas are the fountains drawn up by the moon (i.e. our mistress, Hecate).
33. Read *steeples*.
36-8. Read *nor* . . . *nor* . . . *nor*(?). Some weight attaches to the cumulative testimony of the later versions.


## II

*A Charme Song: about a Vessell*

Black Spiritts, and white: Red Spiritts, and Gray,
Mingle, Mingle, Mingle, you that mingle may.
 Titty, Tiffin: keepe it stiff in
 Fire-Drake, Puckey, Make it Luckey.
 Liand, Robin, you must bob in
 Round, a-round, a-round, about, about
 All ill come runing-in, all Good keepe-out.
 *I. witch* heeres the Blood of a Bat.
 *Hec.* Put in that: oh put in that.
10  *2.* heer's Libbards Bane
 *Hec.* Put-in againe
 *I.* the Iuice of Toad: the Oile of Adder
 *2.* those will make the yonker madder.
15  *Hec.* Put in: ther's all. and rid the Stench.
 *Fire.* nay heeres three ounces of the red-haird wench.
 *all* Round: around: around &c:/.

3. *Titty, Tiffin*] *Tiffin, Tiffin* Dav.
5. *Liand*] *Lyer* Dav.
9. *Put*] *O put* Dav. *oh put*] *put* Dav.
10. *Libbards Bane*] *Lizards brain* Dav.
11. *againe*] *a grain* Dav.
12. *the* . . . *the*] *Here's* . . . *here's* Dav.
13. *yonker*] *Charm grow* Dav.
14. *ther's all*] *all these* Dav. *and rid*] *'twill raise.* Dav.
15. *of the red*] *of a red* Dav.

*Notes*

3. Read *Titty, Tiffin*. cf. *Tittie* and *Tiffin* in Scot's *Discovery of Witchcraft*.
5. Read *Liard* as in Scot and elsewhere in *The Witch* (184).
10. Read *Lizards braine*, as elsewhere in *The Witch* (1986, 1990).
12. Read *then* . . . *then* . . . (?). Crane presumably misread *thẽ* . . . *thẽ* . . . Davenant's reading is an obvious sophistication.

13-17. The variants were evidently made to render the song suitable for use in
Macbeth. Whether they possess Shakespearian authority is an open
question.

## III

*Song*

In a Maiden-time profest,
then we say that Life is best.
Tasting once the Married Life,
then we onlie praise the wife
There's but one State more to trie
which makes woemen Laugh, or Crie
Widow: Widow. of theis three,
the Midle's best, and that giue me.

3. *Married*] *Marridg'* Bodl.
6. *woemen*] *woman* Bodl.

It is highly probable that errors have crept into the later versions of
these songs, but this does not entirely absolve Crane. His transcript of
Fletcher's *Demetrius and Enanthe*, for which the Folio of 1647 serves as a
basis of comparison, appears to introduce about sixty errors, of which
some twenty relate to stage-directions, into a play consisting of 3,356
typographical lines. For *The Witch*, comprising 2,187 typographical
lines, checking is possible only in respect of the songs quoted and of
sporadic paraphrases of Reginald Scot. Even so, the palpable textual
errors and suspect readings recorded by Wilson and Greg amount to
forty, in addition to which there are five errors in stage-directions. The
implication is that Crane's work was variable and never entirely
reliable, and the foregoing collations are disturbing since, when all
adjustments and allowances have been made, they suggest that he was
capable of one error per ten or twelve lines. In view of the fact that it is
now generally held that at least five Folio texts, *The Tempest*, *The Two
Gentlemen of Verona*, *The Merry Wives of Windsor*, *Measure for Measure*,
and *The Winter's Tale*, were printed directly from Crane's transcripts,
it would appear that yet another form of editorial vigilance is called
for since the need to arbitrate between the corrupting First Folio
compositors and a none-too-reliable scribe now arises.[1]

There is no warrant for extreme pessimism, however. Crane's

---

[1] For the argument that *Timon of Athens* was also set, in part, from a Crane
transcript see H. J. Oliver's edition of that play, *New Arden Shakespeare*, pp.
xix-xxi. *King John* strikes me as a possible addition to the list.

transcripts must clearly have been susceptible of correction at one stage or other of transmission. If, as seems unlikely, they were used theatrically, the book-keeper would doubtless have amended all obvious errors. The same would hold if the transcripts, prior to Jaggard's receipt of them, were collated with such authoritative manuscripts as survived, but the question which arises here is whether it was in fact thought necessary to collate professional copies of this kind. The most natural assumption is that the Folio compositors, whatever their shortcomings in other respects, would normally have corrected palpable errors. It is instructive nevertheless to consider what might have happened if one of the Folio compositors had been faced with the task of setting the songs in *The Witch* from Crane's transcript. In I.33 he might readily have grasped that 'Steepe' was a miscopying of 'steeples'. Correction of 'Libbards Bane' in II.10 would have been distinctly possible since he would twice have set up '*Lizards* braine' in the lines immediately preceding. On the other hand, 'Liand' at II.10, would have gone uncorrected unless the compositor's memory had carried him as far back as 'Liard' (line 184), though even then he would not have known which of the alternatives was the correct one. Most of Crane's more trivial errors would almost certainly have gone uncorrected. Thus 'Ther's' (I.14), 'No. . . . not . . . or' (I.36-8) and 'the . . . the' (II.12) would unquestionably have been perpetuated simply because they do not arouse suspicion.

The strong probability that numerous trivial and unverifiable errors were transferred from Crane to the Folio is something that every editor of the plays in question must now face. Unfortunately there is little that he can do about it since suspicions unsupported by evidence are not in themselves ground for emendation. Errors of a more distinctive kind might well be reconsidered in the light of Crane's habits. In addition to misreading his copy, he often obscured it through his peculiar orthography and his predilection for hyphens. It is, perhaps, in the light of these habits that the resolution of such notorious cruxes as 'Most busie lest', 'An-heires', 'The prenzie, *Angelo*?' and 'I would Land-damne him' might most profitably be attempted.

# Index

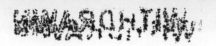